# Dependence and auto.

What are the effects of employment on women's well-being and social position in a Third World city?

Until recently, Calcutta has been notable for having one of the lowest rates of female employment in India. This has been largely determined by strong cultural beliefs that a woman's place is in the home. However, in recent years, the growth of 'female' jobs in the small-scale industry and service sectors, combined with an increase in male unemployment has resulted in a sudden increase in the numbers of women entering the labour force.

Based on Hilary Standing's extensive fieldwork within Bengali households, *Dependence and Autonomy* considers the effects of women's employment on the labour market, the household, and the women themselves. Particular attention is paid to the role of the life cycle and of class position in determining the impact of employment, and the work is set within a historical perspective on gender and employment in Bengali society.

Women's employment in the Third World is undeniably a topic of considerable current interest to academics and policymakers alike. *Dependence and Autonomy* will be of particular interest to undergraduates, researchers, and professionals in anthropology, gender studies, and development.

# Dependence and autonomy

## Women's employment and the family in Calcutta

Hilary Standing

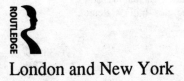

London and New York

For Annie, with love

First published in 1991
by Routledge
11 New Fetter Lane, London EC4P 4EE

Simultaneously published in the USA and Canada
by Routledge
a division of Routledge, Chapman and Hall Inc.
29 West 35th Street, New York, NY 10001

© 1991 Hilary Standing

Typeset by LaserScript Ltd
Printed and bound in Great Britain by
Biddles Ltd, Guildford and King's Lynn

*British Library Cataloguing in Publication Data*

Standing, Hilary, *1949–*
    Dependence and autonomy: women's employment and the
    family in Calcutta.
    1. India. Calcutta. Women. Employment. Social aspects
    I. Title
    305.430954147

*Library of Congress Cataloging in Publication Data*

Standing, Hilary.
    Dependence and autonomy: women's employment and the
    family in Calcutta / Hilary Standing.
    p.   cm.
    Includes bibliographical references.
    1. Women–Employment–India–Calcutta. 2. Sexual division
    of labor–India–Calcutta. 3. Home economics–India–Calcutta.
    I. Title.
    HD6190.C34S73 1990
    331.4'0954'147–dc20                                    90-33510
                                                                CIP

ISBN 0-415-04839-7

# Contents

# Tables

# Tables

# Acknowledgements

All books are the product, in various ways, of many hands. The protracted birth of this one owes more than usual to the help and support of a lot of individuals.

I must first thank the Economic and Social Research Council (previously the Social Science Research Council) for financing the fieldwork and supporting part of the writing of this book with a personal research grant.

In Calcutta, my debts are too numerous to acknowledge in full, but the following people need special mention. My friend and collaborator, Bela Bandyopadhyaya not only organized much of the work, but oversaw it while I was ill. Her expertise, love, care and support have been essential. Anjali Ray, Jharna Bhattacharya and, in its early phase, Kanaklata Majumdar helped to locate and interview the sample households. Mandira Sen pursued a historical odyssey through the first women's journals to be published in Bengal. Meenakshi Chatterjee summarized themes from Bengali fiction.

Professor Biplab Dasgupta, Director of the Centre for Urban Economic Studies, Calcutta University, kindly put the facilities of the Centre at my disposal, helped me in many ways and has been deeply indulgent of my failure to produce promised articles. My friends Nirmala Banerjee and Nripen Bandyopadhyaya, of the Centre for Studies in Social Sciences, have been continuously supportive and wise. Vina Mazumdar, of the Centre for Women's Development Studies in New Delhi, also provided warm encouragement, as did Bina Agarwal.

Mental and physical sustenance are, quite properly, inseparable in Calcutta. All the aforementioned contributed to both, as did the following friends; Mandira Sen and Amit Jyoti Sen, who tolerated lengthy invasions of their privacy with unfailing good humour and kindness, Deepika Basu, Dipali and Sitangsu Banerjee, Rathin Bhattacharya, Arun and Bulu Lahiri, Pushpa Mitter. I should also like to thank Dr Kamal Jalan of the Calcutta Hospital for skilful medical care over a long period. None of this would have been possible without the interest, participation and hospitality of the women and men who form the subject of the study.

Here, I must thank friends and colleagues at Sussex, including the AFRAS secretarial staff, for many kinds of assistance, direct and indirect. My friends Pat Caplan, Naila Kabeer, Tricia Jeffery, Roger Jeffery, Ursula Sharma and Ann Whitehead have all read, commented on or discussed with me various papers or drafts and have been generally encouraging, as has Alice Thorner in Paris. Vanessa Harvey Samuel has been a supportive friend both here and in Calcutta.

I owe to Annie Whitehead a long intellectual debt which is inseparable from an equally long personal friendship. I acknowledge it by dedicating this rather timid book to her.

Hilary Standing

Chapter one

# Introduction
## Issues, methods and empirical background

### Theoretical and conceptual issues

This book examines the effects of women's entry into employment on intra-household relations in an urban Third World context in which there has been little tradition of female employment but where economic pressures have brought a recent increase in the proportion of women entering or seeking waged work. Underlying this account is a wider concern. To what extent can employment for women provide the conditions or pre-conditions for their greater emancipation?

The study was carried out in the city of Calcutta, eastern India, among a representative sample of households which contained predominantly first-generation wage-employed women across a wide range of occupations. It uses a broadly anthropological mode of inquiry, but its starting point lies within a particular feminist conceptualization of the nature of the question.

The premise that economic dependency is the, or at least a, major factor in structuring inequality between women and men in commodity-based economies is one which has been shared by commentators across the political spectrum from Engels to the World Bank. At one level, it is undeniable. Lack of, or inferior access to employment, the social wage or property are the very conditions of powerlessness, albeit ones which are shared by unemployed and assetless men. At another level, it is problematic. The ubiquity of the male 'family breadwinner' ideology and its persistence in contexts where it bears little or no relation to reality suggest that there is more at issue than money or goods. The ideology itself appears to be integral to the way in which male gender identity is constructed in capitalist societies and, hence, how men and women relate to each other. The concept of emancipation thus encompasses more than economic independence. It signifies also the possibility of full social citizenship, of being enabled to act as a person, not simply as a legal and ideological dependant.[1]

The origins of this study lie in more than a decade of socialist

1

feminist re-analysis of women's subordination in the family and in the labour market. Both liberal sociology and Marxism have proved poor predictors of changes in gender relations as a consequence of women's increasing incorporation into waged work. This is because, in the former, the family is hypostasized as a taken-for-granted domain in which women have self-evident and unchanging 'roles', while in the latter, it is ignored altogether or subsumed in the encompassing sweep of class relations. Liberal sociology is thus unable to account for changes in the form and relations of the family and in its gender-based division of labour either historically or across cultural contexts. Marxism cannot deliver a satisfactory account of women's persistent structural disadvantage in the labour market. Neither treat intra-family relations as problematic.

A distinctive contribution of socialist feminism is the insistence on both the materiality and the specificity of gender relations within given contexts. Gender relations are material because they order and reproduce asymmetrical access to resources of different kinds. They are specific because we cannot 'read off' in a prescriptive or a priori way precisely what these asymmetries will be at any given historical or cultural moment. This does not rule out comparison across contexts but does require that the tools of analysis are not, themselves, context bound.

The problematization of the concept of the family has been an essential part of this process of rethinking tools and modes of analysis. As Whitehead (1981) points out, the impetus for this has come both from attempts to grapple with the specificities of household-based petty-commodity production in Third World economies and from attempts by feminists to analyse the relationship in advanced capitalist societies between the particular form of the family, gender subordination and the conditions of capitalist production. In the latter case, this has led to an emphasis on establishing the linkages between women's economic and ideological subordination within the family and their disadvantage in the labour market. In both sets of concerns, families and households are understood as embedded in wider socio-economic processes, not as separate 'institutions'.

Feminist analysis has stressed the need to treat the family as an ideological construct and particularly as a site for the reproduction of specific ideologies of gender; as a locus of economic processes in which women and men are structured into a division of labour; as a site of both shared and diverging interests between the sexes; and as an arena of political struggle in which gender, class and race politics are variously played out. Families are, most critically, about power relations.

It is necessary, first, to make a methodological point. The terms 'family' and 'household' are frequently used coterminously and often coincide empirically. But, as a number of writers have pointed out (e.g. Whitehead ibid, Yanagisako 1979), they refer to conceptually separate domains. For the purposes of this book, households are defined as co-resident units in which the distribution and exchange of commodities and services such as wages and domestic work are organized primarily through relations of kinship. The term 'family' refers both to those kinship-based relations which are located within co-residential groups and to the particular ideological forms taken by kinship relations within the Bengali context. This distinction enables the concepts to be used as analytical tools, while making no a priori assumptions about the specific content of those relations.

Women are associated pervasively with families, both as social beings and as providers of 'domestic' services. Harris (1981) and Yanagisako (1979) have drawn attention to the way in which the household and family are elided and 'naturalized' in everyday discourse so as to render them unquestionable. This naturalization is accomplished through the common-sense link with biological reproduction which provides a seemingly universal language resting upon naturalistic assumptions about women and men as particular, and different, kinds of beings. The language itself, however, is profoundly ideological. Biological reproduction is always constructed within demographic and sociological parameters. (cf. Edholm *et al.* 1977). The meanings of children and childhood, of motherhood and fatherhood, of marriage and sexuality, of maleness and femaleness, vary across socio-economic contexts. Not all women bear children and bearing and nurturing can be, and sometimes are, separated. Deconstructing the universalism of much sociological as well as popular theorizing about 'the family' and about the 'natures' of women and men is an important intellectual and political task.

Households are economic units in which commodities and/or services are produced, distributed and consumed and in which labour is organized and allocated through a sexual (and often age) division of labour. This is as true, albeit in importantly different ways, in predominantly wage-based economies as in 'subsistence'-based ones in that the transition to capitalist forms of production does not remove all productive functions from family-based households but separates out unpaid (use-value producing) labour from paid (wage) labour both formally and, frequently, spatially. It is the persistently gendered aspect of these divisions and the asymmetrical ways in which they structure power relations between women and men, which have particularly concerned feminists.

The 'deconstruction' of the family has also produced a strong critique of popular and academic assumptions about the family-based household as a collectivity of shared interests. Analyses of intra-household income and food distribution (e.g. Delphy 1979, Sen and Sen Gupta 1983, Brannen and Wilson 1987) have demonstrated systematic gender biases. Work on household money management (e.g. J. Pahl 1980, 1983, 1984) has revealed its frequent link to male violence and studies of household-level decision making have shown that women and men may have quite different priorities leading to routine or serious conflicts of interest (Hunt 1980, Roldan 1985). At the same time, the ideological and emotional importance of families in their members' lives, the many forms of support which they provide and their potential as a site of political resistance, have also been recognized, particularly in the literature on black and working-class experiences and survival strategies (e.g. Stack 1974, Humphries 1977). At issue here is the complex and often contradictory nature of the dynamics of gender, class and race struggles, and the valued as well as oppressive aspects of familial relationships.

Recent feminist work on gender divisions in the labour markets of advanced capitalist economies arose out of two major concerns, one theoretical and one empirical. Theoretically, the insistence on the embeddedness of family forms within the wider economy led to renewed interest in the extent to which Marxist tools of analysis could be applied or extended to encompass gender relations and to conceptualize the linkages between reproductive activities within the household and the reproduction of capitalist relations of production. The 'domestic labour debate', initiated by Seccombe in 1974 (and cf. Malos (ed.) 1980, Fox (ed.) 1980), is a major theoretical attempt to specify these linkages. Empirically, the post-war rise in the employment rate of married women in particular, in both Britain and the US, raised afresh questions about the relationship between gender differentiation in the labour market and the sexual division of labour within the home. As Whitehead (1981) points out, the study of gender relations within the household has tended to fall conceptually within the sphere of the sociology of the family, whereas the labour market has been conventionally the province of economic analysis. This has resulted in the reproduction of the disciplinary divide at the theoretical level. The labour market is seen as the site of economic relations, while relations within the family are seen as essentially interpersonal and affective. Recent work has attempted both to transcend this divide and to analyse the links between these domains. For socialist feminists, this attempt owes a much older debt to Friedrich Engels.

Debate on the relationship between oppression and exclusion from social production has been conducted very largely around Engels' famous, century-old dictum that, 'the first condition for the liberation of the wife is to bring the whole female sex back into public industry' (*The Origin* 1884 (1985 edn: 105)). Engels' analysis of female subordination remains a major text despite well-founded criticism of its breathtakingly speculative generalizations and its many empirical errors. Its import-ance, however, lies in its situation of women's oppression 'as a problem of history, rather than of biology' (Delmar 1976: 287, see also Sayers *et al.* 1987 for a revaluation of Engels' work).

Its particular significance for contemporary debates lies in the links which are made between the subordination of women and their location within family structures specific to capitalism. (See Barrett's intro-duction to the 1985 edition of Engels' (1884).) Molyneux (1989) also points out that Engels' thesis has had a major influence on political practice in many socialist societies, where it became the official agenda for women's emancipation. For Engels, it was because the (bourgeois) monogamous family was an economic unit in which the male earner wielded the power that the 'first condition for liberation' was for all women to be earners. This, in turn, would usher in the final condition, which was the dissolution of the (bourgeois) monogamous family based on the legal and economic power of the husband.

Engels' insistence on the historical specificity of the family and marriage under capitalism – its embeddedness in, rather than separation from the wider economy – and on the economic basis of marriage, remain part of the contemporary conceptual currency. Other aspects of the analysis, as well as the prescription itself, now appear inadequate. Engels argued that the power of husbands over wives was a feature only of bourgeois marriage where wives were excluded from the labour force, and that proletarian marriage was an equal partnership as both partners laboured. In short, Engels viewed the family ultimately as little more than a reflection of production relations. What is missing is any consideration of other areas of women's oppression which are not necessarily bound by class and by straight economic oppression, such as gender socialization, sexuality and the unequal division of domestic labour within the home (Molyneux ibid). Equally absent is the question of inequalities in the labour market itself. For Engels, it is class alone which mediates women's relationship to their employment.

Labour markets in urban India are pronounced examples of a more general phenomenon (cf. Dex 1985) in which low wages, lack of access to skills and promotion and concentration in certain kinds of work (often of the low value-added kind) or in certain labour processes characterize the average woman worker's situation and render women, as a category, more disadvantaged than men. Thus, although there are class differ-ences in women's access to the labour market, there are also common-alities which cut across classes to produce relative disadvantage for women in general. Women and men are not, apparently, equivalent as types of labour but enter the labour force as particular kinds of workers.

Attempts to explain gender differentiation within the labour market have come from across the social sciences and from various theoretical positions. These include neo-classical theories of men's comparative advantages as earners (e.g. Becker 1974), dual labour market theories (e.g. Barron and Norris 1976) and Marxist theories utilizing the concept of women as a reserve army of labour (see Beechey 1978, Bruegel 1979, Anthias 1980 for discussions and critiques of this concept). Theories of women's 'dual roles' at home and at work (e.g. Myrdal and Klein 1970) also constitute a form of explanation for labour-market disadvantage. A common problem with most of these analyses, however, is their inability to account for why women should be disadvantaged in these ways. This is because they either locate their explanations within the internal dynamics of the labour market itself and/or predicate them on unvarying assumptions about the nature of women's role in the family. They are thus ultimately descriptive rather than explanatory, and context bound in that they universalize ideologies of dependency which are specific to a particular time and place, usually that of contemporary western Europe.

Much feminist work on the labour market has pointed out that explanations for women's relative disadvantage cannot be found simply by analysing the structure of the labour market itself or by considering women in isolation from men and from their position within specific domestic divisions of labour. This is because the terms upon which women compete for employment are set by the wider social relations into which they are structured. These terms may be dictated by an economic agenda, such as the availability of childcare for women who are mothers. They may be set by a cultural agenda, such as strongly entrenched beliefs about the unsuitability of certain kinds of employment, or of employment for particular subgroups of women, such as young unmarried daughters. They may also be determined in part by political considerations in which the prior right of men to (scarce) employment is upheld. In each case, women are either constrained by their gender roles from competing on the same terms as men, or else attributions about gender roles are made which may have the effect of making it more difficult for women as a category to enter and remain in the labour market on the same terms as men, regardless of their individual characteristics. These attributions often (but not always) rest upon assumptions both about women's primary commitments to families and about the presence of relationships with male providers. Women and men are thus seen as different and unequal kinds of labour.

The attribution of particular characteristics to the genders also permeates the labour market through gender stereotyping. This produces hierarchies of gender-related skills, with women concentrated predominantly in 'unskilled' and 'semi-skilled' jobs and tasks, as well as gender segregation, which results in wholly female or male enclaves of employment. The imputation of intrinsic characteristics to the genders results, again, in naturalized (and thus well-defended) ideologies of 'men's work' and 'women's work'. (See for example Elson and Pearson 1980, 1981 on the notion of 'nimble fingers'). The mechanisms which reproduce these processes need to be sought outside the immediate arena of the labour market by analysing why a particular demand for labour is met by a supply of persons of one gender rather than another.

In a lucid summary and discussion of the problem of defining universals and specificities about women's work, Redclift (1985) raises the question of the applicability of analytical frameworks developed in the context of European industrial capitalism to contemporary Third World contexts with distinctive patterns of capitalist development. She points to the dynamic interplay between the requirements of capital for cheap (and controllable) labour, the specific social relations and cultural practices in any given context and the incorporation of particular categories of workers into wage work. This interplay may produce a predominance of (young) male migrant labour, as in many colonial contexts; or a sudden growth in young female labour, as has occurred in the garments and electronics factories of the newly industrializing countries (Heyzer 1986). It is not sufficient, thus, to rest the analysis of women's incorporation into wage labour at the level of their cheapness to capital. It is necessary to explain why women, or any other category of workers, are constructed at given moments as cheaper, or more compliant, or as having the desired attributes.

These issues require us to recognize 'femaleness' and 'maleness', not as timeless universals but as constituted within historical and social contexts. Their significations vary across time and place. Submissiveness and docility are not essential traits of a particular sex. They are ideologies about gender as a social category. Ideologies can change or be changed by social, political and economic forces and struggles. Any account of the impact of women's entry into employment must, therefore, examine the social and historical terms upon which the genders enter the labour market. This must include associated ideological constructs of the genders as specific, and different, kinds of persons.

In Calcutta, as in other Indian cities, there has been a growth in the number of women entering wage employment since the early 1970s. In Calcutta, this growth has been predominantly in work designated as semi- and unskilled and it has taken place against a tradition of low female labour-force participation and a strongly entrenched ideology of female domesticity and dependency on male kin. In accounting for this phenomenon, it is necessary to examine the changing demands for labour within the economy, why 'women' emerge at a particular juncture as an appropriate category to fill this demand, and the conditions which allow or enable certain women to be released from familial and ideological obligations to take up employment.

The purpose of this book is, then, to examine empirically the background to the rise in women's labour-force participation in Calcutta and analyse its implications for gender relations within a specific context. While much work has been done on this theme in advanced capitalist societies, rather less is known about the effects of women's incorporation into urban wage labour in peripheral capitalist ones, where family structures and familial and gender ideologies have taken historically different forms. The assumption is made that while capitalism always has transformative effects on gender and family relations, those effects cannot be wholly scripted in advance but must be determined by investigation. It follows that there will be no universally generalizable answer to the question posed at the beginning. The aim is rather to reconstitute the question by disaggregating it into appropriate levels of analysis within which the specificities of the context may be caught.

## Kinship, class and gender in urban India

A great deal has been written on the subject of kinship in India. While rural kinship has been largely the province of anthropology, many urban studies reflect a more 'sociological' approach, often signified by a change in terminology from 'kinship' to 'family' and an implicit or explicit use of modernization frameworks to explain changes in kinship patterns and behaviours.

Anthropological accounts have tended to be informed by an interest in kinship theory *per se* and thus to be strongly formalistic, concentrating upon rules rather than upon relations. (The many articles on kinship in both series of the journal *Contributions to Indian Sociology* illustrate this point.) At the same time, there has also been a strong emphasis on the cultural uniqueness of Indian kinship and hence its non-comparability with other contexts. This emphasis has been particularly marked in anthropological accounts of Bengali kinship (Inden and Nicholas 1977, Fruzzetti and Ostor 1976) in which kinship is a quintessentially cultural institution which regulates interpersonal relations and right conduct. From both of these perspectives, kinship emerges as a thing in itself rather than as a historical product. Shah (1974) is a notable exception to this tendency. In emphasizing the relational and developmental properties of households, his work on Gujarat prefigures some of the conceptual concerns of later feminist writing.

The more sociological literature has been dominated by a similar concern with normative rules and also with delineating typologies of household forms. This is because debate in the urban literature has concentrated mainly on changes in family composition as a consequence of urbanization (see for example Ross 1961, Vatuk 1972). Some of this writing is underpinned by a linear conceptualization of change of the kind associated with modernization theories. 'Complex' forms are fragmenting into nuclear families under the impact of modernization. (The paradigmatic account is Gore 1968.)

The differences between these two kinds of account are more apparent than real. In both, kinship and domestic groups are treated as largely autonomous of economic and political relations and thus exist in a sociological vacuum. Where attempts are made to deal with the changes associated with urbanization, as in the literature on the fragmentation of complex families, the treatment of families as ideal types rather than as dynamic processes leaves unspecified the mechanisms by which changes in family forms occur. The kinship literature, in general, reproduces the conceptual division between the family and the economy which was noted on p. 4 in relation to writing on advanced capitalist societies.

Feminist research in India since the beginning of the International Women's Decade has, however, broken new ground in the analysis of the relationship between gender and family relations and changes in the wider economy. This change may be said to have started decisively with the work of the Government of India's Committee on the Status of Women in India. Their report, called *Towards Equality* and published in 1974, is based on extensive empirical investigation across communities and classes. It is notable both for its thoroughness and for its challenge to assumptions that economic development automatically benefits women. Conceptually, it marks a complete break with modernization theories. *Towards Equality* draws particular attention to two major sources of structural inequality between women and men. The first is the adverse demographic regime for women in India and the second is the long-term secular decline in women's labour-force participation.

India is one of very few countries in which female life expectancy at birth (and at all ages below 40) is lower than that of males.[2] This finding has led to important appraisals of the gender biases operating at different structural levels, including that of the household, and the extent to which these are correlated with poverty or are associated more generally with the ideological devaluation of girls and women (e.g. Bardhan 1984, Sen and Sen Gupta 1983, Agarwal 1986).

The secular decline in women's formal labour-force participation rates between 1901 and 1971 has likewise stimulated a major debate on its causes and consequences but has also resulted in a greater focusing of attention on the many different informal or unenumerated economic activities carried out by women, often as a part of family labour. Again, this has required attention to the nature of intra-household relations, along with a clearer conceptualization of the varied socio-economic forms taken by both rural and urban households.

These findings have two major theoretical implications for thinking about gender relations. First, they point to the need to analyse the ways in which cultural practices and understandings about the family, marriage and sexuality which cut across class and other bases of differentiation are modified, reconstituted or remain resistant in the face of wider socio-economic changes. Second, they demonstrate the importance of treating kinship as a resource base, the significance of which varies according to class and context[3] and which has different implications both for women and men and for women of different classes.

One of the major contributions of anthropology to the understanding of kinship ideologies in South Asia has been in relation to cultural codes of status and honour which are specific, but not necessarily unique, to the South Asian context. Women are the guardians or conduits of kin and caste-based honour and status and this is expressed in constraining codes of conduct and in ideologies of female purity (see Yalman 1963 for the clearest exposition of this point). One of the ways in which a woman's, and hence her family's, status is acquired or maintained is through her withdrawal from public activities, usually agricultural work, and confinement to the house. Withdrawal thus has a status-signalling aspect. A household or kin group has or acquires status in proportion to the extent to which it is able to substitute hired male or lower caste female labour for the work which might otherwise be done by higher status women in the fields and in some kinds of household activity. (See Das 1976, Srinivas 1977.)

This 'withdrawal from work' model has been important in drawing attention to the deeply ideological nature of the constraints upon Indian women in a general cultural sense. It has also been utilized by scholars analysing the complex of factors behind the low level of female labour-force participation in India (e.g. Chatterji 1984). As it stands, however, it is analytically and empirically inadequate as a general model of the relationship between cultural constraints and economic processes.

First, it is a model in which synchronic and diachronic dimensions are insufficiently distinguished. Synchronically, it describes a cross section through a system of ranked statuses, while diachronically it indicates a situation of upward social mobility in which lower status groups (families or subcastes) improve their position by emulating higher status ones. The processes which link these two dimensions tend to be unproblematized. Which families/status groups under which combination of circumstances follow this particular pattern? Which women 'substitute' for the ones who are withdrawn?

Second, the model was developed primarily to deal with status ranking among middle and higher castes in rural India. Its generalizability to urban contexts where class formation is marked is questionable. The changing meanings of work and of public activities as well as the increased wage dependency of households alter the nature of 'status' considerations. The assumption of upward social mobility for those sections of the population concerned with the production or maintenance of status is also problematic when transferred to an urban situation where there is evidence that living standards for many are falling.

Recent work on urban India has begun to address some of the issues raised by the persistence or reconstitution of status codes among urban families. Papanek (1979) has characterized what might be an urban equivalent to the 'withdrawal from work' syndrome in her concept of 'status production work'. In this, she suggests that low levels of female employment, particularly in higher status families, do not signify enforced idleness but a productive re-occupation of wives into family status-improving activities, such as the beautification of the home or the supervision of children's schoolwork in an increasingly competitive educational environment. Papanek's model is very helpful in pointing to the materiality of status as an operational code, in its insistence on the productive nature of women's domestic activities and hence in its linkage of cultural codes to family-based households as resource bases.

It does, however, treat these activities in a homogeneous way. In the concept of 'status production work' there is an elision between status-enhancing or maintaining activities and time-filling and income-substituting domestic activities. For example, the participation of some middle- and upper-class women in unpaid charitable work, which carries important political spin-offs for households and kin networks (see Caplan 1985), is not of the same order of activity as flower arranging or knitting. In her study of women's work in Shimla, Sharma (1986) extends and refines the concept of status production by disaggregating its various components and pointing to the ways in which these activities are linked to the strategies of social reproduction of households in different classes. It is necessary to contextualize 'status' and to relate it to changing material conditions in both rural and urban India. If living standards fall, for instance, what kinds of material and ideological adjustments take place in those households caught in the contradiction between economic and status needs? What does this mean for gender relations?

Until recently, Bengali women, with the exception of a small professional group from the upper class, took little part in waged work. The continuing absence of women from many public workplaces remains striking to anyone familiar with Bombay or with urban south India.

11

Bengali values place women, particularly wives and mothers, firmly in the home. Ideologies of family status have meant that the idea of wives and daughters taking up employment and leaving the protection of the family home (and the social control of senior relatives) has been a rather shameful one, reflecting badly on the ability of middle-class men in particular to provide for their dependants but also reaching as an ideological force into working-class families. Urban inflation, falls in real wages and high male unemployment have affected the ways in which households reproduce themselves and have rendered such values increasingly difficult to maintain. This book examines some of the ways in which these processes affect households of different class and composition.

## The nature of the research

It is a general argument of this book that the investigation of the impact of waged employment upon women must be carried out in the context of the material and ideological resources and practices of households and families. Specifically, the book examines the impact of women's employment on intra-household relations and familial ideologies associated with Bengali households. Family-based households, rather than individual women or particular places of employment, thus formed the basic unit of investigation.

Household-level research focused on a range of issues concerned with the adaptations of households and household members to a woman's employment. Women's experiences of employment are also explored both in the context of the kind of work which they obtain and their reactions and responses to it.

An initial question, which is explored in chapters two and seven, concerns the reasons why Bengali women in Calcutta enter wage work. Calcutta has low rates of female labour-force participation when compared with the other major Indian cities and particularly among the Bengali population. Since the early 1970s, however, the rate has been increasing. This points to the need both to examine the structural and historical reasons for the change and to look at the individual constellation of factors for particular women. This approach reveals encompassing features, such as a declining urban economy, high rates of male unemployment and the rise of forms of employment typically seen as women's work. It also reveals a range of factors operating for individual women, such as loss or absence of male support, stage in the life cycle, familial encouragement, familial discouragement, personal aspiration.

In chapter three, women's employment options, conditions and work histories are examined. Options are both limited and highly gender- and class-specific. Home-based piece work or self-employment in sweated conditions forms the lot of many poor women. Middle-class women with college education are predominantly found in the public service sector, rarely in the higher paid positions. Poorly paid factory assembly work is a relatively recent and 'class-neutral' form of employment. Gender disadvantage in the labour market places real constraints upon the potential for employment to provide women with any degree of economic autonomy.

The main concern of chapter four is the effect of women's employment on the household division of labour and on ideologies of domesticity. The customary division of labour in the Bengali household emphasizes strongly men's and women's separate spheres of work and allocates domestic work and childcare fairly exclusively to female members or to domestic servants. This division of labour is allied to historically specific concepts of gender and of women's and men's respective relations to the 'inside' and the 'outside' of the home. This division of labour shows little sign of renegotiation within the household when women enter employment, except between female kin.

The strategies by which women manage domestic work and childcare are considered in detail, particularly in relation to different family forms and to stages in the life cycle. The presence of different combinations of kin in a household or close by can be significant, but there are differences in the availability and accessibility of kin networks for women of different classes. The common finding in European studies that women's levels of employment are determined in part by life-cycle stages and particularly by child-bearing patterns (see Dex 1985: 4–5 for a summary of recent evidence) is not helpful in explaining women's employment histories in Calcutta.

In chapter five, the control and disposal of women's earnings when they enter the household are examined. Several British studies have documented the ways in which different income streams into households are 'gendered' and are thus conceptualized as different kinds of contribution, as well as the ways in which 'culture' mediates monetary resources at the level of the family (see for example J. Pahl 1980, 1983, 1984, Hunt 1980). The organization of financial resources within Calcutta households and the meanings attached to women's and men's financial contributions are explored. These are found to vary with the form in which household income is managed. Forms of management may be more or less collective and this affects the extent to which women's earnings are considered to be separate or different or earmarked for specific consumption requirements.

The degree to which women can claim any part of their earnings for themselves or for purposes which they can specify also varies greatly and is influenced by many factors, among the most significant of which are household income level, marital status and ideologies of appropriation within particular households.

In chapter six, the ideological implications of paid employment for women are considered. For many households, female employment is a phenomenon of the present generation and is being accommodated into familial age and gender hierarchies, as well as into status concerns, for the first time. These are areas of negotiation involving varying degrees of struggle at the level of interpersonal relationships and in the domain of public discussion.

Employment, particularly if it is outside the home, also opens up the possibility of other forms of solidarity and work-centred activity. The meaning of employment for different groups of women and their relationship to the trade union movement are also discussed in this chapter.

Intra-household relations at a particular point in time thus form the main focus. However, in chapter seven, an attempt is made to situate the issues in a wider historical context through an examination of the relationship between changes in family form, the construction of female dependency and women's employment in Bengal.

## Methodology

### Personal note

My association with Calcutta began in the early 1970s when I carried out two pieces of research in rural Bihar. Calcutta was at first the transit point, to be hurried through on route to cleaner air and less obtrusive poverty. Later, it became a place of occasional but compelling escape from the stifling intimacy of village life. During the late 1970s, and influenced by the rapidly developing work on gender issues taking place at Sussex, a research project on women and employment in India began to be conceived but remained to be located. The choice of Calcutta was fashioned, as one suspects with most anthropological locations, out of a combination of personal and intellectual motives. As I wanted a major metropolitan city, I considered working in Bombay but felt handicapped by my lack of knowledge of the very different conditions of western India. Bengali, which I had grown accustomed to hearing in the towns of the eastern region, seemed a less obdurate language into which to move. Finally, Calcutta has certain socio-economic features which make it intrinsically interesting as a site for this kind of investigation. However, the personal element is there – part of the methodology yet eluding its language.

*General Methodological Considerations*

Urban fieldwork methods in anthropology have been, traditionally, fairly primitive. This is because of a tendency in the discipline to compound concrete differences between urban and rural research locations with the form in which a research problem is constructed. As a consequence, the formulation of methodologies appropriate to a particular theoretical objective collapses into the practical constraints of the urban context. This is not to deny that practical constraints affect what is methodologically achievable but to point out that they are not one and the same thing. This elision of the practical with the theoretical has arisen out of the ambiguous status of locality in anthropology. In studies of 'small-scale' societies locality provides, usually quite explicitly, the primary field within which sociologically significant ties are formed and played out (cf. Gluckman 1962 on the concept of multiplexity). The one-person participant observer appears appropriate and adequate to the methodological task.

In such contexts, the empirical and theoretical universes could then be argued to coincide. In more 'complex' arenas (not necessarily only urban ones) this coincidence is broken and the field of visible social relationships based on a locality, whether village, neighbourhood or workplace, cannot provide an adequate basis for a sociological account of, for instance, the effects of state policies on the family or the structure of class in capitalist societies. Urban anthropology, however, remains dominated by a reluctance to disengage the method of participant observation from its embeddedness in locality. Certainly, in urban India, the problem of theoretical boundedness has generally been resolved in morphological terms. Neighbourhoods, caste associations, factories, etc. have been the main units of analysis.

In the urban context, then, this mode of resolution derives from the conflation of a historical preoccupation in anthropology with locality *per se* and the practical difficulties of fieldwork with a scattered set of informants. The status of locality is not, however, self-evident but is itself part of the research agenda. The spatial distance between the subjects of the research changes the content of participant observation but does not invalidate the methodology.

It was clear, from the outset, that a study of the impact of women's employment on households with different socio-economic characteristics could not be carried out on a neighbourhood or workplace basis. What was required was a methodology which could combine quantitative and qualitative data collection and approach some degree of representativeness in terms of the socio-economic profile of the city itself. The case study method, on its own, would not be adequate. It was necessary to specify the universe of the study in sociological rather than simply in locality terms.

## How the Research was Conducted

A three-month visit to Calcutta in early 1979 provided an invaluable opportunity to get to know the city and formulate a more precise research plan. During this initial visit, contacts were made with places of work known to be employing women and with official agencies. At this time, efforts were concentrated on understanding the employment situation for women in Calcutta rather than in researching the social characteristics of employed women (see Standing 1979). The empirical research on which this book is based was carried out between September 1981 and December 1982, but with a four-month break between January and April 1982 as a result of illness. Two further short visits in 1984 and 1985 provided opportunities to check on previous data and take up issues neglected earlier. The study, from 1981 onwards was carried out on a collaborative basis with Bela Bandyopadhyaya, a local Bengali researcher and activist whose intimate knowledge of Calcutta informs the entire research strategy.

The decision to work at household level and to attempt some form of sampling in terms of income and class criteria as well as marital and life-cycle status posed methodological problems which had remained unresolved until I returned to Calcutta in 1981. Researchers working in both rural and urban India are, however, very fortunate in that there is an extremely large statistical data base, albeit of varying quality and level of aggregation. Thanks to the generosity of the Indian Statistical Institute, Calcutta, access was obtained to their 1976 urban poverty survey (henceforth, the 1976 Calcutta Poverty Survey) of the municipal area covered by the Calcutta Corporation and permission given to use it to locate appropriate households.

The objective of this survey was to examine the poverty profile of the city, taking households as basic units and covering social background, family structure, migration and occupational histories, education, health and material conditions. The survey utilized a random sampling frame devised by the National Sample Survey Organisation to cover all urban blocks of the Corporation area. It then combined random and stratified techniques to produce two subsamples, one of households with fixed residential addresses and one of pavement dwellers. The survey was weighted towards lower income households but did not exclude high-income households.[4] This survey yielded a total of 2503 detailed household schedules divided more or less equally between the two subsamples.[5]

All the schedules of households with fixed residential addresses were read and details of all households in which an employed woman was reported were transcribed. A number of exclusions were first made. Pavement dwellers were left out on the grounds that it would be almost impossible to trace non-residential households after a period of five years. Non-Bengalis were excluded because the aim was to look particularly at the cultural context of employed women and this context needed to be standardized for different categories of women. Female domestic servants were also left out except where they had other kinds of employment. It was felt that both the form of employment and the very large numbers of women involved in domestic service from all communities in Calcutta merited a separate study. This procedure yielded a total of 105 households, all of which were revisited to ascertain whether they were still in existence, still had employed female members and would agree to be interviewed. This process was extremely time consuming – many visits often had to be made to each address – however, 59 households were located unchanged and available, 2 more were in areas of recent slum clearance and could not be traced and the remainder had moved elsewhere. These households were then replaced by ones with matching characteristics from the same locality.[6]

Some liberties were taken subsequently with the original sample when it was found that it contained no Bengali Muslim households with employed women, although there were known to be Muslim women concentrated in certain occupations, and no women telephone operators (a comparatively large occupational category in Calcutta). Existing contacts were used to locate these groups. The completed sample size was 114 households, many of which contained more than one employed woman. A few contained active job seekers or unpaid family workers and these were included in the final sample and counted as 'employed'.

A further purposive sample of ten households with only non-employed women was drawn from personal contacts to provide some point of comparison on certain issues. A 10% sample of husbands of respondents in the main sample was also taken up for more extensive, separate interviewing. Many additional neighbours, relatives and friends also formed part of the informal universe of informants. Nirmala Banerjee's pioneering work on a representative sample of women informal-sector workers in Calcutta (1985a) and for which Bela Bandyopadhyaya had carried out the field interviews, provided a further important point of reference.

After initial visits had been completed, a schedule and questionnaire was drawn up, piloted and finalized with the assistance of the two part-time interviewers. This forms the primary data source on all the households and covers a large number of topics from a demographic profile of all household members to qualitative explorations of the questions informing the research. This involved an extensive amount of structured and semi-structured interviewing over a series of visits. Further visits were also made to talk informally with women and other household members. Detailed life histories were gathered from many of the women along with additional written material on household budgets and time use. Almost all interviews and discussions took place in Bengali.

The sample size is smaller than was originally intended. It was at this level that the practical constraints of Calcutta life intervened. Transport and communication systems in Calcutta are perhaps the most over-loaded and chaotic of any city in India. Although the surface area of the city is fairly compact, movement through its streets is arduous and time consuming. This greatly affects the availability of household members to be interviewed as employed members spend long hours travelling to and from work and are often far too tired to be importuned at the end of a working day. During the rainy season, movement is severely curtailed by the flooding of the city's streets in heavy storms and during the period of the fieldwork, there were severe power cuts which caused difficulties with evening interviewing. Plans to increase the sample were thus abandoned.

Beyond the household level, interviews were conducted with trade unionists, women activists, employers and some government agencies. State and central government statistical sources were examined and contemporary newspapers and magazines read. Two small literary studies, one of late nineteenth- and early twentieth-century women's popular journals, and one of representations of femininity in twentieth-century Bengali novels, were undertaken by Bengali researchers. Secondary historical sources in Calcutta and in the India Office Library in London were explored to throw light on changes in women's patterns of employment in Bengal.

This methodology has advantages and limitations. Its advantages lie in a greater degree of confidence about its generalizability and about the nature of the relationship between individual experiences and the wider context. Its limitations are in its reliance on the spoken interview as the main medium of participant observation and its lack of longitudinal depth. It was simply not possible, in a situation of chronic housing and space scarcity, to contemplate living with an informant's family, as anthropologists have been wont to do. At the same time, and as Sharma points out (1986: 33–4), living in the same urban environment brings a researcher face to face with many of the same kinds of problems which afflict the subjects of the research. The absence of time series data is one which affects most sociological studies. Its remedy requires a proper recognition of the importance of re-studies on a standardized basis.

## The city of Calcutta[7]

Calcutta is the capital of the State of West Bengal[8] and the one time imperial capital of British India. There is controversy about when it was founded but it grew largely to serve the British East India Company's trading and commercial interests as these developed from the late seventeenth century. Calcutta's subsequent history and changing fortunes are thus intricately bound up with the historical development of imperialism in South Asia. Calcutta's location near the eastern seaboard of India and on the left bank of the Ganges (Hooghly) River, which flows down into the Bay of Bengal, was responsible for its growth as a major port and commercial centre. Industrial development began in the second half of the nineteenth century and Calcutta became the largest centre of industry, trade and commerce in India, its share of employment and its concentration of private capital outrivalling that of Bombay until into the post-independence period.

Estimates of the current size of Calcutta's population depend upon whether contiguous urban settlement is included and whether temporary migrants, daily or seasonal, are counted. The Calcutta Metropolitan District (CMD) which includes the twin city of Howrah and all contiguous urban development stretching along both banks of the river, has a population of more than nine million. The city of Calcutta itself – the central area administered under the Calcutta Corporation and the subject of this book – has a population of over three million.[9] Calcutta's population is swollen by seasonal migrant labour from the villages of West Bengal after the harvesting season; and by day, thousands of commuters pour into the city's two main railway stations on their way to offices or to hawk produce on the city's streets.

As the only major city in eastern India, Calcutta has traditionally acted as a magnet, drawing labour not only from other districts of West Bengal but also from the surrounding states. Its turn-of-the-century population of rural Bengali settlers was supplemented subsequently by waves of migrants from Orissa, Bihar and the pre-independence United Provinces. In the early twentieth century, Rajasthani traders from western India ('Marwaris') moved into the city in substantial numbers. More recently, there have been major influxes of refugees displaced from East Bengal at partition in 1947 and in subsequent years, as well as some inflow from the 1971 war, which created independent Bangladesh out of the erstwhile eastern wing of Pakistan. Calcutta has acted as a source of employment and sanctuary for many kinds of migrant.

Calcutta's industrial base is in the older manufacturing industries of jute, engineering, textiles, food processing and chemicals, most of which were established during the days of the British East India Company. The early demand for factory labour drew migrants first from the surrounding rural areas and later from the other eastern provinces. The majority of this labour was male and Calcutta has been, historically, a city of single male migrants who generally retained some base in the rural areas and who, in the early stages of industrialization, rarely brought families to the city. This pattern of single male migration has persisted to the present day for some groups of migrants, particularly labourers from the Hindi-speaking states of Bihar and Uttar Pradesh.

This history of male migration has always been reflected in the sex ratio of Calcutta's population. In 1921, the ratio for the municipal area was 487 females to 1000 males (*Census of India 1921* Government of India 1923). The most recent census figures show a ratio of 712: 1000 (*Census of India 1981*, Government of India 1983), giving Calcutta the lowest ratio of females to males of any major Indian city. The rate of migration into Calcutta has, however, been falling since 1951, and more sharply since 1961, reflecting the saturation of employment and living space in this extremely populous city. It is likely that the sex ratio will gradually even out.

Migrants to Calcutta have come from diverse economic and cultural backgrounds and have often brought with them distinctive skills and specializations which produced a degree of congruence between occupation and caste or cultural background. Unskilled labour, initially in industry and later in public sector services has been drawn largely from the Hindi-speaking states but also, in some specific tasks, from migrants from Orissa, bordering West Bengal to the south. Where Bengalis have been involved in factory labour they have been more likely to be skilled labour.[10]

The great movement of Bengalis from rural Bengal into Calcutta from the late nineteenth century was a movement particularly of middle-class and landed elites into opportunities created by the expansion of the imperial administration and into education in the newly opened schools and colleges. Leaving their families on their rural estates in the early years, this group gradually brought their dependants to Calcutta, creating a settled bourgeoisie and petit bourgeoisie rooted in the city (cf. McGuire 1983).

While Bengalis dominated the 'white-collar' services and the professions, the Rajasthani Marwaris increasingly took over trade and commerce and are, today, a major economic force in the Calcutta economy, having capitalized on their traditional strengths as a close-knit mercantile and money-lending community (Timberg 1978).

Other minorities – Armenians, Jews, Anglo-Indians and Chinese – have all occupied particular socio-economic niches in the city and have maintained distinct cultural and linguistic traditions. Calcutta is, simultaneously, a very Bengali city and a meeting point of populations from many different regions and cultural backgrounds.

In 1912, the British moved the capital of British India to its present site of New Delhi, some 6000 miles across the subcontinent. The growing nationalist struggle in Bengal and the successful political agitation for the reversal of the first partition of Bengal carried out by the Viceroy, Lord Curzon, in 1905 lay behind the decision to abandon Calcutta. The consequences of this for Calcutta were far reaching as capital and employment began to leave the city. At the same time, Calcutta's status as the leading industrial and commercial city of India began slowly to be challenged by the growth of other centres such as Greater Bombay and, more recently, smaller cities such as Ahmedabad in the state of Gujarat.

Since independence, public and private investment in the city have stagnated and there has probably been some additional flight of capital during periods of political instability in West Bengal, notably in the late 1960s and early 1970s when mass political mobilization, particularly of urban workers, by the left parties frightened both capital and the Congress Government at the centre. This caused the suspension of the elected State Government and the imposition of President's Rule in West Bengal from 1967 to 1969 and again from 1970 to 1971. The current Left Front Government, which has been elected continuously since 1977, has brought political stability but continues to be viewed with suspicion by the centre.

In 1947, the departing British left the legacy of a colonial metropolitan economy already in decline and heavily dependent on exports with a falling or uncertain demand (such as jute) and on primary commodities (such as tea). Rates of investment were already low and falling and the urban economy was parasitical upon a technologically backward, low-productivity agricultural sector. Silting of the Hooghly has also severely affected the volume of goods handled by the Calcutta Port. Regional development policies initiated by the centre have further exacerbated Calcutta's industrial decline (A.N.Bose 1978: 126).

Between 1963 and 1975, West Bengal's share of all-India production declined by more than 50% during a period in which India's total volume of industrial production had increased by more than 34% (ibid: 132–3). The continual pressure on Calcutta to absorb large numbers of displaced and often impoverished refugees and migrants has strained the city's already declining capacities to breaking point and caused a huge crisis of unemployment among all sections of the population.

That Calcutta is a city in severe crisis is evident to the most casual visitor. Its air of rampant decay, of gross overcrowding and the all-too-painful visibleness of its poor, living on pavements or in huts of patched together cardboard, tin or whatever temporary materials are to hand, present an extreme shock to the senses which exposure to no other Indian city adequately prepares for. Indeed, for most people, Calcutta is summed up in images of abject poverty and Mother Theresa. Like all images, however, it is a representation constructed out of the imperatives of those who observe - the journalists and film makers, searchers after the 'real' India. Calcutta is shocking in its visible celebration of poverty. It is also a city of extraordinary tolerance. Unlike New Delhi and increasingly Bombay, the poor have not been 'tidied out' of the city, their precarious livelihoods finally destroyed by bureaucratic zeal for empty pavements.

Another image of Calcutta jostles with its poverty. Since the nineteenth century, Calcutta has been a major educational, cultural and political heartland. Its output of poets, novelists, film makers, scientists and political activists has been prodigious, its population highly literate, creative and politically aware. Calcutta is simultaneusly shocking and exciting. The one sentiment which it does not generate is that of indifference.

Chapter two

# Employed women

The social and economic background

## Introduction

Women arrive in the Calcutta labour force through a variety of different circumstances and in response to a range of needs which are partly defined by the class position of the family and partly by other social and cultural parameters. The social geography of Calcutta itself reveals some of these parameters. The older, Bengali-settled areas of north and central Calcutta are dominated by West Bengal-originated families, middle class in aspiration if often low in income. On the south-eastern fringes of the city well-defined colonies house many of Calcutta's refugee households. The term 'refugee' generally refers only to those displaced Hindus of East Bengal origin who fled to West Bengal during the violence of the years surrounding the partition of India and Pakistan in 1947. They have tended to form a well-defined social entity in the life of Calcutta.

Dotted interstitially throughout the city, but also concentrated in the very low-lying eastern areas are the most proletarian sections of the population, living in slum or bustee settlements and engaged particularly in the sweated industries and proliferating 'unorganized sector' activities redolent of so many Third World cities.[1] These divisions give rise to somewhat distinctive patterns of labour-market participation and cultures of involvement in waged work.

Women of West Bengal middle-class origins are least likely to be in waged employment and they display the most restricted occupational profile. Of the forty-five employed women living in the thirty-two households which broadly fell into this social category, more than one-third were schoolteachers and a further eight gave private tuition in their homes. A few were professional women in medicine, law and college lecturing. The remainder were mostly clerical workers in public sector undertakings. Only two women, both young, had stepped outside these customary spheres, one to become a bookbinder and the other an actress in a touring company. The latter had initially encountered fierce opposition from her relatives.

Women of this class and cultural background thus face ideological restrictions on the range of employment which they may seek. Their preponderance in what were, traditionally, segregated and thus 'respectable' occupations such as teaching and medicine is a reminder that occupational profiles have a history and a cultural location in specific constructions of 'suitable work' for women. Women of this background were discouraged, traditionally, from entering wage employment. They were expected to be supported by their families and the fact that a woman should need to seek employment did not reflect well upon the status of the family. Something of an ideological legacy remains, in that these families were the most likely to play down or even deny the extent of their dependence on a daughter's or a wife's wage.

The situation in most refugee families is very different. Here, women are frequently under pressure to enter employment, taking whatever job they can find, in order to supplement or sustain the family income. This is reflected in much higher rates of employment among women. Of the 114 households in the sample, fifty-four are refugee in origin and this compares with a proportion of only 15% of refugee households in the general Calcutta population. The bulk of the refugees belonged to the landowning, professional and urban-based middle classes in the then East Bengal.[2] At partition, many lost their property and suffered disruption or termination of education. One generation later, the effects are still apparent and for many it has brought a broader outlook on the question of women's employment. Refugee-originated women have taken employment in a wide range of unorganized sector jobs such as small-scale factory assembly work, food processing and tailoring. Many of the family-imposed restrictions on women entering waged work and on the kinds of employment they may take up have fallen away.

In poor proletarian households there is more likely to be a tradition of female employment, primarily in domestic service and in either home-based, subcontracted piecework for local industries or in petty commodity production and trading. However, even here, the majority of the older women in the sample were first-generation urban workers, although the mothers of a few had been agricultural labourers prior to moving to Calcutta. All the Muslim households in the sample fell into the category of very poor or poor households and despite their poverty, women in these households experienced restrictions on their movement in public which prevented some of them from seeking employment outside their homes.

The concept of class in Calcutta has to be understood in relation to the political economy of the colonial city and the particular cultural

configurations of Bengali society. This had its own hierarchies of social
ranking which were both absorbed and reconstituted by the economic
transformation of Bengal in the nineteenth and twentieth centuries. The
Bengali-dominated middle class arose not from the development of an
industrial bourgeoisie but from the demands of imperial capital for
a service class of bureaucrats and professionals. It is against this
background that the historically strong significance of secondary and
higher education for men, particularly in English medium, must be
assessed.

Members of this class were drawn from a broad status group, known
in Bengali as the *bhadralok* (literally, 'respectable' people). As both
McGuire (1983) and Chakrabarty (1985) point out, the term *bhadralok*
is not a class designation but a cultural term which subsumes historically
specific classes originating in the landed aristocracy and in the category
of small merchants, landowners and shopkeepers. The *bhadralok* have
tended to be almost exclusively Hindu, the costs of a 'western' education having been beyond the means of the predominantly poor rural
Muslim masses. The *bhadralok* are thus a broad cultural coalition of
bourgeois and petit bourgeois class interests which have had considerable significance in the formation and transmission of more
encompassing ideologies of status and respectability, notably in the
context of gender relations.

## Household and family: the composition of co-residential units

With the exception of eight women living in residential quarters who
have been designated as separate households, all the women live in
family-based households, the majority of which contain at least one
married couple or once married member. Households vary in size from
one to fourteen members, with a mean of 5.4 persons. Table 2.1
summarizes household composition at the time of the study. The classification employed is unorthodox by sociological standards and some
explanation for its use is necessary. What is attempted here is a description of co-residential kinship combinations which is not intended as an
alternative typology to ones already employed in the Indian literature
(e.g. Desai 1956, Gore 1968, Kapoor 1965, Kolenda 1968) but as a way
of capturing the variation in co-residence patterns without imposing too
heavy a straitjacket of Eurocentric sociological terms. Thus, the terms
'nuclear' and 'extended' have been avoided because they have no real
equivalents in the ways in which respondents themselves describe
family forms.

*Table 2.1* Classification of household composition

| (1) | Single units (parent/parents + children) | 58 |
|-----|------------------------------------------|-----|
| (2) | Single unit + husband's relative | 10 |
| (3) | Single unit + wife's relative | 5 |
| (4) | Single unit + husband's/wife's relative | 1 |
| (5) | Joint | 12 |
| (6) | Other parent/married/unmarried children combinations | 9 |
| (7) | Single units in joint house structure | 3 |
| (8) | Fragmented joint (through death of spouse(s)) | 3 |
| (9) | Sibling based | 5 |
| (10) | Single person | 8 |
| *Total* | | 114 |

The term 'joint', on the other hand, is used here in a way which corresponds to local meanings, and the overarching distinction between 'single' and 'complex' units conveys something of the locally felt difference between households centred on a conjugal pair and more diverse combinations of kin.

Households in which at least two complete married couples are living and related through the male line either laterally (brothers) or lineally (father–son) are described as joint, the distinction between single and joint families generally being drawn on this basis. However, there is some contextual ambiguity in the term 'joint'. It may be used to refer to complex combinations of kin, such as those described as 'fragmented joint', or to other three-generational combinations where a mother-in-law is present.[3]

What is at issue is the set of meanings accorded to co-resident combinations, not the mere presence of certain types of relationship. In this case, the presence of more than one married couple is a significant marker of jointness as it implies particular forms of authority relationship and intra-household resource distribution which, for many respondents, both distinguishes the joint family and creates the tensions leading to its fragmentation.

Sibling-based households are distinguished on the basis that they are formed predominantly around a group of unmarried siblings or sibling-linked relationships. They tend to be exclusively female in composition and to consist of women who have passed the age of likely marriageability and who have been able to inherit or remain in the parental home. Single-person households consist entirely of women, unmarried and widowed, who live in residential quarters.

In any classification of family-based households, it is necessary to take into account the developmental cycle of the household, the cultural principles which underlie different patterns of co-residence and the diverse set of factors, including class differences which interact with developmental and cultural logic to produce real arrangements of people at given moments.

Thus, although slightly over half of the households in the sample (described as 'single units') are currently two generations only, many have been three-generational in the past and may be so in the future. Few married women set up home separately from their in-laws in the beginning but couples may move away subsequently if they are able to find and afford rented accommodation.

This classification is thus a statement both of current household arrangements and of the possible transformations through which co-residential groups may pass. It also demonstrates a range of variations which diverge from developmental cycle and cultural expectations.

The dominant cultural pattern is for households to form around one or more married males. At marriage, sons are expected to stay with parents, daughters to move to their husband's home. Older widows generally remain within their households of marriage while younger widows sometimes return to their father's households. Unmarried women are expected to remain with their fathers or brothers. Married brothers may or may not stay together depending on such factors as house space, occupation or family tensions.

However, many family-based households do not conform to these cultural principles. In some cases, married daughters reside with their own parents, or else elderly mothers have moved in with married daughters. In others, single units consist of widows and daughters where the daughter(s) have become the sole economic support either in the absence of a male wage earner or when married brothers set up separate conjugal households. Such households should not be treated as deviations from a norm but understood in the context of wider social and economic processes which interact with cultural expectations and developmental cycle processes to produce a variety of possible responses. Housing shortages, the changing construction of kinship dependencies and accompanying ideas about preferred styles of living all play a part.

Women's participation in waged employment is part of these wider interactive processes and chapter seven explores whether women's employment has consequences for family formation. Different patterns of household composition also have varying consequences for employed women, particularly in relation to unwaged work within the household.

**Household incomes, household composition and standard of living**

The assignment of a poverty line within populations is always a conten-
tious exercise, raising difficulties which are both methodological (How
is poverty best measured – by income levels, food intake, etc.? What
should be the unit of measurement – the household, the individual?) and
conceptual (How is poverty to be understood?)[4] This latter problem is
particularly acute in the context of Calcutta where the quality of life for
very many more people than are officially accounted poor, is nonetheless low. Poor and overcrowded housing conditions, environmental
pollution and inadequate transportation affect most of Calcutta's
population in some way, but this is not captured in standard poverty
measurements.

However, arbitrary as such measurements often appear, it is essential
to have some way of dividing up a sample universe and in this study
total household money income has been used to give an approximate
sense of living standards. In the Calcutta context, households rely overwhelmingly or solely on wages for their reproduction. A few have
income from property or have real estate elsewhere in the city or state,
but rent is not a major source of income for those with property as urban
rents are controlled and vacant land is often illegally settled and difficult
to regain. Wage income is thus generally the household's total income.
The use of household income as a measurement does not, of course,
imply that it is shared equally among members.

Table 2.2 provides a breakdown of household income levels by units
of Rs 500. In its August 1983 issue, the magazine *India Today*
calculated that, at current prices a Calcutta household of five persons
would need to spend Rs 465 per month on main food items to achieve a
good standard of diet exclusive of meat and fish consumption (both of
which are eaten in Bengal). As this is exclusive of all other expenditure,
all households with incomes of Rs 500 and below have been categorized
as very poor by urban standards. Households with incomes between Rs
501 and 1000 are considered poor, and households in the range Rs 1001
to 2000 are not, by official standards, in poverty but may be struggling
very hard to maintain a lower-middle-class lifestyle. By Calcutta
standards, households with incomes of more than Rs 2000 must be
ranked as prosperous, and only 1% of the Greater Calcutta population
lives in households with incomes in excess of Rs 3000.

*Table 2.2* Gross monthly household incomes in rupees

| 500 or less | 501–1000 | 1001–2000 | 2001–3000 | 3001+ | Total |
|---|---|---|---|---|---|
| 33 | 25 | 15 | 19 | 22 | 114 |

*Note:* In 1982, Rs 14 = £1 (approximately)

In terms of per capita income, the sample may be compared with the all-India findings of the Indian Economic Intelligence Service (1984), which assessed the urban poverty line at 1977–8 prices as below Rs 75 per capita per month and the proportion of the urban population below this line at 38%. Adjusting for inflation, the comparable urban India poverty line for 1982 would be a per capita income of Rs 104 per month. Thirty-nine households in the sample have per capita incomes below this level as opposed to thirty-three households in the category of below Rs 500 per month. In 1982, the Calcutta Metropolitan Development Authority calculated that the average per capita annual income in the Metropolitan District was Rs 1900, but the average in the city itself (which is the basis for this sample) was much higher, at Rs 3000.[5]

Although these figures are fairly crude and aggregative, they tend to suggest that poor households are not greatly underrepresented in proportion to their representation in the general urban population (estimated at 38%, in 1977–8, cf. Economic Intelligence Service 1984). However, the Calcutta poverty survey on which this sample is based, found that rates of employment for women were significantly higher among the poorest household expenditure groups. The lack of a bias towards low-income households reflects the exclusion from the sample of maidservants and of non-Bengali groups, some of which are poorer on average than the resident Bengali population.

There is a distinct bias at the other end of the income range towards richer households in that as many as twenty-two are in the income categories of Rs 3001 and upwards. This bias reflects an important feature of women's employment – namely its greater preponderance at the highest as well as the lowest income levels. These twenty-two households are middle class, mainly professional households containing at least two high earners, one of whom is a woman.

The effects of the addition of one or more women's earnings to the household can be seen in Table 2.3. If female earnings are discounted, the number of households which would be in severe poverty would nearly double and the number in the very high-income groups would drop to negligible proportions.

In income terms, therefore, women's employment affects most markedly the living standards of households at the top and bottom of the income range. In the highest income groups, it enables some households to achieve an upper-middle-class lifestyle, while in the lowest, it prevents complete immiseration.

Average household size shows a slight tendency to increase with income levels, from 4.7 members in households of Rs 500 and below to 5.4 in households with incomes over Rs 3000. This increase does not, however, correlate with a greater tendency to jointness or complexity.

The majority of households depend on at least two or three earners, and households with multiple earners are somewhat more common in the highest and lowest income groups. Households dependent upon one female earner are all in the poorest income groups.

*Table 2.3* Total household income/household income net of women's incomes

| Monthly income | No. of households (less those with non-contributing women and single-person households) | | | |
|---|---|---|---|---|
| (Rupees) | Gross income | % | Income net of women's incomes | % |
| 200 and below | 2 | | 23 | |
| 201–400 | 12 | 21 | 13 | 46 |
| 401–500 | 7 | | 10 | |
| 501–750 | 14 | 24 | 10 | 18 |
| 751–1000 | 10 | | 8 | |
| 1001–1500 | 9 | 16 | 9 | 21 |
| 1501–2000 | 7 | | 12 | |
| 2001–2500 | 11 | 17 | 9 | 14 |
| 2501–3000 | 6 | | 5 | |
| 3001–4000 | 16 | | – | |
| 4001–5000 | 4 | 22 | 1 | 1 |
| 5001–6000 | 2 | | – | |

Income level and class position do not necessarily coincide, and this means, effectively, that two measures of living standard are employed in this study; one based on income and the other on a class-derived concept of needs and wants. In the higher income categories the two do tend to coincide – there are no proletarian households with incomes above Rs 2000 and very few with incomes over Rs 1000. However, there are many income-poor households which are self-described as 'middle class' or 'lower middle class' (*maddhyabitta sreni*), and only the Muslim households described themselves as belonging to the 'poor class'. These self-descriptions are rooted in the historical legacy of class formation in Bengal. Despite their apparent divergence from contemporary realities, they act as a powerful cultural mediator of behaviour and expectation.

The condition of the housing stock in Calcutta is generally very bad, particularly in the older central and northern neighbourhoods and in the lower lying eastern settlements, which are prone to monsoon flooding. Because of the rather peculiar topography of the city, lying between the Ganges (Hooghly) River on the western side and salt marshes on the eastern fringes, Calcutta lacks space to expand except in an attenuated northerly and southerly direction. Its population is squeezed into an area with a population density more than double that of New Delhi, the Indian capital. A detailed account of the housing conditions and assets of households in the sample can be found in Standing (1985a) and a few points only will be made here.

The majority of low-income households live in slum settlements ('bustees') in one-room dwellings usually with some space such as a verandah or shared courtyard where food is cooked. Toilet and washing facilities are present but are generally shared by several households. Overcrowding is a serious problem which persists well into the higher income groups and reflects the city's chronic housing shortage. Major improvements in access to running water and bathing facilities and in general housing condition appear only in households having a gross income exceeding Rs 1000 per month.

The proportion of house ownership increases with income but falls off sharply in the highest income households, resulting in a low overall owner-occupancy rate (24% compared with an all-India urban average of 47%). This is explained by certain features of the housing and rental market in Calcutta. A number of the highest income households live in rented accommodation while owning property elsewhere in the city from which rent is derived. Rent controls, security of tenancy and shortage of building land also dispose households to remain in rented property, and higher income households have been able to secure the better housing at comparatively low rents and at almost the lowest percentage cost in relation to their incomes.

Only thirty-eight households have gas connections for cooking. The majority of the poor use a combination of kerosene stoves and coal, and a few use only coal, or cowdung shaped and dried into cakes, which are the least efficient methods of all. Seven households are effectively assetless in that they possess only a string bed, some bedding and clothes and a few cooking pots. The consumption profile otherwise shows that the most common items owned by the poor are radios, followed by clocks or watches.

Only a quarter of households in the Rs 501–1000 group own a pressure cooker. Fridges are rare in all but the top two income groups, and food mixers, which would relieve the drudgery of much cooking, are most uncommon. The poor material condition of much of the housing and the lack of time and work-saving devices have major implications for women's domestic workloads.

Table 2.4 Place of birth, age and marital status

(a) Place of birth and family origin

| 1 Calcutta-born and originated | 2 East Bengal-born, refugee-originated | 3 Calcutta-born, refugee-originated | 4 Born elsewhere, refugee-originated | 5 East Bengal-born, non-refugee | 6 Calcutta-born, family from elsewhere | 7 Born and originated other districts of W. Bengal | 8 Born other states of India, origin-ated Bengal |
|---|---|---|---|---|---|---|---|
| 73 | 36 | 38 | 1 | 3 | 4 | 13 | 3 |

(b) Age profile of all women in the sample

| 14 and under (%) | 15–24 (%) | 25–34 (%) | 35–44 (%) | 45–54 (%) | 55–64 (%) | 65+ (%) |
|---|---|---|---|---|---|---|
| 6 (3.5) | 39 (22.8) | 39 (22.8) | 44 (25.7) | 33 (19.3) | 10 (5.8) | –(–) |

(c) Marital status of all women

| Single (%) | Married (%) | Widowed (%) | Separated/divorced (%) | Total |
|---|---|---|---|---|
| 81 (47.0) | 64 (37.4) | 22 (12.9) | 4 (2.3) | 171 |

**Demographic and social characteristics of employed women**

It can be seen from Table 2.4(a) that the sample is composed not of migrants of relatively recent urban origin who have come to Calcutta looking for employment, but of a population which has a fairly long history of urban settlement and dependence on the wage sector.

The majority of the women in the sample come either from Calcutta-originated families and were themselves born in the city, or are from refugee-originated families. These latter women were born in East Bengal before or shortly after Partition, or in Calcutta after their families had moved to India. There is only one case of a proletarian household moving to Calcutta within the last generation. This is a Muslim household which, unusually, moved into Calcutta from a neighbouring district during the pre-partition riots of 1946 and remained in the city rather than moving to the newly created East Pakistan.

Table 2.4(b) and (c) gives information on age and marital status. There are no currently married women under the age of twenty, but one 17-year-old was married and living apart from her husband at her parents' home. Rates of separation and divorce are low, as in India generally, but may be underestimated because of the social opprobrium attached to divorce.

*Table 2.5* Numbers of children by income group

| Nos of children | <500 | 501–1000 | 1001–2000 | 2001–3000 | 3001+ | Total |
|---|---|---|---|---|---|---|
| 1 | 1 | 6 | 2 | 10 | 9 | 28 |
| 2 | 6 | 1 | 3 | 4 | 8 | 22 |
| 3 | 3 | 1 | 2 | – | – | 6 |
| 4 | 4 | 4 | 2 | – | – | 10 |
| 5 | 4 | 3 | 1 | – | 1 | 9 |
| 6 | – | 1 | 2 | – | – | 3 |
| 7 and over | 1 | 2 | – | – | – | 3 |
| Average for each group | 3.4 | 3.4 | 3.25 | 1.3 | 1.7 | 81 |

Eighty of the women, or just under half, had borne children. Table 2.5 shows the numbers of living children of women in different income groups. Average fertility levels fall by half in the highest income groups, reflecting the different costs and benefits of children across the different classes. For proletarian families children provide an important source of family labour. In middle-class families, children are a 'cost' on parents in respect of their education and welfare, and one-child families have become common.

*Table 2.6* Educational level of all the women

| | 1 Illiterate | 2 Can read | 3 Can read/write | 4 Up to primary level | 5 Up to middle level | 6 Up to secondary level | 7 Graduate and above | Total |
|---|---|---|---|---|---|---|---|---|
| Number | 23 | 2 | 18 | 17 | 21 | 20 | 70 | 171 |
| Percentage | 13.4 | 1.7 | 10.5 | 9.9 | 12.3 | 11.7 | 40.3 | 100 |
| ISI Survey% 1976 (all females in labour force) | 49.27 | 8.76 | | 4.37 | 9.22 | 9.98 | 17.66 | 100 |
| ISI Survey % (general female population) | 38.85 | 17.18 | | 11.08 | 17.18 | 9.68 | 5.22 | 100 |

Table 2.7 Educational level of women by household income group

| Income group | 1 Illiterate | 2 Can read | 3 Can read/write | 4 Up to primary level | 5 Up to middle level | 6 Up to secondary level | 7 Graduate level |
|---|---|---|---|---|---|---|---|
| 500 | 17 | 1 | 6 | 11 | 6 | 3 | 4 |
| 501–1000 | 6 | 1 | 7 | 4 | 14 | 6 | 3 |
| 1001–2000 | – | – | 5 | 2 | 1 | 7 | 13 |
| 2001–3000 | – | – | – | – | – | 1 | 21 |
| 3001+ | – | – | – | – | – | 3 | 29 |

It can be seen from Table 2.6 that the women in the sample are, on average, more educated than the female populations sampled in the 1976 Calcutta Poverty Survey (which includes non-Bengali women). In particular, the current sample has a very high proportion of graduates and a far lower proportion of illiterate women. This reflects the sampling biases noted in the methodology. Table 2.7 shows some relationship between illiteracy and poverty in that all the illiterate women are poor. But by no means all poor women are illiterate and the households of a number of educated women are in some degree of poverty. These households are largely female-supported, and their poverty reflects the relative disadvantages of all women in the labour market, whether educated or not.

When the completed educational levels of employed women are compared with other members of their households, some interesting findings emerge. Three sets of comparisons were made: wives with husbands, unmarried sisters with brothers (employed or unemployed) and girls and women with still-living mothers or mothers-in-law. The matched sample of spouses showed very little overall difference in educational qualifications, although husbands did have on average very slightly more years of education than wives. The average for both was somewhere between middle and secondary level, with younger couples more likely both to be graduates. Graduate wives were married to graduate husbands except in two cases where the wives had completed secondary education. In only one case was a wife more educated than her husband. The matched sample of siblings showed the reverse, in that sisters averaged slightly more education than brothers – midway between middle and secondary level while brothers just averaged middle level. Sisters had reached higher educational levels than brothers in fourteen households and brothers had reached higher levels than sisters in twelve. However, illiterate unmarried women were at a pronounced educational disadvantage in relation to their brothers who had averaged primary-level schooling.

There is little indication of systematic educational discrimination against female children within this sample except among young illiterate women. This may reflect simply the greater accessibility of employment for educated women, rather than being generalizable to the wider population. Yet again, the slight educational advantage of employed sisters over their brothers may also reflect the differing social evaluation of education for female and male children. Education for girls is not necessarily geared towards an expectation of employment but may form an important part of their marriage prospects (cf. Mies 1980, U. Sharma 1986).

Moitra's survey of educational attainment by gender in Calcutta schools and colleges (1983) suggests the possibility that the educational strategies of urban families may well be changing in response to a perceived need to put daughters into the labour market. It was found that in higher income groups, there was a greater enrolment among girls than among boys in all age cohorts, and in the older cohorts this was true also for households in lower income groups.

Intergenerationally, there has been a major increase in educational levels among women. The mothers and mothers-in-law of working girls and women generally received far less education, having completed on average primary schooling only. Almost half had received no formal education, and among the oldest of these women, as well as among the grandmothers of young women in the sample, there had been little possibility of formal schooling whatever their social background.[6]

## Religion and caste

Three religions, Hinduism, Islam and Christianity, are represented in the sample. The majority of the Bengali population in Calcutta is Hindu, and 106 of the sample households are Hindu. Of the remaining households, six are Muslim and two are Christian. In 1971, Muslims (including non-Bengalis) were 14% of Calcutta's population and Christians were 1.4%.[7]

The six Muslim households are, on average, poorer and have lower educational levels than the average Hindu household. Two of the households have gross incomes exceeding Rs 1000 but these incomes are achieved only by several wage earners on individually low wages living in complex family households. Educational levels are low particularly among the women. None of the eight employed Muslim women had reached primary level although five of them could read or write. This profile accords with the findings of the 1976 Calcutta Poverty Survey, in which educational and skill levels were significantly lower among Urdu speakers (who are Muslims, but mainly non-Bengali), suggesting that religion does have some correlation with socio-economic position.

The two Christian households are both middle-income professional households where the women are employed as school teachers.

Table 2.8 gives caste membership. The great majority of the Hindu households, including one based on an intercaste marriage, belong to the Brahman-Kayastha-Baidya bloc of castes which has dominated Bengali society and Calcutta in particular since the late nineteenth century. Of the three castes, Kayasthas are the most numerous and this may reflect some tendency for claims to Kayastha status to be laid by upwardly mobile sections of lower castes. Kayastha is thus a fairly elastic category (cf. *Census of India 1931*, Government of India 1933, vol. 5, part 1, chap. 12).

*Table 2.8* Caste membership of Hindu households in order of numerical
frequency

| | |
|---|---|
| Kayastha | 47 |
| Brahman | 25 |
| Baidya | 7 |
| Mahisya | 7 |
| Scheduled caste | 4 |
| Gope | 3 |
| Teli | 2 |
| Ugrakshatriya | 2 |
| Baidya/Kayastha | 1 |
| Goala | 1 |
| Malakar | 1 |
| Napit | 1 |
| Namasudra | 1 |
| Sadgope | 1 |
| Subarnabanik | 1 |
| Tanti | 1 |
| Vaishya | 1 |

Of the remainder, all except six 'scheduled caste' and Namasudra
households belong to blocs of castes which are part of the Sudra division
and therefore considered to be 'clean' castes within the traditional caste
system. Scheduled castes are those formerly 'untouchable' castes
which, together with non-Hindu 'scheduled tribes' were first identified
as a disadvantaged minority in an Act introduced by the British in 1935
as a legal basis for discriminatory action. Special legal provisions for
reservation of jobs and political office were extended in independent
India and the formal abolition of untouchability was written into the
Indian Constitution. Since 1931, scheduled caste and tribe statistics are
the only ones to be recorded in the census.

Both the caste composition of Hindu Bengal and the role of caste in
Bengali society have shown marked historical differences from other
parts of India. In particular, distinctive patterns of social mobility, the
absence of a Kshatriya (warrior) division of castes and a comparatively
weak stress on untouchability and pollution have been considered by
scholars to be the hallmarks of the caste structure in Bengal (cf.
Bhowmick 1969, Inden 1976, J. Sharma 1980, *Census of India 1931*
op.cit.).

The contemporary significance of caste in Calcutta does not lie in the
economic specializations associated with castes, which were rapidly
eroded in most cases in the urban context. The 1931 census noted the
erosion of caste occupations in all but a few artisanal and service
occupations such as barbers, launderers and sweepers. Among the high

castes, only 7% of Brahmans were engaged in providing priestly services on a full-time basis and the most common occupation of Brahmans and Kayasthas ('writers' by tradition) was in clerical and related services. This high-caste bloc which, in 1931, formed almost half the Hindu population of Calcutta, was also found across the whole range of occupations, including domestic service, trade, artisanal and labouring work. This was also true for Mahisyas, the next most numerous caste, who were traditionally cultivators (*Census of India 1931*, Government of India 1933).

Although caste ceased to be a reliable indicator of occupation early in the century it has partly shaped the occupational contours of its members. The hierarchy and functional specialization of the caste system has been absorbed, to some extent, into contemporary forms of class differentiation. The Brahmans, Kayasthas and Baidyas formed a group of highly literate castes in Bengal which became closely involved in colonial political and administrative structures. This group, which formed the nucleus of the expanding middle class in the later nineteenth century, was well placed to exploit the limited openings offered by the expansion of the imperial bureaucracy with its demand for lower level administrative personnel (cf. McGuire 1983). Attracted by these employment opportunities and by the growth in colonial educational facilities, members of these castes came to Calcutta in very large numbers in the early part of the century (*Census of India 1921*, Government of India 1923, vol.VI, part 1, chap.5).

Their preponderance in the city and their monopoly of the professions and services (a general category of employment known as 'service' in colloquial Bengali), which was only gradually challenged by upwardly mobile castes such as the Mahisyas[8] has set a particular cultural stamp upon the Bengali petit bourgeoisie, immortalized in many Bengali plays and novels.[9] Membership of these castes does not form any guarantee of 'service' employment, still less of prosperity. (See also Ul-Awwal 1982 on the crisis of educated Bengali unemployment in the earlier decades of the century.) Nor is it now necessarily an essential prerequisite for membership of the *bhadralok*. But the monopoly of service occupations and the traditions and aspirations associated with it, particularly educational attainment, remains strongly entrenched in these castes.

The education of women is no longer a high-caste monopoly. Except among Mahisya women, whose educational levels are very low, women of the non-elite castes, including the scheduled castes, have a mixed educational profile. Current class position, or perceptions of it, rather than caste *per se* determines women's educational prospects, and the correlation between caste status and wealth is weak both in the sample and in the wider Calcutta population. Banerjee's study of poor informal-sector women workers (1985a) noted that the majority of them belonged to middle-ranking castes and a substantial number to high castes.

Caste retains its greatest significance in the arena of marriage. When questioned about the significance of caste in their lives, few women considered it to have any relevance. Those who did, were women from scheduled castes who pointed out its continuing importance in the marital prospects of their children. Inter-caste marriages remain fairly uncommon, although there is evidence that Kayastha-Baidya unions have been quite acceptable historically (*Census of India 1931*, Government of India 1933). The majority of marriages continue to be arranged and it is unusual for caste boundaries to be breached. Where inter-caste marriages do occur they are most likely to be within the high-caste bloc where caste and contemporary class attributes intermesh and where caste continues to play a role in the circulation of property between families. Inter-caste marriages are more common where the couple have made their own choice.

## Why do women enter the labour force?

The disparate socio-economic backgrounds of the women in the sample suggest a probable diversity of reasons for their entry into employment in a situation where female wage workers are a minority of the adult female population and are not expected, customarily, to be wage earners.[10]

Personal histories reveal that decisions to seek employment in the first instance were sometimes a straightforward response to contingencies, such as the death of a husband or male breadwinner, and sometimes the result of interwoven economic and ideological factors. Equally, the reasons for remaining in employment may have undergone changes as circumstances have changed. An economic necessity solidifies into an active commitment to paid work.

The main parameters within which such decisions are set are those of marital status, financial circumstances and the particular ideological nexus within which women's employment is interpreted. Women gave overwhelmingly economic reasons for their decisions to take employment or to remain employed. Only three women considered their decision to be wholly non-economic, in that they felt their family situation was such that their earnings could be forgone without any hardship to the household or to themselves.

However, the meaning of 'economic necessity' varies with the class and income position of the household. Needs are class defined and the entry into, or presence, particularly of married women in employment is important to the reproduction of middle-class living standards. As one woman, a graduate librarian in her 40s and married with two children and a husband earning over Rs 2000 per month, said, 'It is impossible now to maintain a family with a single earning member.' For low-income households, needs are defined in terms of the most basic requirements of food and shelter. Some households would not survive if female members did not earn.

Reasons for entering paid work fall into four broad kinds. Women became employed because they needed to maintain themselves or to provide some element of their own living expenses; to maintain their families either wholly or partly; to improve the existing standard of living of their families, and because of a strong commitment to personal independence or to using their educational and vocational skills.

The married women in the sample may be divided into those who entered employment before their marriage and then remained in paid work, and those who took up paid work during marriage. The majority of the women who entered employment before marriage were either very poor women for whom employment has always been a matter of survival, or women in professional and white-collar occupations who entered wage work primarily because they were strongly committed to personal economic independence and in some cases came from backgrounds which encouraged girls not only to be educated but also to take up employment. This commitment continued into marriage and became transformed for many into a commitment to improving the standard of living of the family into which they had married. The following examples illustrate these various paths into employment.

Aruna Ghosal[11] is 27 years old and has worked as an untrained hospital aya (nursing assistant) for the last ten years and since before her marriage to a clerical worker. She has two young children and the combined incomes of herself and her husband (Rs 440) put them into the lowest income category. She has always worked from economic necessity and her present household would be hard-pressed to survive on her husband's wage of Rs 300 per month.

Asha Ganguly is 34, a graduate and worked first as a telephone operator and now as a clerk. Her husband works for a private firm and her father-in-law, who lives in the same household, has income from part-time legal work. Their gross monthly income is Rs 5540, putting them into the highest income category, and they live in a spacious apartment in a new upper-income suburb of Calcutta. Asha has been employed since she graduated eleven years ago and since before her marriage. Although she is not particularly happy with her job she has resisted fiercely her husband's attempts to make her give it up on his complaint that she is 'neglecting' her children and household duties. She is adamant about her need for some degree of economic independence and her right to employment.

Manisha Sen is a 42-year-old graduate clerical worker in the Post and Telegraphs Department. Her husband is similarly employed and their combined incomes, which are similar, amount to Rs 2200 per month. She has one daughter who is in her final year at school. She has been employed for twenty-two years and never considered giving up at marriage. Her income is both essential to the maintenance of their standard of living and to her own sense of personal economic independence.

Women entering waged work after marriage do so generally as a response to a particular crisis or change in circumstances. An example is Mani Das, who is a 39-year-old nurse married to a fruit seller twenty-three years her senior who is in poor health and whose income has become increasingly irregular. Her two sons are in casual employment and draw low wages and Mani, who earns Rs 200 per month, is the highest earner. The household income fluctuates around Rs 500 per month. She started nursing fourteen years ago, a few years after her marriage, as the family was unable to manage on her husband's earnings. She did so reluctantly as she had wanted to remain at home with her young children, and she continues to want to give up her employment in order to manage the household.

Widows and divorced or separated women have usually entered the labour force through routes similar to those of married women, especially in those cases where there was loss of a male 'breadwinner' through illness and incapacity. Some were already in employment when their husbands died and carried on with a greater economic impetus born from having to take over the maintenance of dependants. Others were precipitated into employment by widowhood or a husband's incapacity preceding death, either because they had no other source of security or because they were concerned not to be a financial liability to their relatives.

Rita Ghatak is an example of the latter. She is a 42-year-old graduate who was widowed in 1975. One month after her husband's death she took up a post in the State education service where she earns Rs 900 per month. She lives in a joint family of thirteen members, consisting of her parents-in-law, two brothers-in-law and their wives and children. One of her children lives with her and the other stays with her own parents. The combined income of the household is high – Rs 2900, but Rita took employment out of a felt necessity to maintain herself and her children and not be a 'burden' on the wider family.

Single women enter employment by four main routes which often overlap. They take up paid work because it is their own or their parents' expectation that a person with skills or qualifications should look for employment, or because they are living alone and have no other means of support, or, like widows and married women they may find themselves seeking paid work because of an economic crisis or chronic poverty in the household. Finally, they may take a job because they feel the need to be economically self-supporting in a context where other earners are perceived to be under pressure from the needs of other dependants.

Renuka Majumdar is 20 years old, has only primary level education and works in a plastics factory. Her parents are refugees whose fortunes have deteriorated since they left East Bengal. Her father works in a clothes shop for Rs 250 per month and her two younger siblings are still in school. Her mother had been a factory worker for nine years but had given it up because of poor health. This job was then taken by her daughter, whose income of Rs 150 per month is essential to the family's survival.

Sudha Mandal is a 45-year-old hospital matron who earns Rs 300 per month and receives free accommodation. She is the youngest of six siblings, the rest of whom are married, and she looked after her father until his death in 1978. She then took up her present job and left the family home as she did not wish to burden her married brothers and wanted to use her education.

As well as the major contribution made by women's incomes to household survival, the theme of economic independence runs strongly through women's accounts of their movement into paid work. This sense of independence ranges from the married woman who 'does not like to ask her husband for pocket money' to the single woman, not anticipating marriage, who does not want to be a burden on relatives who would be expected, customarily, to support her. The opening up of employment and its greater acceptability for women are part of the wider changes which are redefining familial obligations in urban households.

Chapter three

# Working lives
Women in the labour force

### Women's employment in Calcutta

The history of women's employment in Calcutta is a chequered one. There has been expansion in some spheres and contraction in others. Further, as in the rest of India, it has often been rendered invisible by methods of accounting and by changing and narrowing definitions of productive work. Official statistics tend to reveal more about the assumptions of the data collectors than they do about the productive activities of women.

An understanding that productive work is equivalent to regular paid employment permeates most official data collection on labour-force participation in the national accounting procedures of all countries. This causes acute problems in measuring women's economic contribution, particularly in the Third World where proletarianization has been uneven and much productive work is hidden as family labour in agriculture or petty commodity production (cf. Young *et al.* 1981, Munslow and Finch 1984).

There is now a substantial literature on problems of enumeration, particularly in relation to changes in census definitions, and the apparent decline in women's labour-force participation in India for most of this century.[1] In the context of Calcutta, the most salient issues are the extent of women's involvement in the unorganized sector and the decline in female employment in manufacturing industry.

In India, establishments are not classified as part of the organized sector unless they are either public sector establishments or non-agricultural sector private establishments employing at least ten workers and using electrical power. Establishments above this limit are required to observe various forms of labour protection, depending on size, and to provide facilities ranging from toilets to creches and pension funds. Workers in such establishments are automatically enumerated in employment statistics, which means that statistics on organized sector employment are reasonably reliable.

Unorganized sector workers in small-scale establishments are frequently unrecorded either because of definitional exclusion or because of their invisibility to enumerators. The term 'unorganized sector' is also often used to describe the many forms of unregulated and unrecorded self-employment providing goods and services to the urban poor, such as hawking, liquor brewing and prostitution.[2]

For urban wage workers, the unorganized sector generally marks a distinctive deterioration in wage levels and working conditions, in that it is distinguished by casualized forms of labour contract and an absence of bargaining power (Banerjee 1985a).

Estimates of the extent of women's participation in the unorganized sector can only be speculative. The Status of Women Report (Government of India 1974) has argued that as much as 94% of the female workforce in India is in this sector, mainly in agriculture. Banerjee (op.cit.) estimates that in 1977, 60% of women workers in Calcutta were in the unorganized sector. These figures echo wider perceptions that women are found disproportionately in the informal sector in developing economies (cf. Moser and Young 1981), and underline the importance of looking at the role of gender in structuring the options of the poor.

The secular decline in Indian female labour-force participation in the formal sector, particularly in manufacturing, is a notable feature of Calcutta's employment history until recently. Rates of employment for women in Calcutta and Bengal as reported in the censuses this century, declined up to 1971. The 1981 provisional figures show a slight rise.

However, in view of the known increase in the numbers of women employed in unorganized sector industries in Greater Calcutta, the figures cannot be taken as a reliable guide to the extent of contemporary female employment. The 1976 Calcutta Poverty Survey, with a definition of employment which includes most unorganized sector workers and a bias towards poorer households, found that the level of female employment in 1976 was double that recorded in the 1971 census.

Nevertheless, there have been some spectacular losses of female jobs over the last sixty years as a consequence of the displacement of women from the traditional manufacturing industries based in and around Calcutta. In 1911, these industries together employed a quarter of the entire population of Calcutta and its suburbs, including substantial numbers of women.

The jute mills around Calcutta were by far the largest employer of female labour in undivided Bengal. In some mills, probably up to a quarter of the workforce was female. The labour process in jute was highly gender segregated – women were in demand for specific tasks such as preparation and hand sewing and they were also paid much less than men. In 1921, the Annual Report of the Indian Factories Act in

Bengal recorded 44 705 women working in the jute industry out of a total adult labour force of 252 613. By 1972, the figure had fallen to 6642 out of a workforce which has remained fairly constant in size. Large numbers of women's jobs were also lost in textiles and food processing over this period. There was, in other words, a massive displacement of women by men. Some of the processes involved in this displacement, together with their implications, are discussed in chapter seven.

The census of 1911 for the city of Calcutta gives an interesting insight into the forms of employment available to women during this period of industrial and commercial expansion, as well as into the modes of classification used at that time. Utilizing a more liberal definition of employment than subsequent censuses, the census found that 20% of the total female population was employed or self-supporting. Table 3.1 shows their distribution across the different categories. Domestic service was by far the largest source of employment, followed by prostitution and then by industry and trade. This census also shows the very beginning of the growth in employment for newly educated middle-class women. Also recorded in the census figures are more than 8000 female 'beggars and vagrants' – five times as many as among males.

This early record of female labour raises the question of who were these women who worked in factories, traded foodstuffs and sex and entered professional occupations at a time when middle-class women had limited access to education, let alone employment. Unfortunately, the history of early female proletarianization in India is yet to be written and official records only hint, tantalizingly, at the backgrounds and characteristics of these women.

Historical accounts reveal dispossessed agriculturalists and artisans forced increasingly to sell their labour to the new factories, but the high levels of prostitution and female beggary suggest that the process of proletarianization had different consequences for women and men. The Indian Factory Commission Report of 1891 gives a vivid indication of the extent to which early capitalism had already severed the industrial and urban labour force from traditional means of support (cf. Misra 1975). The consequences for poor women appear to have been an even greater degree of personal destitution.[3]

From the scattered evidence available, it seems that the early female industrial labour force came mainly from three sections of the population. The first was the low-caste labouring poor who formed the bulk of unskilled factory labour. The second was families of artisans displaced from their craft occupations by British imports. Large numbers of labourers came from weaver castes, particularly from Muslim groups. Men, women and children who had produced cloth on a household basis were absorbed into the early jute and textile mills (Misra 1975).

46

*Table 3.1* Female employment in Calcutta in 1911

| | |
|---|---|
| Domestic Servants | 22 409 |
| Prostitutes | 14 271 |
| Industries: | |
| Jute | 3360 |
| Building | 1623 |
| Dress and Toilet | 1595 |
| Food processing | 1147 |
| Sweepers, etc. | 1073 |
| Trade (mostly foodstuffs) | 8449 |
| Professional and Liberal Arts: | |
| Religious | 1661 |
| Medicine | 836 |
| Midwives, nurses etc. | 753 |
| Letters, Arts | 581 |
| Teachers | 502 |
| Living on own income | 2808 |
| Insufficiently described | 4055 |
| *Total* (including beggars and vagrants) | 72 914 |
| Total female population, 1911 | 364,570 |

*Source: Census of India 1911*, vol. VI City of Calcutta, part 1 Report (Government of India 1913)

The third group of women, came from 'respectable' (i.e. *bhadralok*) backgrounds and were either widows lacking any other means of support, or women who had been ostracized by their families for 'offences' against their class or caste. Most contemporary writers insisted that Bengali women (by which some meant only *bhadralok* women) did not work in factories. A report by a woman doctor in the colonial medical service on the conditions of women workers in Bengal industries in 1921–2, stated that 'respectable Bengali Hindu women do not undertake industrial work and practically all such Bengalis found in the mills are degraded women and prostitutes' (Curjel 1923: 2). However, she also found local Bengali artisan families, both Hindu and Muslim, employed regularly in some mills. The 'degraded' women were apparently from *bhadralok* backgrounds. She comments on their 'fine physique' and concern to provide for their children's education.

Colonial reports are interesting for the perhaps unintended light which they throw on accelerating processes of class formation in urban Bengal and on the cultural attitudes which accompanied them. The language of 'respectability' is pervasive in contemporary accounts of

Bengal from the late nineteenth century onwards, dividing the population morally and ideologically along class lines and focusing particularly on women as symbols of newly emergent social statuses. Impoverished *bhadralok* women who sought employment as wage labour, were rendered 'unrespectable' and thus invisible. Proletarian women were allied with prostitutes.[4] Respectable Bengali caste Hindu families and families aspiring to respectability sought to curtail female involvement in paid work or to limit it to a few select occupations, the parameters of which were the subject of continuing public debate.

Of the background of prostitutes at this period, little is known except that the great majority were Hindu and some were practising a traditional caste occupation. One in five were said to belong to the Mahisya caste (*Census of India* 1911, Government of India 1913). As Mahisyas were a cultivator caste, it may be speculated that dispossession of cultivator families played a part in swelling the numbers of prostitutes in a city with a large migrant male population. Similar processes probably underlay the influx of women into domestic service in Calcutta.

The extent of Bengali women's involvement in these various occupations is difficult to gauge but there are grounds for suspecting that it was greater than has been suggested. The majority of Bengali women wage labourers were almost certainly from lower and scheduled castes, but there appears to have been a submerged tradition of wage work for caste Hindu women, and particularly widows who had no other means of support.

At the same time, women from middle-class Bengali families were gaining a foothold in those occupations which were deemed respectable, notably teaching and medicine, where increased demands for educational and medical services for women had opened up a small category of acceptable, gender-segregated employment (Borthwick 1984). Such occupations continue to be regarded as ideal employment choices for middle-class Bengali women to the present day.

From 1921 onwards, the censuses show a steady decline in the proportions and numbers of women employed in domestic service and prostitution, fluctuations in the proportions and numbers in trade and industry and a slight upward trend in professional and more recently, clerical occupations. Changes in occupational classification, particularly after 1931, and also in the nature of the employment being described, make comparisons through time extremely difficult, as can be seen in Table 3.2 which gives the 1981 figures for female and male employment in Calcutta. What is immediately striking, however, is the absolute decline in the number of women recorded as employed, even though the female population has more than tripled since 1911. This points to the likelihood of a combination of processes of displacement and underenumeration.

*Table 3.2* Male and female employment in Calcutta city, 1981

|  | M | F |
| --- | --- | --- |
| Manufacturing, processing, servicing and repairs | | |
| (a) Household | 7105 | 605 |
| (b) Non-Household | 309 919 | 6230 |
| Construction | 27 715 | 406 |
| Trade and commerce | 332 588 | 5251 |
| Transport, storage and communication | 155 650 | 2453 |
| Other services | 257 683 | 54 185 |
| *Total* | 1 090 660 | 69 130 |
| (Total population | 1 930 320 | 1 374 686) |

*Source: Census of India 1981*, part 11 B (i) Primary Census Abstract (Government of India 1983)

In industry, there has been a real loss in women's share of organized-sector manufacturing jobs. From the 1960s, however, there has been a rise in female employment in small-scale, mainly subcontracted manufacturing work, much of it unenumerated. Again, there are reasons for suspecting that the very small numbers involved in 'household' industry are an underestimation of the real extent of family labour in home-based manufacturing. Banerjee (1985a) points out that the unorganized sector is expanding at a much faster rate than the organized sector.

She also points out that before the early 1970s, domestic service was one of the few employment options available to women in Calcutta and that the expansion of opportunities since then has had the effect of bringing a new group of women into the labour force rather than simply causing a straight substitution between domestic service and the newer opportunities (ibid.: 65–7). However, it also appears to be the case that when other employment opportunities do become available, women will move out of domestic service. Contractual wage labour relations are greatly preferred to the long hours and personalistic control inherent in householder – domestic servant relationships.

Now, as in 1911, the majority of women are engaged in the service sector in a wide range of personal services usually located within the unorganized sector. There has been an increase in women's employment in clerical work and in areas of the social, health and educational services. These opportunities have benefited middle- and lower-middle-class women whose access to education has been much greater since independence.

In summary, there has been a restructuring of women's labour-force participation in Calcutta over the course of the century, entailing both major losses and some small gains for women. This restructuring has involved cultural and ideological as well as economic and technological factors. For some groups of women, it has meant their displacement from regular wage employment, probably into casualized forms of income generation in the unorganized sector and hence into greater destitution. For others, it has meant the withdrawal from or withholding of work opportunities as part of the code of family respectability.

Over the last two decades, increasing immiseration of the poor, declining living standards among the middle class and the crisis of male unemployment have forced more women to seek employment. Women's share of employment in Calcutta is now increasing in a stagnant labour market (Banerjee 1985a). Employers can hire women for lower wages and they are perceived as a more quiescent labour force in a context where some groups of male workers have been able to organize increasingly effectively.

## Current occupations and working conditions

Table 3.3 lists the occupations of women in the sample, including secondary occupations where applicable. There are both continuities and discontinuities with past employment patterns. The continuing predominance of service-sector employment, much of it poorly paid, is clear. Teaching, private tutoring and clerical work are the most common occupations. Private tuition has flourished fairly recently as an income earning activity for women who have completed at least school final examinations. This is in a climate of increasing educational competition brought about by high levels of unemployment which force an ever greater need for formal qualifications. Teaching of all kinds continues a tradition of preferred employment in services which are considered 'respectable' and 'honourable' spheres for women.

Tailoring and needleworking is the next most common source of employment for women of all classes. For the most part, it is home based and constitutes a disguised form of wage work in that the materials and orders are supplied ultimately by an employer and work is performed on a piece-rate basis. Some women do, however, own sewing machines purchased out of loans from relatives or employers.

The women factory workers are mainly in small manufacturing units producing mica, soap, electrical goods, plastics, pottery, leather and leather goods. Some of this employment is in the newer small-scale manufacturing sector, but some represents older manufacturing concerns in Calcutta. Seven of the eleven women factory workers are from refugee families, while one is a Muslim from a background of long involvement in the tannery industry.

*Table 3.3* Occupations of women in the sample

| Primary/secondary occupation | Primarily wage workers | Self- and semi-self-employed | Unpaid family labour |
|---|---|---|---|
| Teacher | 26 | | |
| Private tutor | | 14 | |
| Teacher/private tutor | 3 | | |
| Researcher/private tutor | 1 | | |
| Newsreader/private tutor | 1 | | |
| Office Assistant/private tutor | 1 | | |
| Runs own music school | | 1 | |
| Lecturer, researcher, librarian | 6 | | |
| Clerical, receptionist and telephone operator | 22 | | |
| Executive officer | 2 | | |
| Bank clerk | 4 | | |
| Businesswoman | | 1 | |
| Doctor | 1 | | |
| Lawyer | 1 | | |
| Air hostess | 1 | | |
| Actress | 1 | | |
| Nurse | 7 | | |
| Aya (nursing assistant) | 5 | | |
| Aya/surgery assistant | 1 | | |
| Hostel matron | 1 | | |
| School peon (orderly) | 1 | | |
| Factory worker | 11 | | |
| Factory supervisor | 1 | | |
| Bookbinder | 1 | | |
| Craft worker | 1 | | |
| Tailor, needleworker | 14 | 3 | |
| Tailor/cook | 1 | | |
| Tailor/private tutor | | 1 | |
| Incense stick maker | 4 | | 2 |
| Garland maker | 5 | | |
| Biri (cigarette) maker | 3 | | 1 |
| Paper bag maker | | 2 | 3 |
| Pulse grinder | 1 | | |
| Pulse grinder/private tutor | | 1 (part self-employed, part family labour) | |
| Button fitter | 1 | | |
| Cotton bag maker | 1 | | |
| Betel nut cutter | 1 | | |
| Doll painter | | | 1 |
| Masseuse | | 1 | |
| Cowdung fuel maker/domestic servant | | 1 | |
| Tea stall worker | | | 2 |
| Liquor maker and seller/domestic servant | | 1 | 1 |
| Total | 130 | 26 | 10 |
| Number seeking work | 5 | | |
| Number in sample | 171 | | |

Nursing, traditionally frowned upon by middle-class families, has become more common and more acceptable for women in recent years. One nurse, a graduate in her mid-40s said that when she was young, nursing was considered akin to prostitution. Borthwick (1984) describes attempts at the turn of the century to persuade *bhadralok* women to take up nursing and midwifery, in line with imperially inspired ideologies of women's pivotal role in the caring and nurturing professions. Such occupations had been, traditionally, the province of low-caste women because of the pollution from contact with bodily functions. Increased competition for scarce employment, together with the process of professionalization with its accompanying hierarchization, has rendered nursing gradually more acceptable. Ayas (nursing assistants) carry out the more routine and less acceptable tasks. In this sample, all the ayas are from families which would not be considered *bhadralok*.

In Calcutta, large numbers of women are home-based workers, a category which combines disguised wage work, forms of self-employment and family labour. Some of this is in personal services, such as massage, laundering of clothes, serving of food and prostitution.[5] Others manufacture goods on a piece-rate basis, getting their materials through an intermediary.

Eleven women have secondary sources of income, mostly from private tuition at home, but two women each hold two outside jobs. In all cases, secondary occupations were taken up to supplement low wages or irregular incomes.

Wage and income levels are shown in Table 3.4(a). The disparity between professional salaries and the incomes of home-based workers is enormous. Home-based personal services and the production of goods on a contracted-out basis are mostly extremely poorly remunerated. Factory wages are somewhat higher on average, but some small-scale units pay no more than can be earned in home-based piece work. A notable feature of some occupations is the wide range of remuneration for the same job. Nurses, distinguished from ayas by their formal training, may nonetheless draw salaries as low as or lower than some ayas, depending on the type of institution for which they work. These range from small private nursing homes, some of which pay very poor salaries, to public hospitals with recognized pay scales.

A similar situation occurs in teaching, where private, non-recognized schools have mushroomed to cater to unmet demand for educational facilities. These schools employ large numbers of qualified and unqualified women on a casual basis at very low rates of pay. There are also small schools in bustees, raised or aided by voluntary subscriptions, which have inadequate funds to pay proper salaries. Such initiatives depend on the availability of female labour able or willing to work for an 'honorarium'. Women working on this kind of basis often do so in the hope of achieving a better paid position in a government-recognized institution or of being regularized in their existing jobs.

A further area of fairly poorly paid employment for educationally qualified women is that of private tuition. Graduates can ask higher fees than school finalists, but rates per pupil are still extremely modest.

Women employed on a regular basis in government and public sector institutions and in large firms, as well as in the professions, receive salaries in accordance with official pay scales. These salaries, though not particularly high for many categories of employee, are greatly in excess of incomes in the unorganized sector.

Table 3.4(b) shows the proportion of women at different income levels. Nearly a third of the women earn below Rs 100 per month and nearly two-thirds are earning Rs 1000 or less, while only three women earn over Rs 2000 per month despite the bias of the sample towards graduates.

How do women's earnings compare with those of men? Because of the gender-segregated nature of the labour force, direct comparisons are difficult. Comparisons were therefore made on an intra-family basis both between wives and employed husbands, and between employed unmarried women and a brother closest to them in age. The average monthly wage of women in the seventy households which allowed for either comparison, is Rs 635, while for men it is Rs 1009. Women are thus earning an average of 62% of the wages of their husbands or brothers. However, the range of variation at different income levels is very considerable. Among women earning less than Rs 200 per month, incomes are on average only 28% of the incomes of their husbands or brothers. As they go up the income scale, the disparity remains consider-able but becomes less dramatic. Women earning between Rs 501–1000 earn 53% of the comparable male figure. It is only when women are in professional jobs that they either level with their male counterparts or may overtake them. Thus, the three highest paid women in the sample earned 115% of their comparable male relatives' incomes.

It is evident that women as a category are disadvantaged system-atically throughout the occupational structure unless they can break into the most highly paid professions. They are disadvantaged in different ways, however. In the seventy households compared here, thirteen husbands or brothers earned salaries in excess of Rs 2000 as against three wives and sisters. In the poorest households, women without skills and training are frequently unable to obtain employment which pays them more than a pittance, and their position in the labour market is much worse than either poor men or educated women (cf. Banerjee 1985a: 16).

*Table 3.4* Monthly wages and incomes by occupation and income level
(a) Monthly wage and income levels of women in different occupations

| Occupation(s) | Average or actual remuneration in rupees | Range |
|---|---|---|
| Teacher | 750 | 40–1500 |
| Private tutor | 72 | 20–250 |
| Music school owner/tutor | 700 | |
| Lecturer, Researcher and Librarian | 990 | 0–2100 |
| Clerical, receptionist and telephone operator | 770 | 300–1200 |
| Executive officer | 2035 | 1270–2800 |
| Bank clerk | 1375 | 1300–1500 |
| Businesswomen | 500 | |
| Doctor | 1500 | |
| Lawyer | 1000 | |
| Air hostess | 3000 | |
| Actress | 200 | |
| Nurse | 455 | 107–700 |
| Aya | 219 | 75–150 |
| Hostel matron | 300 | |
| School peon | 150 | |
| Factory worker | 163 | 60–300 |
| Factory supervisor | 800 | |
| Bookbinder | 80 | |
| Craft worker | 150 | |
| Tailor, needleworker | 127 | 20–300 |
| Incense stick maker | 57 | 48–60 |
| Garland maker | 20 | |
| Biri maker | 50 | 42–65 |
| Paper bag maker | 25 | |
| Pulse grinder | 50 | |
| Button maker | 150 | |
| Cotton bag maker | 120 | |
| Betel nut cutter | 50 | |
| Masseuse | 59 | |
| Cowdung fuel cake maker | 20 | |
| Liquor maker/seller | not disclosed | |

(b) Income levels of employed women (where applicable)

| Monthly income (rupees) | No. of women | % |
|---|---|---|
| 100 and below | 49 | 31.4 |
| 101–200 | 26 | 16.6 |
| 201–400 | 13 | 8.3 |
| 401–500 | 7 | 4.5 |
| 501–1000 | 42 | 27.0 |
| 1001–2000 | 16 | 10.2 |
| 2001–3000 | 3 | 2.0 |
| *Total* | 156 | 100.0 |

Using the official definition of the organized sector, eighty-four, or nearly half the women in the sample are employed in this sector. Twenty-six women are mainly self-employed workers, mostly in the unorganized sector, and ten are unpaid family helpers. The remainder (apart from employment seekers) are unorganized sector wage workers, with the exception of two women living and working in a charitable institution, the status of which is ambiguous.

The dividing line between the two sectors is not, however, as clear for some women when the question of wages and working conditions is considered. The poor employment status of some teachers in non-recognized schools has already been instanced. They share with unorganized sector workers both insecurity of employment and low wages.

Of the eleven women factory workers in the sample, six work in registered factories and five in unregistered units. The two best paid workers (one in electronics earning Rs 250, the other in a nationalized pottery factory, earning Rs 300) are both organized sector workers, while the lowest paid earns Rs 60 in an unorganized sector mica factory. But there is little difference in the wage levels of the remaining workers and some of the unorganized sector workers earn slightly more than other women in the registered units.

As important for workers is the nature of their employment contract. Cutting across the sectoral distinction is the issue of permanent or regular employment and casual or temporary hiring. Being in a registered unit does not guarantee a regular contract and many women are hired and rehired as temporary workers for long periods of time. Such contracts have important implications for their rights to a range of benefits.

The majority of organized sector workers are in the public sector and are entitled to pensions, maternity leave, paid leave and holidays. The most generous conditions of service in the public sector are among bank employees, the least generous among staff hired on a temporary basis. Altogether, sixty-seven women have pension or provident fund arrangements.

Organized sector employees mostly work a standardized working week of forty-two hours including some Saturdays. Teachers usually work a five-hour day, often teaching morning school, starting from seven. Factory hours are long with eight- or nine-hour days and a six-day week. There is little concept of part-time work within the organized sector in India, in contrast with the expansion of service sector employment for women in Britain, which has been largely a growth in part-time work.

Most of the unorganized sector workers in this sample are home based and work on piece rates, which means that their incomes, low by any standards, are subject to fluctuation by the non-availability of work, sickness or domestic disruption.[6] They are also heavily dependent upon the 'goodwill' of intermediaries for their supply of work and for the maintenance of existing rates of remuneration as it is common for goods to be rejected on often spurious grounds of quality. Home-based workers also depend frequently on other family members for casual or regular assistance to meet their targets.

Working hours of women in unorganized sector piece-rate work vary greatly. *Biri* workers work up to ten or twelve hours every day for a pittance of about Rs 60 per month, while others may only manage three hours. Those employed in small factories or workshops generally work an eight- or nine-hour day with Sundays off.

Many women have problems finding sufficient work on a regular basis. A woman making flower garlands complained that she could only get work for ten to fifteen days every month. Generally, women will do as much work as they are able to get, even if it means working continuously.

Although rates of pay in this sector of employment are extremely poor, there is nonetheless considerable variation. While a pulse grinder's hourly rate (including her daughter's labour) works out at almost Rs 1.00, the *biri* maker's hourly rate is one fifth of this. This points not just to fierce competition for work which maintains very low rates but also to the structural isolation of home-based workers who have no organizations of their own and no access to wider knowledge of market conditions and wage rates.

Except in the area of personal services, few of the women are genuinely self-employed, and the opportunities for female self-employment in Calcutta are fairly limited (cf. Banerjee 1985a: 68–70). The main type of self-employment in this sample is private tutoring. Although limited to women with educational qualifications, it has the advantage of being in quite high demand and of otherwise having low entry costs. It rarely becomes a viable independent source of livelihood, however, as there is little scope for turning it into a formal enterprise.

For women lacking sought-after skills and capital, self-employment is restricted to the production of very poorly remunerated goods and services in the unorganized sector. The returns to labour, often encompassing family labour, are extremely low. For instance, the two self-employed paper bag makers, both of whom had initially to take their small starting capital from their husbands, each depend on family labour. In one case, young sons provide two to three hours labour per day and in the other, three daughters work for one hour per day each. The total income per month in these two cases is Rs 40 and Rs 100 respectively.

Tailoring and stitching provides a possible source of self-employment. In practice, most such workers take orders on a piece-rate basis through intermediaries of wholesale and retail outlets. In practice, tailoring involves different degrees of self-employment. One woman does piece-rate work for a clothing merchant along with taking her own orders from neighbours and making some items with the help of her children which her husband hawks in local markets. In marriage and festival seasons she gets more orders than she can meet herself, so employs women in the neighbourhood on a casual basis to finish the orders.

Tailoring work holds out slightly better prospects than other forms of unorganized sector self-employment for women who can acquire reasonable levels of skill and speed and obtain machines. One household of five sisters working partly in a tailoring shop and partly at home on piece-rate orders had been able, on a revisit in 1985, to become self-employed by obtaining a loan from their previous employer and credit in goods from an old family contact, to set up independently at home.

Most self-employment is carried on from home. Only the two businesswomen rent premises elsewhere. Personal services do not require much in the way of extra space and private tuition is done either in the family's living quarters or at the homes of pupils. Cowdung fuel cakes are plastered onto any available outside wall and are a familiar sight in Calcutta streets. Liquor brewing for sale must be carefully concealed within the house because of its illegality. Tailoring and garment enterprises do require space but none of the self-employed women or families were able to afford additional rooms. They lived around the sewing machines and accumulated piles of garments, cloth and half-finished piece goods. Tailors and garment makers and finishers are dependent on both casual and regular family labour both to maintain daily output and to cope with fluctuations in demand.

Although poorly remunerated and limited in scope, self-employment could be said to allow more flexibility in working hours. On average, self-employed women do work shorter hours than wage workers. However, in some cases this is because of absence of work rather than choice. Private tuition is done usually for between one and four hours per day, although one woman managed to find pupils to fill a five-to six-hour day. Self-employed tailoring work depends on the season. One woman who works only two hours per day for most of the year, works a twelve-hour day during peak periods of demand.

Discussions of working conditions and practices brought to light a large number of examples where women had been or had felt themselves to be discriminated against or harassed on the basis of gender. Table 3.5 summarizes the main complaints, made by a total of fifty-five women.

*Table 3.5* Discrimination and harassment complaints

| | | |
|---|---|---|
| (1) | Being paid lower wages | 45 |
| (2) | Being expected to work harder | 38 |
| (3) | Denial of compassionate leave | 29 |
| (4) | Verbal abuse | 26 |
| (5) | Denial of training or promotion | 18 |
| (6) | Physical harassment | 5 |
| (7) | Sexual insults | 4 |

There is a clear hierarchy of occupational risk. Proportionately, the greatest magnitude and range of complaints comes from nurses and ayas. All the nurses and four out of six of the ayas cited examples both of discriminatory practices and of various kinds of harassment from patients and from other staff. Nurses are the group most likely to experience sexual harassment. Aruna Brahmachari, a 40-year-old unmarried nurse, spoke of a long history of harassment by senior staff and doctors and of a number of 'promises' of marriage in return for sexual favours.

Home-based piece-rate work carries the next highest risk. Two-thirds of these women complained of being paid lower wages than men in comparable work, of being expected to work harder than men and of being verbally abused. Women *biri* workers pointed out that they were paid only Rs 3.50 per thousand *biri*, while male workers in the factory were paid Rs 12.00 per 1000. A woman making flower garlands at home echoed a common complaint when she said that employers take advantage of women's 'quiet nature', knowing it is difficult for them to refuse greater demands or argue for their rights in front of male employers. Similar complaints were made by half of the factory and sweatshop workers.

Only four of the twenty-four teachers complained of discrimination and none of harassment. Of these, wages, denial of compassionate leave and being expected to work harder were the main areas of complaint and they came from teachers in non-established schools with irregular pay scales. Seven of the twenty-two clerical workers complained of similar problems. Telephone operators were the only public sector employees to complain of sexual harassment. This included routine verbal and sexual abuse from subscribers prone to unleash their frustrations with Calcutta's inadequate telephone system onto the hapless operator.

Of the women employed in the more senior administrative and teaching positions, only one - the doctor - complained of discriminatory treatment, giving instances where compassionate leave to cope with family responsibilities had been denied. She also felt generally that she had been expected to work harder as a woman just to 'prove' herself competent.

It is notable that the league of complaints corresponds almost exactly to the general social evaluations of different occupations. Apart from home-based piece work, which is rarely a 'choice' for the women concerned, teaching, academic and administrative jobs are the least likely to produce complaints, while clerical work is slightly more likely, factory work more likely still and nursing the most likely of all. The pressure on women both to remain within fairly segregated 'women's occupations' and to pay heed to wider evaluations of suitability is thus not simply ideological, but based on the realities of workplace practices.

It is extremely difficult for women and men to find jobs in Calcutta and employment seekers may have to try various strategies over long periods of time. Table 3.6 shows how the wage-employed women in the sample obtained their existing jobs.

*Table 3.6* Method of recruitment to wage employment

| (1) | Formal application/exam/interview | 54 |
|------|-----------------------------------|-----|
| (2) | Employment exchange or agency | 2 |
| (3) | Training institution/women's assoc. | 4 |
| (4) | Local contractor | 1 |
| (5) | Neighbours | 30 |
| (6) | Friends | 17 |
| (7) | Household member | 11 |
| (8) | Relatives | 10 |
| (9) | 'Connections' (nature not disclosed) | 7 |
| (10) | Inherited from mother | 4 |
| (11) | Inherited from husband | 1 |
| (12) | Through local doctor | 1 |
| (13) | Combination of methods | 10 |
| (14) | Found job herself | 2 |
| (15) | Unspecified | 2 |
| Total | | 156 |

All the organized public sector employees and most of the nurses had made formal applications. A number, such as the bank workers, had taken the appropriate competitive examination. Not all organized sector employees had relied on formal procedures alone, however. The two temporary clerical workers and eight of the teachers, particularly the ones in private schools, had been assisted in the first stage by relatives or personal connections who were able to 'put in a word' for them.

The importance of social networks to the acquisition of a job is clear from Table 3.6. Neighbours and friends provide the most significant sources of information and assistance, surpassing that of relatives and other household members. This is true particularly for home and sweat-shop workers who rely solely on neighbourhood information networks, thus reinforcing the tendency for piece rates to be highly erratic.

Jobs had been inherited in only a few instances. One young woman had taken over her mother's tailoring orders when she could no longer work. Another had inherited her retiring mother's factory job. A third had managed to take over her mother's public sector clerical job after her death, but 'only after a big struggle.' A young widow had been given a job in her husband's factory after his early death.

At the time of the study, five women were seeking jobs and another twenty-six, all in temporary employment or working as family labour, were looking for better ones. Thirteen women had registered their names in the employment exchange and two were taking further vocational courses in an attempt to increase their employability.

Most had narrow but realistic expectations. Young unemployed women graduates and those doing private tutoring at home were attempting to get teaching posts at the lowest scale. Some were also attempting to get clerical jobs and others said they would accept 'any respectable job.' Home-based workers and non-graduates were trying to get factory employment or tailoring work. Apart from one graduate, none expected salaries greater than Rs 500 per month and some were prepared to accept as little as Rs 150 or 'any wage'. Most appeared to be following a procedure which could be characterized as 'one step at a time'; in which those with no employment at all would take any kind of work, while those with temporary work would then begin to search for more secure employment.

Women were divided as to whether or not they faced greater problems than men. Many felt that high levels of unemployment made the struggle equally difficult for both sexes. Others pointed to three specific ways in which women are potentially disadvantaged. Illiterate women all felt strongly that their illiteracy handicapped them in the labour market to an extent greater than for men. The findings of this study bear out this perception. Many women also pointed to the heavily gender-segregated character of the labour market and the inability of women to break into male spheres of employment. Women were, however, divided in their opinions as to whether segregation was a consequence of women not being capable of doing 'male jobs' or of social prejudice.

A further disability mentioned by women at all class and income levels and emphasized particularly strongly by Muslim women, was the greater restriction experienced by women on their personal movements. As a consequence, a lot of women spoke of their ignorance of labour-market conditions and of opportunities in general. It is notable that only six women had gone searching personally for jobs by contacting employers directly. Unmarried women particularly are discouraged from 'roaming around' unsupervised to look for work. This pressure joins with what is often a self-imposed restriction. Shanta Ghosh, a temporary clerical worker trying to find a permanent post, commented that unscrupulous men frequently harass young women in the guise of finding them jobs.

Women's employment histories reveal a high degree of continuity of employment with few breaks and changes of job. Thirty-one women have changed or left employment at some point, of whom only six had changed more than once and none more than three times. Table 3.7 gives the reasons for the thirty-eight changes made by these women.

More than two-thirds of these changes were in response to work-related reasons. Poor remuneration was the most likely cause, followed by retrenchment and poor conditions of service. Four of the twelve who gave low wages as their reason for changing were teachers and two were private sector clerical workers moving into the public sector. Of those moving because of their conditions of service, three telephone operators moved into routine clerical work to avoid night shifts and irregular hours and one nurse moved to avoid living in. Two women complained of ill treatment by superiors, and in one case, a librarian resigned because she was made to sign for higher wages than she actually received.

Eight women left jobs because of family-related reasons and then returned to the labour force after periods ranging from a few months to three years.

Women's employment histories suggest that they are very stable workers who, once they enter the labour force, are likely to remain in it. As the sample covers only women currently in employment it is not possible to reconstruct the extent to which marriage or childbearing and rearing does remove women permanently or for long periods from the labour force. From this sample, it seems that the common contemporary pattern in Europe for married women to leave the labour force temporarily at the birth of the first child and to rejoin at a variable later stage (cf. Dex 1985: 3–4) is not the pattern for Calcutta women. Childbirth itself rarely affected women's employment histories. The degree to which this may be due to greater childcare alternatives for these women is explored in the next chapter.

Table 3.7 Reasons for changing or leaving previous employment

| Low wage/ unprofitable/ better offer | Employer transferred/ establishment closed | Poor conditions of service | Casual contract ended | Change of residence | Looking after sick relative | Marriage | Child-bearing/ rearing | Relatives created difficulties | Illness | Other | Total |
|---|---|---|---|---|---|---|---|---|---|---|---|
| 12 | 6 | 5 | 3 | 1 | 1 | 3 | 2 | 1 | 2 | 2 | 38 |

Chapter four

# Working lives
## The domestic arena

What is the prime duty of women? *grihadharm*. Today, disorder and revolution will be unleashed if women abandon their households. What is *grihadharm*? To run a peaceful home, not to waste time, not to gossip maliciously.

(From *grihadharm* ['Duty to the household'],
*antahpur* journal May/June 1899)

In the scheme of this household every activity of each member, high or low, was directed and subordinated to one great purpose, namely the comfort and convenience of the gentleman who presided over it.

(Tagore, *Two Sisters*, 1964 edition: 55)

### Changing concepts of domesticity in Bengali society

The growth of an urban wage economy in Bengal in the nineteenth and early twentieth centuries with its accompanying class differentiation brought radical changes in the organization of households and in the ideologies which gave meaning to their day-to-day activities.

In the demarcation of the domestic arena, three major elements in this transformation can be detected. First, there was the transformation of pre-existing, 'inside – outside', female – male divisions of space into a distinction between the private, familial world of the home and the world of employment and public affairs. Second, there was a reconstruction of gender ideologies in relation to the duties of the sexes in their separate worlds. Third, there was the rise of the 'housewife' both as consumer and as conveyer of the new values and attitudes that were essential to the reproduction of the new middle class.

Pre-colonial Bengal was not an undifferentiated entity. High caste Hindus and their Muslim counterparts practised forms of purdah which rested upon the spatial segregation of the sexes within the inner and

63

outer living quarters of the home. Only close male relatives had access to the inner courtyard (*antahpur*) where the women spent their lives from a very early age.

Borthwick (1984) suggests that the establishment of the *bhadralok* in Calcutta from the late eighteenth century onwards, with the gradual increase in the numbers of female dependents brought to the city, had the effect, initially, of sharpening seclusion practices. Stricter controls were seen to be necessary in a potentially corrupting urban environment. Purdah practices were to become a major target for social reformers later in the nineteenth century.

However, as Borthwick points out, in the segregated women's quarters, 'domestic life constituted social life and was not something separate from it' (ibid: 13). The spatially segregated women's world of upper-caste and wealthy Muslim households in early nineteenth-century Bengal was not the parallel of the private, domestic sphere associated with the separation of the home and the workplace under capitalist relations of production (cf. Davidoff and Westover 1986).

Household work was carried out in a form which was at once more communal and deeply hierarchical. In the larger and more complex households which provided the model for the *bhadralok* style of living, the duties of its individual members were clearly structured by age and kinship status. At the same time, the boundaries of the 'domestic', as the quotation suggests, cannot be so precisely drawn. Although increasing in extent, the norm of salaried employment was not firmly established and many men continued to be engaged in traditional occupations like estate management or lived-off land rents. The continuing rural connection involved women in more communal activities such as food processing and ceremonials. The slow growth of professional specializations such as medicine allowed women to maintain their position as first-resort healers through their knowledge of the properties of plants and herbs. Women also played a key role in arranging marriages.

Thus, though segregated, the women's sphere did not mark out a set of activities which could be labelled exclusively 'domestic'.[1] The distinction between female and male spheres embodied rather honour and status codes which centred most crucially upon the control of female sexuality. Onto this were mapped ideologies of domesticity derived from Bengal's encounter with and response to imperial ideologies, and from the rapid restructuring of its social relations as households were incorporated into wage relations.

By the late nineteenth century, the separate spheres of men and women were becoming established ideologically as the worlds respectively of employment and public affairs, and household duties. Men increasingly undertook 'service' (*chakri*), or paid work, while women devoted themselves to household work (*sansar*) and to motherhood. The content of these spheres, and the gender identities appropriate to them were subject to public and private struggle and debate.

The ideological offensive mounted by the British against local custom and practice had provoked fierce debates about the position of women in Bengali society. Some of these debates paralleled those of nineteenth-century Britain. Were women's natures essentially different from those of men? Were women to be educated and, if so, what education would be suitable? Should women be allowed to take up careers and which ones would be appropriate? Equally, in certain respects, the answers which emerged were similar. The general social condition would be improved by educating women, but education should be tailored to and limited by their first duty to be devoted wives and mothers and, in the Bengali case, daughters-in-law. Employment was not appropriate for married women but could be countenanced under certain circumstances for widows and indigent women.[2]

The engagement with imperial ideologies was marked by resistance and ambivalence. Conservative Hindu leaders mounted a defence of tradition against British interference, particularly in the sphere of the family, turning the Victorian notion of the home as the private domain answerable only to the family patriarch back onto the colonial power. There was resistance to Christian proselytizing and the greater 'audacity' of converted women. Indian nationalism was gathering force. The achievements of 'the Victorian woman', admired as more 'advanced' and seen by some as the domestic power behind the rise of Britain as a major industrial and political power, had to be offset against the arrogance and racism of British women and men in India. While facets of western civilization were recommended for emulation, other aspects were deplored. Western dress, too free a mixing of the sexes and smoking and drinking were all considered examples of moral decadence. There was fear that the forces unleashed by rapid social change would precipitate social disintegration or revolution.

The models of womanhood which emerged as dominant were a product of the convergence of middle-class Victorian ideals and models derived from Hindu textual and mythical inspiration. While Victorian Britain had the 'angel in the house', Hindu Bengal had its own images of the sacrificing and suffering wife/mother (Roy 1975a).[3] This encounter reached its apotheosis in the late nineteenth century with the growing influence of the Brahmo Samaj, a sect heavily imbued with puritan Christian ideas and practices which became the religious progressivist alternative to orthodox Hinduism. The Brahmos, while emphasizing a vision of equality between the sexes, constructed equality as an exclusively moral, and thus private issue, rather than as a political and economic issue as well. The emphasis was thus less upon bringing women into the public sphere on the same terms as men (although they did attack purdah traditions) than on making women equal to men within their own sphere of activity. This religious-cum-social reformism thus reinforced the image of women as primarily dutiful wives and mothers while emphasizing a new vision of marriage as one of companionship and mutual respect.[4]

There was at this time an efflorescence of Bengali journals aimed at a small but growing number of literate middle-class women. The quotation on *grihadharm* at the head of this chapter conveys well the hortatory tone of much of this writing. This term carries the connotation of duty as a sacred act, not simply a set of daily chores. The household was a kind of shrine, to be worshipped with the proper observances (and cf. Chakrabarty 1989b). These concepts draw potently upon Hindu traditions. At the same time, the article quoted on p. 63 goes on to extol the Victorian example of Mrs John Bright – 'an accomplished woman who ran a perfect household, providing a peaceful environment for her husband'.

Gradually, there crystallized the model of the ideal woman who was self-sacrificing in the cause of the comfort and wellbeing of the other members of the household, a good manager of household affairs, including finances, skilful in all the domestic arts and never idle. She was also sufficiently educated to be able to provide companionship to her husband and instruction to her children, but was morally pure in that she centred her existence on her household duties and was not deflected by external interests or by trivial activities such as reading novels or 'gossiping'. The journals of the period constantly held aloft examples of women deemed to fit this ideal. It is doubtful whether the new emphasis on marital companionship and the stress on the home as a haven for men from the public world could be translated into practice by many middle-class families. Joint family living, with its different authority structure, emphasized intergenerational ties, often at the expense of marriage. Contemporary accounts suggest that men spent rather little time in their homes which, due to the chronic housing scarcity in Calcutta and the often low remuneration of salaried employees, were frequently overcrowded and probably uncomfortable, judged by the 'new' standards. The home remained the sphere of women. Men spent most of their time with other men, returning only to eat, sleep and avail themselves of the services provided by their kinswomen.

Motherhood also underwent some redefinition during this period. Although the mother figure has always occupied an important place in Indian cultural traditions (Roy 1975a, Hershman 1977), in the later nineteenth century there are signs of the influence of the Victorian concept of motherhood as a sacred duty to build up the nation (and 'race') by producing and rearing 'good citizens'. (Borthwick 1984 chap. 5).

Manuals and articles on childcare started to appear, advocating strict childrearing regimes and castigating lax mothers who spoiled their children by feeding them between meals or breastfeeding them beyond the first year. The crucial role of the mother in the moral development of the child was heavily emphasized, as was her importance in supervising their educational progress. There is less sense of a corresponding reconceptualization of fatherhood, except perhaps among Brahmos; and the redefining of middle-class childhood evident in the new childrearing regimes can only have had the effect of placing greater burdens on mothers themselves; burdens which were, however, mitigated by the less privatized nature of mothering in a context where other female kin played an important role in childcare.

The 'housewife' was a product of the rise of the urban Bengali petit bourgeoisie. Borthwick (1984) argues that it was women who had to mediate the change from non-capitalist social relations where status depended on ceremonial expenditure and traditional forms of gift giving to one in which prudent expenditure, savings and investment came increasingly to underwrite class position. Wives had to learn management and financial skills appropriate to the maintenance of a middle-class household dependent increasingly on a salaried income. This was not always easy. New needs, such as education and medicine, as well as household consumer goods, had to be purchased from often inadequate salaries. Women rarely had independent means to contribute to the household. Their role was to use their managerial skills to transform the contributions of male earners into forms of consumption which reflected the family's social position.

Again, literature was on hand to provide direction in this task by stressing the need for thrift and through practical discussions of prudent housewifery, such as how to save money by stitching the family's clothes at home instead of sending the cloth to the tailor. The growth of more elaborate patterns of consumption added to the housewife's workload. Cooking styles became more varied, with western and regional cuisines added to the repertoire of the accomplished wife. Western-style furnishings and house decoration became common and required new management skills (Borthwick 1984).

From the 1880s, employment of household servants increased. Cheap labour was abundant in the city, elaborated domestic lifestyles produced more work but little gadgetry was available to lighten the burden, and the employment of servants became a mark of status for *bhadralok* families and for those aspiring to that status. Nonetheless, popular journals of the time were quick to lampoon the women of such families for their 'idleness'.

As among the Victorian middle class, the new wife and mother was pivotal to the consolidation of class identity. The many debates during

67

this period on how to improve women's position, reflected partly an urgent need for wives who could manage this new lifestyle, who were sufficiently educated to ensure their children's proper socialization and who had sufficient knowledge of the world not to 'shame' their husbands on public occasions when new protocols demanded that wives should appear with their husbands in public. The 'domestic' was being transformed for middle-class women, but with little encouragement for that avant-garde minority which, like its radical counterparts in Britain, had begun demanding a wider role for women in the public domain.

Changing ideologies of domesticity in Bengal were located in the emergent middle class created from the expanding professions and bureaucracy. They served also to mark off this class both from the upper-class elite, where women often broke social conventions - a tiny minority of women has always been prominent in public life (see Forbes 1975, 1982); and from the growing urban proletariat.

Caste divisions did not lose all significance in this ideological restructuring. Brahmans were more likely to take a conservative view of women's role – Brahman respondents to the 1931 census questionnaire on social issues described women's participation in public life (including employment) as 'humiliating', 'positively harmful' and 'absolutely ungodly' and prominent women were considered to be actuated by a 'discreditable desire for self-advertisement' (Government of India 1933 vol. V, part 1, Report: 401). Those very few respondents who favoured women taking up employment and appearing in public were all Kayasthas and Baidyas.

How did these ideological changes affect working-class and lower-caste women? Historians have yet to tackle this question, but a few tentative remarks may be made. Early proletarianization precipitated many artisanal and agricultural caste women into factory employment. The effect of the consolidation of a petit bourgeois ideology of women's place in the home was to reinforce the image of women in the public or 'male' domain as sexually permissive and to construct them as poor wives and mothers and, increasingly, as subjects for moral reform (Borthwick 1984). Victorian respectability meshed with Hindu and Muslim concepts of purity and shame, of male and female space.

This complex intermeshing of class, caste and religion is well illustrated in the example of the Mahisyas, a fairly low ranking agricultural caste which, in the early decades of this century made a concerted bid to raise its status by a combination of Brahmanization – the observance of orthodox religious practices, and more secular means such as the uplift of women through education. At the same time the theme of purity and chastity for women was constantly emphasized and treated as coterminous with their duties to the home and the family. The implication was clear: women who entered the public domain were 'impure' in the double sense of sexually impure and of not fulfilling their rightful destiny within the home.

This set of associations operated strongly upon upwardly mobile but conservative castes such as the Mahisyas and upon other groups which were being incorporated into the urban petit bourgeoisie. It provided a powerful model for 'respectable behaviour', a careful partitioning of the public and domestic, which discouraged families from contemplating employment for their daughters unless *in extremis*. Although this effect has never been quantified, it probably operated to remove some women from employment as a mark of status aspiration as has occurred in other parts of north India (cf. Das 1976, Srinivas 1977, and chapter seven). However, poor women and women from families which experienced economic decline, remained a submerged constituency of the Bengal labour force.

The effects of the ideological restructuring of the domestic domain have been far reaching for Bengali women as they were for women in Victorian Britain. A rigid sexual division of labour was reconstituted, sanctioned both by recourse to religious and cultural traditions and by an appeal to the new modalities. While the ideological sanctions against women's employment became increasingly contested from the early twentieth century onwards by highly educated women from progressive bourgeois families, the Calcutta-based petit bourgeoisie kept its wives and daughters within the home. But even where women did succeed in obtaining employment, or were forced into it by their circumstances, their responsibility for domestic labour, and its construction as a wholly female domain, remained inviolate. The remainder of this chapter examines this continuing responsibility for contemporary women and considers what, if any, changes have taken place in response to increases in employment among all classes of women.

## Negotiating the housework

### Household chores

Housework is thus produced historically. Its content and amount are not fixed entities but vary with material conditions, classes and cultures. This is not how it seems to the women themselves. 'Housework' has the property of appearing as an eternal burden, never completed and never diminishing. One respondent, asked to fill in a daily work schedule, commented that it would look like the *mahabharat*, a famous and very long Hindu epic poem. Yet although housework appears as a constant, private burden borne by women in all classes and contexts, the content of this responsibility and its relation to paid work differs.

As Nirmala Banerjee points out (1985a: 9), poor women in particular are engaged in household activities which contribute in a very direct way to the household's real income, such as processing cowdung and other gathered materials to make fuel for cooking which would otherwise have to be purchased. For middle-class women, higher standards of consumption tend to entail correspondingly more elaborated, if less physically onerous domestic tasks such as more varied menus and higher levels of home comfort. As will be seen, the substitution of women's labour by domestic servants in households which can afford it changes the content of women's household tasks but does not necessarily reduce their domestic burdens.

In India, the minimal state provision of services in health, welfare, housing and childcare also has profound implications for women's domestic burdens. Many of the tasks which are to varying degrees performed by the state in advanced capitalist countries must be provided privately by households through a combination of wage expenditure, such as on health and educational provision and through unpaid domestic work, such as caring for the sick, handicapped and elderly. Although some of the heaviest of this burden may be mediated by paid domestic help, responsibility for its management usually devolves wholly upon women.

All women in Calcutta, however, experience the effects of a low level of domestic technology and an underdeveloped market for prepared foods. Apart from childcare, which is examined separately, food preparation is by far the most onerous task to be confronted each day. For most women, this takes up two periods of the day, the longer being usually in the morning before leaving for work, while a shorter session takes place in the late afternoon or evening. Husbands and schoolchildren often take cooked food from home. Where families can afford to, two full cooked meals must be provided each day. The majority of women in the sample thus rise extremely early – some married women reported rising at three in the morning, but around five was more common – and do the bulk of their daily chores before they leave for, or begin, paid work. For poor women and women in poor housing conditions, water must be collected from outside taps or wells. Nineteen households have no water supply in the house or compound. Fuel supply problems and the absence of reliable cooking stoves among poorer households add to the difficulties of daily food provision. The low incidence of items such as pressure cookers and fridges means that there is little scope for saving time or fuel or for storing cooked food.

House cleaning and washing utensils are likewise made laborious by the lack of domestic appliances and cleaning aids and, where they are employed, these are the tasks most likely to be performed by domestic servants.

Detailed information was collected on the precise division of labour between members of the household and on the total daily amount of time spent by employed women on household chores, including childcare and servicing of other family members. Most women were able to state, very precisely, how their days were divided up among different activities – a consequence of the need to have a highly organized routine in order to manage their various responsibilities. Ten literate women also filled out daily work schedules over two-week periods and these confirmed the high degree of organization needed to maintain household and employment commitments.

The division of labour within the household is one between female members and between female members and domestic servants, not between women and men. Along with gender, kinship-based seniority plays a major role in determining tasks and responsibilities. Mothers-in-law, except when very elderly, elder sisters-in-law and elder daughters generally have heavier responsibilities than younger women, particularly in relation to cooking and to overall supervision. This customary weighting of responsibility has not dissolved for most employed women.

A continuing supply of very cheap labour, female and male, means that the employment of domestic servants is more widespread in Calcutta than in the other major cities of India where alternative employment has become increasingly available. With one exception, the lowest income households employ no servants at all. The exception is a household consisting of a young married couple with two very young children and no extended kin network, where the wife works full time as a hospital aya. She is nominally resident in a hospital quarter and her casually employed husband mostly takes care of the children during her working hours while the servant does most of the daily housework. If the roles of husband and wife were reversed, it is unlikely that a servant would be employed.

Households with incomes above Rs 800 per month almost all employ at least one servant on a part-time basis. In the lower-income households, this is a woman who comes in for two to three hours daily to wash cooking utensils and clean floors. High-income households generally employ a full-time servant of either sex who may live in and be more or less continually on call, and about a third of the highest income households also employ a part-timer.

Despite the prevalence of servants, the average number of hours spent daily on household duties recorded by women across the income groups is virtually the same. Women in households which do employ servants do not show any time advantage over households which manage without. This is for several reasons. First, servants are rarely left to work without supervision and women spend a lot of time 'managing' their work. Menus and marketing have to be organized, usually by the

71

senior woman. In only two households was there a housekeeper who was trusted with responsibility for managing the domestic arrangements, as opposed to executing tasks under supervision.

Second, the greater elaboration of domesticity among middle-class families means that the employment of servants only 'frees' women for other aspects of social and cultural reproduction, while poor women must, of necessity, cut their domestic chores to a minimum and do not have the means to provide more elaborated standards of consumption. Domestic servants do not greatly affect the time burden but do alter the content of women's domestic workloads by relieving their employers of some of the heaviest and dirtiest daily chores.

The data reveal a complex relationship between household composition and the life cycle in respect of employed women's daily work burdens (cf. Roldan 1985 for similar findings on urban Mexico). Table 4.1(a) illustrates the effects of the life cycle and of kinship status on the hours spent on housework. Unmarried daughters who are either the only employed female member in households with other adult women, or are the younger or youngest employed sister are the least burdened. In some cases, a working daughter is relatively cossetted by being 'let off' regular housework. Seeta and Deepali Majumdar, two sisters in their mid-twenties who are the main providers for their family of seven persons from their wages as factory workers, do no housework at all, having assumed the role of 'breadwinners'.[5]

Where more than one daughter is employed, her household responsibilities will depend upon her seniority and the presence of other female relatives in the household. Elder daughters can be heavily burdened. Twenty-four-year-old Jayanti, who combines home-based tailoring with giving private tuition, also spends up to four hours each day on housework. Her mother is an invalid and her two younger sisters both work as private tutors. As the eldest active woman, she is responsible for the cooking and thus spends twice as long on household chores as her younger sisters.

Employed mothers carry the heaviest burdens. Table 4.1(b) shows, however, that workloads for employed mothers vary with the composition of the household. The presence of husbands or sons makes little difference and it is rare for either to undertake domestic work on a regular basis. Thus, it is mothers in single-unit households, with or without servants, who spend the most time each day. Arati Majumdar, a 32-year-old clerical worker whose husband is similarly employed and who has a 4-year-old-son, calculated that she spent seven and a half hours each day on household tasks plus morning and evening childcare. This was in spite of the employment of a full-time aya for the child. Her husband spent most of his time outside the office with his friends and she has no close kin nearby to help her out.

*Table 4.1* Daily hours of selected working women by kinship status, and of working mothers by household composition

(a) Regular daily hours of housework by different categories of working women

|  | Less than 2 hours | 2–2½ hrs | 3–4 hrs | 5–6 hrs | 7–8 hrs | 9–10 hrs | More than 10 hours | Total | Average hours |
|---|---|---|---|---|---|---|---|---|---|
| Working mothers | 3 | 12 | 22 | 20 | 4 | 3 | 2 | 66 | 4.5 |
| Elder working daughters | 1 | 7 | 9 | 1 |  |  |  | 18 | 3.0 |
| Younger working daughters | 5 | 8 | 5 |  |  |  |  | 18 | 2.2 |
| Sole working daughter | 5 | 7 | 8 | 2 |  |  |  | 22 | 2.7 |

(b) Average daily hours of housework by household composition of working mothers only

|  | No other adult household members present except employed husbands or sons | No other adult household members present except daughters aged over 10 years | Other employed and non-employed adult females present | Other non-employed adult male members present only | All households in which no domestic servants are employed |
|---|---|---|---|---|---|
| Average daily hours | 5.1 | 4.9 | 3.6 | 6.0 | 5.3 |

As her children grow older, an employed mother may get some help from her daughters. This is more common in poor households where daughters are less likely to be in school. Mothers of school- and college-attending daughters may try not to impose too heavy a load on them and daughters in middle-class households are not invariably expected to help with domestic chores.

It is the presence of other adult women in the household, whether employed or not, which provides the best likelihood of a reduction in the employed mother's domestic burden. Resident mothers-in-law, mothers, sisters-in-law or other relatives may substantially relieve employed women. Anjali Shah, a 35-year-old clerical worker with two young children, spends only between two and three hours per day on housework. Her mother-in-law and her husband's brother's unemployed 22-year-old daughter manage the household and childcare. Similarly, Jyoti Das, a 43-year-old nurse with a teenage daughter and living in a joint family, has a non-employed sister-in-law who runs the household and cooks.

At a later stage in her life, an employed woman may be able to utilize her seniority advantage to devolve much of her domestic responsibility on to her daughter-in-law. This had happened with Ayesha Begum, a widowed hospital aya living with her sons and one daughter-in-law to whom she had relinquished all the household management. On the other hand, Sandhya Chatterjee, a 59-year-old teacher living with her son, non-employed daughter-in-law and grandson, faced the opposite experience as her son and traditionally minded daughter-in-law are hostile to her continuing employment. Her daughter-in-law has signalled her disapproval by insisting that all the housework should be divided equally between herself and her mother-in-law on the basis of total responsibility for fifteen days each in every month.

In households where there are two or more employed women, burdens are often reduced by explicit sharing mechanisms such as alternation of the morning and evening cooking shifts. Households consisting of several unmarried sisters organized their housework quite differently. One, which could afford to do so, employed a full-time housekeeper who was given complete responsibility for running the household. Others organized the work either in terms of who had the most time to spare, regardless of the age hierarchy or had a system of rotation. Five professional sisters employed full-time help and took it in turns of a month at a time to manage the household, a process they described humorously as a 'change of ministry'. It seems that the absence of husbands makes a significant difference, not simply in terms of extra numbers to service but in terms of the kinds of demands which are made both in relation to consumption standards and to ideological conventions surrounding the division of labour.

In households where the only other adult non-employed members are men, the burdens of an employed wife and mother are greatest. This is because the men tend to be fathers-in-law who expect to be cared for by their daughters-in-law rather than to contribute to the housework.

Although many employed women seem to spend a large proportion of their day on household chores, they do spend less time than that recorded by their non-employed counterparts in the small purposive sample, who averaged seven and a half hours per day. Employed women have had to make adjustments to their domestic work loads, at least on weekdays for those whose employment is regular. Given the very long working days for women who have to depend on overcrowded public transport or who have to maximize their hours as piece-rate workers, it is understandable that it is in the most time-consuming tasks of food preparation where most adjustment has been made. 'Short cuts' in cooking were frequently described. The number of dishes served and the elaborateness of meals is minimized despite considerable consumer resistance. Women reported cutting down on cleaning and clothes washing, and some described their households as having moved to a 'self-help' system with respect to individual needs. For some employed mothers, however, this only applied to weekdays. On Sundays and holidays they reverted to a much heavier work load, seeing these days as an opportunity to 'catch up' with what they did not have time to do in the week.

Male participation in domestic work is largely casual or sporadic. The exception is marketing which, as a consequence of the historical legacy of the 'inside–outside' division between male and female spheres of activity, has remained a strongly male task. The majority of husbands and some sons did at least some of the marketing, daily shopping and queueing at government ration shops. They also fetched water in households with no internal water supply. Only one husband, who was mentally ill and permanently unemployed, cooked regularly. Five more husbands or adult sons cooked 'sometimes' either when illness prevented their wives or mothers from doing so, or on 'special occasions'. One husband did some regular house cleaning. A few fathers took responsibility for supervising their children's school work. In eleven households in which there were no non-employed female members, the men did nothing at all. Women were asked for their views on the existing sexual division of labour in their households and on men's responsibilities when female members are in full-time employment. Only two women felt strongly that men should not do housework, and one of these qualified her opposition by admitting that she did not encourage her husband and son to do so because 'men are so unreliable'. Most insisted that men should at least help or even take an equal share, but when asked why this did not happen in their household, they generally replied that men had 'no time' or that their employment kept them 'too busy'. These replies are illuminating in the context of the extreme shortage of time from which most employed women suffered, and suggests that men's time is valued differently from women's time by both women and men.

A further deterrent to shared domestic responsibilities was pointed out by some perceptive women and men, who remarked that women often prevent or discourage men from doing household chores on the

75

grounds that it is, after all, 'women's work.' For young married men particularly, non-participation in household chores is maintained by the strong peer-group pressure against men who do 'women's work' or who are seen to spend 'too much' time with their wives.

Husbands were also asked about their participation in and views on housework, childcare and the division of labour in their households. Responses were engagingly frank. Most of the husbands claimed to do some housework, but it was, again, mainly in the sphere of marketing and financial management. The husband of Rita Mukherjee, who herself works a seven-hour day in a government office and spends up to another six hours each day on housework, said, 'I only do marketing and daily shopping. I don't do any other housework because I do some intellectual work as well as my photography hobby.'

Some husbands were quite unaware of the length of time spent by their wives on housework. Arati Majumdar's husband said, 'I cannot say. I haven't noticed. When I stay at home she seems to be engaged in housework but I don't know what she does in my absence.' Both husband and wife work identical hours in a bank, but he spends up to twelve hours each week visiting friends by himself. Others had a clear sense of the burdens of housework but some greatly underestimated its extent. Gouri Sen Gupta's husband suggested that she spent two hours each day on housework while, with a small son and no other assistance from relatives, she estimated that she spent six hours on weekdays and ten hours on other days.

All but one of the husbands agreed in principle that, when wives are employed, domestic work should be shared between spouses but this agreement was heavily qualified with reasons why equal participation was not possible. One husband argued, 'Cooking and childcare cannot be done by men. These are specialized tasks for women.' Another said, 'Men should do housework except cooking and cleaning – these are women's jobs'.

Taking a rather different tack, Arati Majumdar's husband felt that he did more than his fair share anyway: 'I think I do the major part of the household work. I am earning money. If I did not do that, no household tasks could be done smoothly. I spend the major part of my time earning.' His wife's full-time and comparatively well-paid job are conceptually invisible. She remains a housewife because that is where her duties lie. As her husband commented, 'There should be a division of labour. If a woman works she should appoint a helping hand.'

For these husbands, then, their wives' employment carried no particular implications for their own participation in domestic work. The only signs of change emerge among retired men with still employed wives who generally assume a more managerial role in the household: organizing budgets and supervising servants, though rarely doing the cooking.

For male members of the household, the impact of female members' employment lies in its effects on a wife's or mother's capacity to organize the running of the household and to service their needs: 'She cannot organize her household work very smoothly and sometimes she cannot find time to look after her daughter properly', said one husband and father. Another commented, 'My father doesn't like to see his daughter-in-law going out to work. He thinks he has been neglected by her, but she cannot find more time to take care of him.'

Others mourned the 'short cuts' inflicted upon them: 'We cannot have delicious food. We cannot keep our social commitments due to lack of time, and my daughter is less well cared for.' Thus, employed women can expect little assistance from husbands and other male members with household chores and management, but must depend on other female relatives or on paid help. Where neither is available or affordable, women simply work an even longer day.

## Childcare

Eighty-one women in the sample are mothers, of whom seventy have to make arrangements for the care of young children during their employment. Of these, sixteen women have children under the age of five years and another thirty-two women have children who are of an age where they need care and attention. This age cannot be defined in absolute terms as definitions of childhood vary by social class. The mother's own definition was thus used.

Childcare arrangements loom large in the lives of employed mothers, whose employment involves a long daily absence from home. Most childcare arrangements remain centred on kin. There are few facilities available to women either in the neighbourhood or the workplace, although there are some small signs of a growth in private creches in the middle-class suburbs of south Calcutta. The most likely carers of young children are non-employed adult members of households, unless they are very elderly or infirm. These persons may be husbands, or dependent relatives in the case of the two households where the woman's father's sister and husband's father's brother are the chief carers.

More usually the carer, or carers, will be female in-laws in joint or three generational households. Mothers-in-law are the relatives most frequently involved, but women's own mothers also figure significantly as carers, often in combination with other relatives or helpers. Shanti Sen left her baby with her own mother for the first five months of its life, taking it there each day on the way to work. She then employed a full-time aya to look after the child at home. Rita Ghosh's mother and mother-in-law divided the care of Rita's son between them, an arrangement made possible by the close proximity and good relations of the two families. Mira Das Gupta and her husband live with her mother. Both women are employed, but her mother teaches morning hours only in a government school so the two women are able to cover the childcare.

Employed mothers with no access to a wider kin network, have to resort to a variety of strategies. There are two contexts in which husbands emerge as significant carers. One is where both husband and wife work somewhat shorter hours outside the home enabling childcare to be alternated, such as teachers and college lecturers whose hours fit better with school timetables. The other is where husbands are unemployed or casually employed. In only one case did a woman take her children to her place of work when they were very small. This was the hospital aya with residential accommodation whose husband subsequently took on the main responsibility for the children. However, Banerjee (1985a) reports that the practice is common in small-scale unorganized-sector units.

In a significant number of households, children are left largely to look after themselves, or older children are expected to look after younger ones. Without exception, these are poor households, but in all except one case where the children were described as 'looking after themselves', the mother is or was a home worker who is on the premises, if unable to spare much time for her children. The age of the children is of particular relevance to the home worker's productivity. If she has young children who are close in age, she has to care for them alongside her employment. As the children get older they increasingly take care of themselves, and when they reach the age of about ten, particularly if they are girls, they become an important resource for poor mothers. They may take on the household chores or contribute unpaid labour to their homeworking parents. If there are further births they are likely to take on the additional childcare.

The other major resort of mothers with no kin to assist them is to paid servants or ayas. These vary from very young girls, or sometimes boys, who work as servants performing, for little more than their keep, general household tasks including childminding, to ayas who are paid exclusively to take care of children. This latter arrangement is restricted, because of cost, to high-income households. Neighbours are more likely to be resorted to by poor women and are quite frequently a first resort in emergencies such as sickness. Only one mother, a professional woman with a reasonable salary, uses a private creche.

Illness or other emergencies provoke crises for many women. Eleven women reported that, whatever their usual arrangement, they, or sometimes their husbands, took leave from work. This was not very difficult for public sector employees with fairly generous casual leave provisions, but women in casualized employment who stood to lose

Table 4.2 Current and past childcare arrangements by gross monthly household income

| Main caretaking category | Rs 500 and below Current | Past | Rs 501–1000 Current | Past | Rs 1001–2000 Current | Past | Rs 2001–3000 Current | Past | Rs 3001+ Current | Past | Total |
|---|---|---|---|---|---|---|---|---|---|---|---|
| Wife/children | | 1 | 1 | 1 | | 1 | | | | | 4 |
| Husband/children | 2 | 1 | 1 | | | | | | | | 4 |
| Husband/wife alternate | | | | | 1 | 1 | 1 | | | | 3 |
| Husband | 1 | | | | | | | | | | 1 |
| Children themselves | 1 | 7 | 1 | 5 | 1 | 1 | | | | | 16 |
| Wife's in-laws | | | | | 1 | 1 | 3 | 2 | 5 | 5 | 18 |
| Wife's natal family | | 1 | 1 | 1 | 1 | | 2 | 1 | 1 | | 8 |
| Servants/ayas | | | | 2 | 1 | | 2 | 2 | 4 | | 12 |
| Neighbours | 2 | | | | | | | | 1 | | 3 |
| Nursery | | | 1 | | | | | | | | 1 |
| Total | | | | | | | | | | | 70 |

wages, said that sick children generally had to fend for themselves.

Table 4.2 gives childcare arrangements according to income group. The class differences between households in terms of their capacities to command secure arrangements for their children show quite clearly. The poorer the household, the less likely it is to have wider kin to call upon, and it has to fall back upon the limited resources within the household itself or on neighbours. In-laws are conspicuously absent from poor women's lives and any wider assistance from kin tends to come from a woman's own natal family.

Childcare arrangements also reflect the different value and opportunities of children in different classes. Middle-class children at school are a greater 'cost' on parents, in terms not just of a longer period of dependency but also of the need for certain forms of intensive supervision, such as coaching them for schoolwork and organizing the numerous extra-curricular activities.[6] Middle-class children are schooled in an extremely competitive environment and most families provide extra supervision during evenings and holidays. This burden falls mainly on mothers, although some fathers also do evening coaching of children. Arati Shah is fairly typical of this pattern in better-off, middle-class households. A headteacher herself, she spends two hours each evening supervising the schoolwork of her two teenage sons.

Women were asked about their level of satisfaction with their childcare arrangements, past or present. Fifteen women said they were fairly or very dissatisfied, but others, while not expressing themselves as actively dissatisfied, pointed out that the question was immaterial as they had no other alternative. The greatest dissatisfaction was expressed by those who employed paid assistance. Six of the twelve women dependent on this mode were 'very unhappy' with it. Hired helpers were described as 'unreliable' and 'lacking training'. Servants and ayas are mostly working-class women employed by middle-class families and such statements often conceal conflicts over childrearing methods.

With the exception of paid helpers, women were happiest with arrangements which involved one constant carer such as a mother or mother-in-law. More contingent combinations caused anxiety. Jaya Ghosh, whose mother-in-law, sister-in-law and an aya were all variously involved in the care of her children, was unhappy because she felt that her mother-in-law was too elderly, her sister-in-law was unwilling and the aya was untrained. Male carers were also rated fairly low in the estimation of mothers and it may be that this reflects the strong cultural preoccupation with the view that childcare is properly women's work as much as the standard of care provided by male carers.

As was pointed out in chapter three, women who obtain employment tend to remain in it through the childbearing and rearing years. The data suggest, however, that availability of kin substitutes, mainly female, may not be the major factor determining this pattern of continuing employment for women in all classes. Assistance from kin was available to only 40% of the employed women in the sample. The other 60% had to make what *ad hoc* arrangements they could. Even when kin were available the care given was not always considered satisfactory.

A more potent reason for mothers remaining in employment is the extreme scarcity of employment. Even where families can manage without their financial contribution, women are not prepared to give up these hard-won jobs in the knowledge that they would be unable to regain their position or obtain similar employment in the future.

## Waged work, domestic work and contemporary ideologies of domesticity

Strong ideologies of the appropriate place and activities of women and men in Bengali society, together with low formal female labour-participation rates, have resulted in a clear division of labour and separate male and female 'spaces', which associate men particularly with activities 'outside' the home and women with activities within it.

Thus, men's spare-time activities are much more often located outside the home in places such as tea shops or liquor stalls where animated discussions are carried on.[7] Middle-class men may also visit each other's homes but sit in a separate part of the house such as a verandah. Wives and daughters may be expected to provide them with refreshments but less often to join in. Women's spare-time activities, on the other hand, are often an extension of domestic routines, such as cooking and sewing.

The 'culture of domesticity', highlighted by sociologists of contemporary Britain (e.g. R. Pahl 1980, 1984) in which the home is, for married couples, both the location and the focus of leisure activities such as 'DIY' repairs, decorating and refurbishment, is almost entirely absent in Calcutta. It forms part, neither of the economics nor the culture of household reproduction. The low proportion of house ownership, the continuing availability of cheap skilled labour and the culture of segregated activities for men and women means that the concept of 'the home' must be understood in a contextually distinct way.

These patterns have not been substantially modified by the entry of women into paid employment. In terms of the domestic division of labour, while in some households, there has been some substitution of one woman's domestic labour for another woman's paid employment, there has been no restructuring of the division of labour between the sexes. Where husbands or sons do 'help out', they are usually doing just that, leaving wives or sisters with the general managerial responsibility which is carried continuously. In many cases, men continue to play no part, even of an occasional kind, in domestic work. Arati Shah, the head teacher with teenage sons and a school teacher husband and who is one of the few women in the sample to earn more than her husband, described the very busy period of her day between six and eight in the evening as the period of husband and childcare. Husbands are part of the problem rather than part of the solution.

These conclusions are strikingly similar to those of Hunt (1980) in her study of British families and Roldan (1985) in her study of proletarian families in Mexico city. In explanation, both note the strength of ideological constructions of men's and women's work with their power to confer a taken-for-granted quality upon the existing sexual division of labour. This quality rests ultimately upon the language of the natural order to reproduce these divisions, transcending divisions of class and culture. Women may complain about their domestic burdens as the non-employed sister-in-law of a young employed woman said, 'My husband has holidays. I am on duty twelve months of the year' – but find it more difficult to articulate an argument against 'nature' and often find themselves trapped by the same language to explain why men are unfitted for housework.

At one level, ideologies of domesticity in class society appear similar, but at another level they must be located in specificities. The 'domestic' is not only about a set of mundane, repetitive chores. It also embodies a statement about what kinds of persons women and men are and how this is translated into specific activities.

In the section on the historical emergence of an ideology of domesticity, it was pointed out that this took place at a particular moment of class formation and entailed a reconstruction of gender ideologies which fused Bengali, and to some extent, pan-Indian notions with ones derived from Victorian values. This fusion, together with major differences in the material conditions of urban Bengal as compared with those in advanced capitalist societies, gives Bengali ideologies of domesticity a distinctiveness of their own as well as a similarity to those operating across contemporary capitalist societies.

Manisha Roy, a Bengali sociologist, has argued that for Indian women, being female is defined more by role than by personality traits and personal attributes (Roy 1975b). Although the term 'role' is a rather confused and ambiguous one, compounding a sociological concept with a cultural construct, Roy is pointing to what seems to be an important area of difference in the cultural construction of gender in the Indian context:

> A woman is not more or less feminine. She is feminine simply by
> virtue of being a woman... What makes a woman feminine and

attractive depends on what point she is in her life cycle and how well she is playing her roles.

(ibid: 221)

Exemplifying this, comments from both women and men in Calcutta which touched upon gender characteristics always conceptualized the issue as one of what the genders do as opposed to what they are. This is not to deny the existence of ideas about the mental or psychological attributes of the genders or the influence of contemporary non-Indian writing, but to point to what may be a dominant cultural mode of constructing gender in terms of duty. Thus, to be a good wife and mother is to discharge in exemplary fashion the duties of a wife and mother. Further, this does not necessarily mean that these duties must always and only be carried out by the woman herself, only that it is her responsibility to ensure that they are accomplished 'smoothly' (a term used frequently). This concern was articulated by all the husbands who were interviewed. When asked their views on the qualities most desirable in a wife, 'efficiency in running the household' and 'attachment to the family' were most often mentioned. More 'personal' qualities, apart from physical beauty, rated little concern.

The particular cultural emphasis on 'duty' and the forms in which it is carried out have a bearing upon the way in which the relationship between women's waged and unwaged work is seen. There appears to be little evidence of a guilt-inducing psychological conflict between the two, as much of the sociological and psychological writing on European employed wives and mothers has emphasized (see Wilson 1977 for a critical historical review). Rather, conflicts arose over non-fulfilment or neglect of duties, or failure to ensure that a reliable other person, preferably female, carries them out. Such conflicts tend to be precipitated by complaints from other members of the household, particularly husbands, as some of their comments, noted previously, demonstrate.

Asha Ganguly, a 34-year-old telephone operator, said, 'My husband and I are always in conflict. He thinks that I am not doing my family duties and caring for the children properly.' Asha herself, however, has not internalized any guilt about this. She went on to say,

> Generally, if the children are sick my husband looks after them. I am not so attached to my children. If I became too attached I could not do all my other activities such as organizing women's associations and cultural functions.

Asha is unusual in her determination to maintain this degree of personal autonomy and the rest of her family consider her to be a 'bad' wife and mother as a consequence, but she is not unusual in her lack of personal conflict. Her failure is seen as one of organization rather than of

83

personal inadequacy. Bengali women have been less assailed by pyschologistic ideologies of gender and motherhood which place the emphasis on the person of the woman/mother. Bengali ideologies place more stress on the distinct duties and activities of the genders. It follows that there is no reason for women's waged work to alter the sexual division of labour or to cause guilt. Women who are employed must simply become more efficient organizers. It is also important not to assume that the undeniable existence of a double burden on employed women takes the same form, or creates the same conflicts, as among women in the capitalist west.

There are signs, however, of the appearance of a view among some middle-class mothers that the biological mother is the only appropriate caretaker of young children. This may well lead to the development of feelings of personal guilt.[8] Deepa Bhattacharya, a schoolteacher with a teenage son, described her worries about leaving him with a servant when he was small. Using an unexpected English phrase, she said she felt that young children with employed mothers were always 'hankering after the mother' and not receiving proper care. It may be significant that this view was expressed by a woman with no female relatives to sub-stitute for her, and an increase in the use of paid childcare may perhaps encourage a further ideological shift in the conceptualization of mother-hood from a more collective activity of women in general to a private concern and burden of the biological mother.

## Conclusion

Domestic work, and hence the relationship between paid and unpaid work, is historically and class specific. This chapter has noted the emergence of an ideology of domesticity in middle-class Bengali society with the attendant rise of the 'housewife' devoted to the manage-ment of increasingly elaborated forms of consumption. A rigid sexual division of labour allocated this management to women, while men operated 'outside' in the world of employment and public life.

The growth of employment among women has had little effect on this division of labour. Among middle-class employed women, female kin and domestic servants provide the main sources of assistance. Proletarian women can expect little help except from older children and neighbours. There are similarities with accounts of employed women's (and especially mother's) dual roles elsewhere. However, men's and women's roles are also constructed in a culturally specific way among Bengalis. The content and meaning of women's 'dual roles' should not therefore be assumed to be universal across capitalist societies.

Chapter five

# Employment and autonomy
Women's wages and the distribution and
management of household income

> ...in the domestic dyarchy all management was in Sarmila's
> control....Whatever her husband earned was delivered into her
> hands to the last copper. If any special need arose he had no
> alternative but to go and beg from the Annapurna of his home.
>
> (Tagore: *Two Sisters* 1964 edn: 14)

> I can exercise my opinion on any matter such as politics, art or
> family affairs, but on financial matters I cannot say a word. If I
> need to buy a book or a sari, I have to ask for it from my husband.
> At the end of the month, only if all the bills have been accounted
> for, can I have anything.
>
> (Dipali Ghosh, 46-year-old college lecturer, Calcutta 1982)

## Some theoretical issues

These two highly contrasting accounts of middle-class Bengali
women's relationship to money highlight the crucial importance of
familial power structures in determining women's access to resources
such as money or wages. This chapter examines both the contribution of
women's wages to the household economy and explores the control,
disposal and conceptualization of women's incomes within households
across classes and income groups.

In posing questions about disposal, access and control in relation to
household income resources, feminists have begun to uncover important
ways in which family-based households structure access to resources
unequally between their members, a finding which has run counter to
some of the development orthodoxies of the past two decades (cf.
Brannen and Wilson 1987).

For many writers and planners across the spectrum from institutional
to Marxist approaches, the 'household' has been the unquestioned
bottom line for strategies aimed at redistributing resources more

85

equitably. Once resources could be made to reach that level, it was assumed that all members would benefit - or rather, there was no assumption that distributional relations within the household might be problematic.

For others, the deconstruction of the household has been accomplished through a recasting of neo-classical paradigms, as in what has become known as the New Household Economics (Becker 1965, Schultz 1974, Ben-Porath 1982). In these paradigms, the basic unit of analysis is the individual, and the family (or household - they are treated as one and the same thing) is a variable which intervenes to maximize the individual's capacity to acquire scarce resources. Neo-classical models assume a disembedded individual voluntarily exercising a rational choice over whether to marry or to be employed. The family is thus a product of the voluntary choices of individuals who, with their varying endowments of human capital, have chosen to cooperate in their individual best interests. Apart from its tautological limitations (it must follow that the family, by which is assumed a western nuclear type centred on marriage, is always consistent with maximum economic utility because that is the *raison d'être* of its existence), neo-classical economics, despite its focus on distribution, cannot encompass those inequalities of access within families which derive from the structure, ideology and power relations of the family itself.

Cultural practices which discriminate systematically against categories of persons, such as Indian widows and often against female members generally, in the distribution of familial resources are rendered invisible because the family is conceptualized as a voluntary contract, not a set of power relationships. Thus, there can be no real conflict of interest within families over resource allocation.

Despite their different theoretical premises, all these approaches share a tendency to use the language of equity in relation to family distributional practices. Ben-Porath, writing within a new household economics framework, describes families as 'the major non-market mechanism through which incomes are jointly generated, *pooled* and *redistributed*' (1982: 1, my emphasis). Similarly, the non neo-classical literature is littered with the terminology of 'pooling' and 'sharing' as descriptions of intra-household distribution practices (for examples and discussion, see Harris 1981, Whitehead 1981). Analysis has often tended to replicate uncritically the ideologies of family members themselves. These may disguise a considerable degree of inequality in the structures of distribution.

Delphy (1979) has pointed to the ways in which culturally constructed theories of needs can mask different levels of consumption within families, particularly in relation to female members. She points out, further, that unequal distribution exists at all levels of income and that rising standards of living may allow for the emergence of new forms of consumption which provide fresh arenas for differentiation. Resource distribution can take unequal forms in middle-class families as in poor ones.

The effects of the insertion of women's wages into the complex redistributional processes of families can thus only be addressed in the context of specific ideologies and material conditions. Certainly, no assumption can be made that the capacity to command a wage automatically guarantees women access either to a major or an equal share of the fruits.

The effect of women's wages and incomes on family-based households outside the context of the advanced capitalist countries has only recently begun to receive attention. The comparatively low level of female wage labour in many contexts explains only partly the lack of concern. The 'invisibility' of women's direct and indirect income contributions has been a potent reason. A recent collection arising from a Population Council workshop has, however, produced some much needed empirical accounts (Dwyer and Bruce 1988). The major issues are summarized in Dwyer (1983). Starting from the premise that there is considerable variation in income management at the household level by culture, history and class, Dwyer reviews the existing literature and concludes that in general, women's incomes (however small) are critical to the survival of poor households; that pooling of incomes is not the norm in many societies and that both obligations to the household and priorities for it may differ systematically by gender. She also points out that women's contributions are often culturally evaluated as less important than those of men and that this may produce conflict rather than unity in decision making.

The recent rise in modern-sector employment opportunities in export-oriented industries located in some of the newly industrializing countries has also yielded up important information. The majority of these women are young, unmarried and newly but fully visible wage workers, which perhaps explains why they have generated particular interest. Salaff (1981), Kung (1983) and Mather (1985) on Taiwan, Hongkong and Indonesia respectively, have all touched upon the role of unmarried daughters' wages in sustaining a family economy and its existing power relations.

With the exception of Roldan (1985) on urban Mexico, discussion of the effects of married women's wages on the family has received more attention from British sociologists, doubtless following the rise in married women's employment in the post-war period. Early sociological accounts tended to reproduce popular stereotypes of the 'working wife.' Conceptions of married women's wages as supplementary or as 'pin money' have been shown historically to derive from the 'breadwinner–dependant' conceptualization of the marriage contract which has its roots in the restructuring of the labour market and of ideologies of gender and work in the late nineteenth century (Barrett 1980). The understanding which this subsequently generated of married women's wages as 'non-essential' and facilitating the purchase of 'luxury' goods or holidays meshes with the conceptualization, found in earlier literature, of married women as secondary earners whose wages supplement those of a primary earner (cf. Cunnison 1966 Jephcott *et al.* 1962, Klein 1965). These understandings are also reinforced in some areas of state legislation, such as social security benefits (see Hunt 1980: 83–9) and can be self-fulfilling in that employers may utilize such arguments to justify the payment of low wages to women in general.[1]

Jan Pahl is one of the few researchers to study the relationship between money and power within marriages and to point to the ideological forms within which monetary transactions are embedded and the potential which exists for conflict. Her studies in Britain uncover considerable variation in styles of money management within households and she found that class, life cycle and cultural factors are all implicated in the production of different patterns of management (J. Pahl 1980, 1983, 1984).

Pahl's work shifts the terrain of the discussion into questions of control and management of resources within the household, such as to what degree of control women may have over the disposal of their own income, what it means to say that they have control and to what extent having the status of a wage earner may lead to changes in family power structures.

The way in which such questions are answered is crucial to how the liberatory potential of wage employment for women is assessed. I have argued elsewhere (Standing 1985b) that discussion of these issues has often been conducted at an overgeneralized level. Some writers have argued that women's entry into waged work has had no significant impact on women's condition or on existing power relations within families because women are trapped into low-paid work with little possibility of freeing themselves from familial and marital dependency (e.g. Salaff 1981). Additionally, their wages are often appropriated by other members of the household, leaving them with little or no personal income or control over its destination. Others have argued that, however small, a money wage is a powerful weapon which, whatever its destination, does affect the bargaining capacity of women within the family (e.g. Omvedt 1980). In so far as these views tend to utilize different parameters ('objective' constraints versus 'subjective' experiences) both are valid at a general level, but it is important to disaggregate the many issues raised here into more precise analytical and empirical questions.

It is equally important to employ a common terminology for analysing these issues. J. Pahl (1983) distinguishes usefully between 'control', which concerns major intra-household decisions of a 'policy-making' kind; 'management', which puts policy decisions into action, and 'budgeting', which is concerned with manipulating available resources to keep within pre-determined expenditure decisions. The distinction between control and management is particularly crucial when analysing women's relationship, not only to wages, but also to other forms of property where it exists, such as land, housing and non-monetary forms of saving. Control here signifies a capacity to enforce rights of direction and disposal over property against competing claims. Middle-class Indian women are sometimes involved in property management but less often have control in this sense.

Bengali family forms are often complex and the level of state intervention and support in the familial domain is much less than in western Europe with developed welfare states. These differences do affect the redistributional processes within households and the manner in which women's wages are inserted into them. Most of all, the control, management and disposal of women's wages are directly related to the empirically specific ways in which household income is conceptualized and managed. An understanding of this requires some consideration of the historical context of Bengali patterns of household resource management and their associated ideologies of distribution.

## Household income management: the historical background

The previous chapter charted the emergence of the 'housewife' among the Bengali *bhadralok* and the increasing need for married women to learn household management skills appropriate to the transformed economic and social base of urban Bengali society. According to Borthwick, the common pattern of management became one in which 'the husband gave his wife a portion of his earnings to manage according to her own judgement of priorities' and that 'the ability to keep accounts was a quality sought after in the new housewife' (1984: 190).

Articles and lectures gave practical advice on how to manage accounts and draw up a balance sheet. Women were exhorted to save money and forego personal expenditure on 'non-essentials'. The idealized picture of women's control over the domestic arena sketched in Tagore's *Two Sisters* has a basis in the system of domestic management which arose with the transformation of landed households into increasingly wage-dependent ones. The new emphasis on the role of the wife as housewife and manager through an allowance given to her by her husband was tempered, however, by previous traditions of management and by the continuing presence within many households of

89

extended kin relations which meant that household responsibilities were defined in culturally specific ways.

In his discussion of this period of transformation, Broomfield argues that, for the Bengali middle class, rural – urban links were sustained through the institution of the joint family 'maintaining a village home for a number of generations of kin, and pooling income from landed rents and the salaries of its professionally employed members' (1968: 11). A strict division of labour assigned men to the external economy, to culture and to politics, and women to the internal organization of the household. The age and kinship hierarchy delegated the overall management of this to the senior-most married woman. This included the management of a common fund, the payment of servants and the management of gift giving and charitable obligations. Young married women would generally only have authority within the household if there were no older married women. Men were usually physically absent from the domestic arena.

The household's financial resources were usually managed through a common fund (*joutha bhandar*) within which incomes were pooled and out of which members were entitled to funds according to a conception of their personal needs. The fund thus embodied a redistributive ideology which did not distinguish between earners and non-earners in resource allocation. As with land, money incomes – from whatever source – were vested in the kinship group as property-in-common. This did not signify equal access or equal rights for individual members. Gender and kinship status structured these in unequal ways. Just as women held inferior rights to landed property, their claims to other resources were circumscribed by pre-defined concepts of rights and needs. Hindu widows, for instance, were expected to eat a meagre, vegetarian diet and have few items of clothing. But these structured inequalities in the redistributional process were not based on the distinction between individual wage and income earners and dependants, or between productive and non-productive members.

This common fund pattern of management appears to be a historically specific mode of managing household finances which was particular, if not exclusive, to family forms based in jointly held property and linked to a distinctive ideology of redistribution. Senior married women were generally responsible for its management. To what extent any form of common funding and associated ideologies reached into propertyless households is, unfortunately, unknown.

The growth of wage dependency introduced new sources of tension into middle-class households, in that it brought about incipient differentiation between earners and non-earners, and precipitated a clash between competing ideologies of resource distribution. Not coincidentally there appears, from the turn of the century, a wave of comment on the subject of the 'breakdown' of the joint family. The 1911 Census ascribed the 'insanitary' conditions prevailing in north Calcutta partly to the constant partitioning of dwelling houses due to the division of joint families. The causes of division were said to lie in the rising rate of property litigation and the tensions between earning and 'idle' members. The Census writer quotes the case of 'an officer in government employ who obtained a large increase in pay but was poorer than before because his elder brother at once threw up his own post and ceased to contribute to the family income' (Government of India 1913 vol.V, part 1: 50).

Women were, however, considered to be equally at fault in causing the demise of the joint family:

> Devoted to their husband's interest, the wives are jealous of their earnings being used by others, particularly by those who do not contribute to the family income. More petty feelings, less disinterested motives, such as the mutual jealousy of the brothers' wives, the quarrels of their children etc. also contribute to the breaking up of the family.
>
> (ibid: 50–1)

A cautionary tale of a selfish wife in the journal *mahila* for July 1902 concludes by warning that 'the wife must never let her head be turned by her husband's salary if it is the largest in the household'.

These comments, expressive of a colonial discursive and regulatory concern with the nature of the 'family' at this period, illustrate at the same time the magnitude of the ideological clash and the ways in which the growth of the wage economy challenged traditional mechanisms of intra-family distribution and their basis in a different conception of dependency. Male non-earners became defined as 'idle' and a burden to their earning relatives. Degrees of dependency emerged within the wider household collectivity as the conjugal tie came to pre-empt or challenge other claims.

As Hunt (1980: 47–8) has pointed out in the context of contemporary Britain, in capitalist economies the wage becomes associated with an ideology of personal appropriation. It 'belongs' to the wage earner and is allocated to wageless dependants as a personal dispensation. A related ideology of individual occupational achievement underlines a wage earner's 'right' to use the fruits of his labour for his own personal consumption and the maintenance of 'his' dependants. Tension arises between ideologies of pooling and redistribution among a complex range of kin and the ideology of the wage, which emphasizes private accumulation, personal achievement and personal ownership through individuating mechanisms such as banking, savings and insurance policies.

In the Bengali case, it is commonly argued by observers and respondents alike that when brothers living in a joint family which pools resources, earn different wages but have the same number of immediate dependants, tension emerges between the obligation to redistribute the additional income, and the wish of higher earning members to appropriate it for themselves and their immediate dependants. This is not, however, in itself a sufficient explanation for individuation and the ensuing breakdown of complex family forms as it renders the construction of kinship dependencies unproblematic. Definitions of dependants and ideologies of marriage have also changed. Some important elements of these changes are well captured by respondents to the 1931 Census 'Questionnaire on Hindu Public Opinion':

> Many correspondents commented on the fact that the presence of a widow in a family was always welcomed because she would cheerfully undertake the drudgery of the family whilst the extreme self-denial expected of a Hindu widow makes her support very little of a burden. But where she is unprovided for and has children there are bound to be heartburnings on account of the differences in the treatment which her children and those of her husband's relatives receive.
>
> (Government of India 1933: 402)

This statement acknowledges an important breach with the principle of non-differentiation between family members on the basis of earning capacity and it also reveals the extent to which narrowing definitions of dependency had begun to operate. There is no 'natural' reason why a man should feel less responsible for his deceased brother's widow than for his own wife, nor why a woman should consider her sister-in-law's children less deserving than her own. These understandings of dependency are social in origin, and the apparent tendency for complex families to fragment both materially and ideologically into conjugally based units around an individual male 'breadwinner', his wife and dependent children, is a social and historical, not a natural and inevitable process. It is also one which is uneven and non-linear in its effects and a subject of ideological struggle, as will be seen in the next section.


## Contemporary patterns of household income management

As was pointed out in Chapter two, p. 28, money enters the household largely in the form of wages or in some cases as pensions from previous employment or as remittances.

Table 5.1 Patterns of household income management

| | Eldest ever-married employed woman | Eldest ever-married non-employed woman | Joint, husband-wife | Joint, other female-male | Eldest never married female | Joint unmarried female | Ever-married male | Unmarried male | Joint married male | Total |
|---|---|---|---|---|---|---|---|---|---|---|
| Col. | | 1 | 3 | 5 | 7 | 9 | 11 | 13 | 15 | 17 |
| Common fund management | 18 | 10 | 2 | 1 | | 1 | 6 | – | 1 | 40 |
| Col. | 2 | 4 | 6 | 8 | 10 | 12 | 14 | 16 | 18 | |
| Individual management | 15 | 4 | 18 | 4 | 1 | – | 19 | – | | 61 |

Note: Excluding single-person households and 5 households with incomplete information

Table 5.1 attempts to capture the different modes through which income is managed by households, excluding those of single persons which are considered separately. The table distinguishes between styles of management and, within those, the member or members responsible for their administration. The overall distinction is between those households which reported having a common fund and those where the management of money is either delegated to or appropriated by one or more members without the intervention of a pooling mechanism such as the common fund. Altogether, 38% of households operate a common fund and in three-quarters of these households, the management is a solely female responsibility.

The common fund refers both to a concept of household income management and to a physically discrete sum of money put aside to cover a somewhat variable set of needs to which each member of the household is entitled by virtue of that membership. It consists usually of a fixed amount of money contributed by all wage earners in proportion to their incomes and deposited generally as cash in a small safe or tin box. The person who administers the fund keeps the key, if there is one, and usually takes responsibility for the payment of the fixed expenditures which are allocated to the fund. In some households, the money is accessible to household members to take from as necessary. The ideology of the fund is that all members, earners or not, have an entitlement to the fund according their personal needs.

The common fund thus continues to embody a redistributive ideology which does not differentiate earners from non-earners or high earners from low earners. In practice, the extent to which all wages are distributed through the fund is variable and this is particularly the case with women's wages. Equally, the kinds of expenditure covered by the common fund vary. The minimum is that of basic food and housing costs, but it may also cover clothing, medicine and 'non-essential' expenditure such as entertainments.

The amount of the wage kept back for personal use also varies. In some households, essential daily expenditure such as bus fares or meals, is kept back by individual earners. In others, it is taken back from the fund on a daily basis. This sum, (*byektigata kharach*) is a separate item from 'pocket money' (*hat kharach*), which may also be kept back in different amounts by wage earners. Again, although earning members contribute in proportion to their level of earnings, the redistributive effect tends to be blunted by the wide variations in individual earning power, particularly between women and men. Husbands' and wives' 'pocket money' is rarely of the same magnitude. Nonetheless, the language of the common fund remains the language of pooling and non-differentiation.

Likewise, the language of common-fund management is that of caretaking rather than controlling. The person responsible manages funds which are disbursed or taken from according to already determined concepts of personal need and household priorities. The management presupposes an existing structure of decision making. As one husband explained: 'A common expenses fund is kept in a common place, from where all of us three (including our daughter) spend whenever necessary and while the fund lasts.'

Responsibility for the common fund tends to be female, and age and kinship status continue to be significant in the management of common funds, as can be seen from Table 5.1, columns 1 and 3. In twenty-six out of these twenty-eight households, the most senior ever-married woman, whether employed or not, was responsible for administering the fund. Only in two cases, have younger married employed women taken on the responsibility despite there being in both cases a resident mother-in-law. Unmarried women only have responsibility in households of unmarried siblings and in no household did an unmarried man carry this responsibility although in one case (col. 7) the senior widowed woman and her married son administered the fund jointly. Male management of common funds does occur (cols 13 and 17) but is not the common pattern.

Is there a historical link between this form of financial management and the common fund associated with joint families of previous generations? There are few systematic differences between households with a common fund and households without except that common-fund households tend to be larger, containing on average 7.4 persons as against 4.9 for households with individual management styles. They are, however, only somewhat more likely to contain complex combinations of kin (61% as against 42%) than other households. There is some correlation with income level in that poorer households are less likely to have a common fund (22% and 50% in the lowest and highest income groups respectively). However, this may reflect practicalities such as irregularity of income and lack of house security, rather than demographic and ideological differences. The common fund is not a straightforward function of income level, occupation or household complexity. Nor does it seem to be associated with a particular stage in the developmental cycle of households.

The redistributional ideology of the common fund does seem to have some ideological continuity with the concept of income as property-in-common to which all members have some customarily determined right of access, albeit differentially structured. Income inequalities, however, have almost certainly wrought changes in the meaning of the common fund and having a common fund does not mean quite the same thing in low income households as in high income ones.

In low income households with a common fund, where women's

wages are generally crucial to survival, married women's earnings tend to go into the fund in their entirety. Unmarried daughters may keep a small amount for personal expenditure, and male members almost always have some pocket money, but on the whole there is little differentiation of earnings. Whatever is earned is pooled to ensure survival.

In high income households, far less of the wage is pooled in the common fund and there are several areas of expenditure, such as clothing, medicine, education and leisure, which may become an individual responsibility. The implications of this increasing differentiation of incomes in higher income households are considered in the next section but clearly, the significance of the common fund differs with the financial circumstances of the household. (See also Dwyer 1983: 3–5.)

The question also arises as to whether the common fund form of management is declining. Although systematic information on the financial arrangements of previous generations was not collected, some hints emerged of a possible switch from common funds to more individual styles. The link between complex families and the common fund was made by Asha Ganguly, a 36-year-old telephone operator:

> Now we are a single family. Originally, we were a joint family but my mother-in-law died. Now only my father-in-law is living with us. When we were a joint family we had a common fund and every earning member used to contribute to it. My father-in-law and mother-in-law managed everything. This covered all necessities for every earning member except their personal expenditure. Now my husband manages the household finances.

This household had switched, not only between styles of management but to a different structure of responsibility entailing more individual decision making on the part of the husband.

Common fund arrangements may, however, also disguise a considerable degree of individual decision making within the household. In one, where the common fund was described by both husband and wife as jointly administered, the husband explained their arrangements thus: 'I make a budget and give money to my wife according to that. She manages all domestic expenses with that money. I only keep money in my hand for the establishment charges like house rent.' This arrangement appears, in practice, to be much closer to an allowance system (see p. 100) than to the principles of the common fund despite being described in that language.

It is the role of individual decision making which marks the apparent difference between the common fund and individual management of household finances. Operationally, it has been suggested that the common fund manager is more like a caretaker who oversees the disbursement of funds according to already determined understandings of need. The locus of decision making lies elsewhere than with the manager. By implication, in systems of individual management, the manager may play a more active role in the determination of intra-household income distribution.

In fact, styles of individual management vary widely. There is considerable variation in the extent to which those nominated as financial managers can or do determine the disposal of household income and the degree to which they refer to other members. In other words, there is variation in the degree to which they are controllers or managers. Styles range from the autocratic to a caretaking responsibility similar to that found in most common fund management. Within this range of variation, three main styles can be discerned.

The first is that exemplified by households in Table 5.1, cols 2 and 4. Here, the senior woman, who is generally a wage earner herself, is handed a proportion, or sometimes the whole, of the wages of earning members and takes responsibility for paying bills and organizing the budget according to the inflow of wages into the household. Major expenditure decisions may be taken in consultation with a variable range of household members, but day-to-day budgeting is the woman's responsibility. In most respects, this style of management is much like that in common fund households, the only difference being in the physical form in which money is held. It is notable, also, that twelve of these nineteen households are either all female or are ones in which women are the only or major wage earners. They are also disproportionately low income households.

Shabala Das, a 48-year-old school teacher with one dependent child, is the only wage earner in her household as her husband is sick and unable to work. She manages the household finances entirely by herself from her earnings, keeping no money for personal expenditure. Malati Biswas is a 50-year-old widow living with her four unmarried children, married son and his wife. Their combined income of Rs 625 comes from the home-based manufacture of incense sticks by herself, her 10-year-old daughter and her son's wife, together with the unskilled employment of three of her sons. All earners give their wages to her to manage, keeping only essential expenditure and sometimes some pocket money for themselves.

This pattern of management and budgeting has similarities with the pattern described by J. Pahl for some British families, which she calls the 'whole wage' system (1983: 245). Here (assuming a nuclear family unit with one main male wage earner) the husband hands over his wage packet to his wife and either keeps back or is given personal spending money. Pahl suggests that this system, which tends to be region specific, is characteristic of proletarian households on low incomes where the management and 'stretching' of money is an onerous task allowing for little exercise of choice and conferring no independence of action on the manager. It is not, therefore, a task which male members would wish to take on. This may also be the case for some poor households in Calcutta, where a culture of female management of household income combines with poverty and the frequent loss of male income support to place responsibility upon women.

The second pattern of individual management is jointly by husband and wife. This may take two different forms. In one, the contributions of all earners are pooled and the married couple then assume joint responsibility for management and budgeting. In the other, which is more common, the wages of husbands and wives are earmarked for different purposes.

This pattern of management, where there is no intervening common fund, is limited to single-unit family structures. It is not found at all in joint families and in all but five of the households, the structure was 'nuclear', while in the remaining five, there was just one other resident dependent elderly or young unmarried relative.

Again, in practice, the meaning of joint management is variable. Some couples in the higher income groups reported that they sat down together on pay days to discuss their budget and expenditure priorities for the month. In other cases, either husband or wife did the major planning but consulted their partner. Ranjana Bose's husband said:

> My wife does not find time to organize financial arrangements. She is overworked with her school teaching load. As I am a retired person I make a monthly budget, consulting with my wife, and then I deal with the expenses.

Where both have regular (usually salaried) incomes, there is more likely to be a division of financial labour. Subodh Sen, an accountant whose wife is a librarian, explained, 'I keep money for house rent, electric bills, fees for school. My wife manages day-to-day expenses.' The division of labour usually takes this form, with husbands bearing responsibility for housing and establishment costs while wives spend their own earnings on food, clothing and daily household expenditure. It is a division which reflects, less the disparities in male and female incomes (rent costs are generally lower than food bills), but a more ideological sense of what women's and men's wages mean and which is discussed on p. 105. But nor is it invariable. Bela Ghosh, a 31-year-old clerical worker whose salary is exactly half that of her husband, uses her own earnings to pay the house rent and school fees as well as the daily household expenses.

Again, joint management cuts across income groups and occupations, but high income professional households are characterized by a self-conscious model of shared decision making which is less in evidence in poor households.

The third pattern (Table 5.1, col. 14) is one where a senior male member manages the finances individually. These nineteen households are not, for the most part, the mirror of those where a senior woman is the manager. It was suggested that individual female management is ideologically quite similar to female common fund management in terms of the structure of decision making and the role of the woman as 'caretaker' of household funds. By contrast, male managers are much more likely to be the main decision makers as well. Male managers often control incomes as well as manage them and in a few cases they did the daily budgeting as well.

While there are no cases where husbands give their whole wage to their wives except where there is a common fund, in six of the nineteen individually male managed households, women reported handing over their whole wage to their husband or father. Malabika Datta, a 32-year-old clerk, said, 'I give all my money to my husband and ask him for some when I need it.' Shaila Majumdar, a 20-year-old factory worker who is one of the main earners in her very low income household, gives her wage to her father, keeping back only sufficient for her daily bus fare. The husband of Deepali Ghosh, whose unhappy description of monetary arrangements in her household appears at the head of the chapter, maintains a precise record of household income and expenditure in which every paise (one-hundreth of a rupee) is accounted for. Expenses are doled out daily in small amounts to his wife and teenage children and written up in a large ledger each day.

In the two households in this category of management in which a family business operates, both of which are low income households, male control is absolute. Mohan Pal runs a tailoring business with family labour. His wife and daughter also earn independent incomes from contracted-out piecework and have some personal income of their own, but the household finances are run by the husband, who has outstanding bank loans against the business.

In other households, the degree of individual male control varies. In some, earning members give a proportion of their wages to a husband or father and manage their own personal expenditure on clothing and other needs, as in some common-fund and female-managed households. Male responsibility for finances may also result from practical contingencies. Shanti De and daughter, both clerical workers, are the main earners in their households as Shanti's husband has retired. They both deposit a share of their earnings, which are larger in Shanti's case, with him and he manages the finances because he has more time than his wife.

Yet again, both the incidence of male management, and the different styles which it may take, cut across income groups. Nor is it associated with particular family forms. Male managers, autocratic or otherwise, are found in both high and low income households and in complex families as well.

Finally, the situation in households where there are no employed women may be considered. The small sample of these households yielded two patterns of money management. One is that of the common fund managed by the senior married woman, which operates in similar ways to those found in the main sample households. The other is the allowance system which is also common in British families with non-employed wives. The husband, or breadwinner, takes responsibility for certain elements of fixed expenditure and gives his wife, or the woman responsible for daily budgeting, a fixed amount from his wage. This was how Muni Patnaik, a 50-year-old housewife, described her arrangements:

> My husband gives me so much each month and I have to manage,
> If I run out before the end of the month I have to ask him for extra.
> He then demands an explanation of how I have spent the money.
> If he is satisfied then he gives it out of his own pocket, If not, then
> I have to manage without.

This form of management, though nominally female, is notable for the lack of control which it bestows on the manager, the absence of any area of autonomy over even small amounts of money and the sense of personal ownership of money associated with the male earner.

Styles of management and their implications for decision making are thus quite varied and do not correlate straightforwardly with demographic, life-cycle and income effects. There is a critical area of ideological mediation which also explains why the entry of women into waged employment does not automatically mean an enhancement either in women's share of household income resources or in their decision-making capacity in relation to those resources. J. Pahl, while suggesting that wives who earn in their own right are more likely to have some power over how the money is spent, points out that '. . .this power is still shaped by ideologies about the nature of marriage as held by husband and wife and by the social worlds in which they live' (1983: 252). Several different ideologies of marriage and of familial obligation underpin the various patterns of management discussed previously.

The ideology of the common fund entails a particular conception of sharing and needs which de-emphasizes marriage as the major conduit through which resources are allocated. Male management and fixed allowances, on the other hand, bring the marital relationship to the fore, emphasize the male breadwinner/decision-maker role and may also throw into relief the power inequalities within the marriage contract. Joint wife and husband management can embody an ideology of marriage as an exclusive and equal partnership in which decisions are shared only within the couple.

In terms of the general direction of change, common funding may be giving way to more individual styles of management. Most significantly for women, this may also entail an increase in male control of household income if female common-fund managers relinquish management to male members.

The form in which money is distributed within the household does affect the impact of women's wages and the extent to which the bringing in of a wage alters the balance of power within households. Where there is a common fund managed by a senior woman, the employment of a female member does not directly affect the existing financial arrangements although it may strengthen her voice in household decision-making processes. In common fund households, the significance of women's wages lies more in the potential to generate further intra-household differentiation by exacerbating income inequalities, as is discussed on p. 103.

In other households, the effects of women's employment on their capacity to command increased power and resources will depend to a great extent on the nature of the marriage, or the relations between parents and children. In households where husbands and wives see themselves as joint managers, the ideology is often that of a 'modern' marriage, which includes an emphasis on the importance of women as wage earners, not simply because of their financial contribution but because of their 'equal right' to be earners and decision makers.

In households where husbands or fathers appropriate the earnings of wives and daughters, women's employment tends mainly to raise the level of conflict among household members. Employed women whose husbands take control of their wages are structurally in a position little better than that of non-employed women dependent on an allowance system.

## The disposal of women's earnings

It has been pointed out that in many contexts, women's earnings are often treated differently from those of men when they enter the household. This section examines the extent to which earnings are differentiated along gender lines in Calcutta households and what are the implications of such differentiation. Three intersecting variables largely determine what happens to women's wages; the form in which household income is conceptualized and managed, the income level of the household and the stage in the life cycle of the woman earner.

In common fund households, where an agreed proportion of each person's wage enters the fund there is, in principle, no differentiation of incomes, whether between high and low earners or between women and men. Among this category of households, there are only two cases where incomes are allocated to specific forms of major expenditure. In both households, the woman earner sets aside money from her wage to pay the rent, while in one, the husband purchases the food and in the other, employed sons and daughters buy food and fuel. This is unusual in common fund arrangements as these items are generally taken from the fund.

As was pointed out, unequal earning power can nevertheless lead to inequalities of access to money, and one potential inequality is that of personal spending money. Generally speaking, the larger the number of items purchased separately from the fund, the greater the likelihood of higher earners having more personal spending power than lesser earners. Where all except essential daily expenditure is put into the common fund, women earners are formally in the same position as non-earners and as male earners. Any inequalities in their rights to call upon the common fund derive from their position as women rather than as inferior wage earners.

Common fund households where money is kept back for personal expenditure, do tend to adjust the shares of wage earners so that they give fairly equal proportions of their wages. Parbati and Shanta Mukherjee, unmarried sisters in their 20s, live with their mother, four employed brothers and the wife and children of one brother. They earn Rs 75 and Rs 50 respectively from private tuition and generally keep all their earnings for personal expenses while their brothers' salaries provide the common fund. This gives them personal spending money, unlike their mother and sister-in-law, although it remains less than that of their highly paid brothers. However, they sometimes feel compelled to give their mother Rs 20–30 from their earnings to help the household budget, making their personal income quite small. There is one other case where the woman's earnings are so low, and her household reasonably well off that it is treated as personal income and she does not contribute to the common fund, and another high income household in which the married woman earner sometimes contributes and sometimes keeps her earnings for personal consumption and saving.

Differentiation of incomes does, however, enter through categories of expenditure excluded from the common fund. This happens particularly when a third generation is added to the household. There is then a tendency for households to divide into separate consumption units based upon a conjugal pair and in which more and more areas of expenditure become the responsibility of the parental income. The cost of education, clothing (of both children and adults) and medicine are particularly likely to devolve upon the parental unit rather than upon the common fund.

This may be both the first stage in the breaking up of the common fund in complex households, as units usually have different purchasing capacities which are not fully evened out by the fund, and is also the point at which, where there is a financial surplus, differentiation may emerge between male and female incomes. The employed wife's income becomes associated increasingly with the separate provisioning of her own children, while her husband's income goes mainly to the common fund.

Rekha Mitra, a 26-year-old businesswoman, lives in a joint family with her husband and child, her husband's two brothers and their wives and children. She is the only employed woman in the household. Their common fund is managed by the eldest brother and all earners contribute for common food and housing costs. Rekha keeps most of her own earnings, however, which she uses to pay for her son's education in an English medium school and to buy clothing for her own unit.

The emergence of separate provisioning in certain areas of expenditure can be understood fairly easily at one level. At given points in time, the expenditure needs and priorities of different units vary according to numbers of children and expenditure choices. Self-medication and homeopathy are cheaper than consulting a private doctor. English medium education and private tuition add to the costs of education. But this separation of expenditure along more 'nuclear' lines does presuppose the narrowed definition of dependency discussed earlier. Married couples see their priority as providing for and investing in their own children, and the income of wives makes it more possible for them to do so.

This does not mean that intra- and inter- household inequalities are automatically greatly exacerbated when women are employed. While it is common in complex households for some areas to be separately provisioned, a form of redistribution can then take place through a different mechanism. Better endowed conjugal units may 'give' money to the less well endowed specifically to pay for a child's education or for medical treatment.

One set of households which was previously a joint family with a common fund but subsequently split into four completely separately provisioned units, exemplifies these various forms of possible transfer. The seventeen members of the Adhikari family, several generations resident in Calcutta, live in a large dwelling structure built by the father of the three remaining brothers whose units make up the now separate households. Some years ago, they decided to separate financially and spatially, and constructed three separate living quarters out of the existing house. The units all have different numbers of members and earners, and each contains an employed woman. The youngest of the three women earners, a 22-year-old clerk, gives a proportion of her wage to her father, who manages the household finances, and uses the rest to pay for her continuing education and personal spending money. Her father's brother's daughter, a 30-year-old casually employed teacher, gives money to her own parents and also to her cousins in the first unit to help pay for their education. In the third unit, the 46-year-old brother's wife, a clerical worker with one teenage son, sends Rs 200 every month to her own brother to pay for the education of his daughter.

In households with common funds, therefore, increasing income inequalities and the appearance of a financial surplus, together with changing kinship ideologies, lead to pressures on pooling modes of income management and their replacement by other, more differentiated, forms of redistribution such as personal gifts and remittances. Where women have an income, this may contribute to intra-household inequalities and be a factor in the demise of pooling arrangements.

In poor households, the differentiation of women's wages from those of men is usually minimal, whether income is managed through a common fund or by an individual. It is not often earmarked for or conceptualized as pertaining to particular kinds of expenditure but is part of the household's essential survival fund. Apart from single women living independently, thirteen households are in any case entirely female supported and all but two of these are in the lowest income groups. Here, the question of differentiation does not arise.

In households with individual management forms, the extent of differentiation between men's and women's wages varies. In male-managed households, where male control over the household finances may be very great, there is little room for differentiation. In female-managed households, the range of variation is similar to that found in common fund households.

Differentiation is most developed where there is joint non-common-fund management by married couples. In all but one of the eleven households in which there is joint management by a married couple who are both employed, wives could specify precisely what their own incomes provided to the household and this was true for households at all income levels, but probably for different reasons. In low income households, joint management means that husbands and wives hold on to their respective earnings and agree a financial division of labour. In households where the couples receive monthly salaries, some at least of the money tends to be banked in a joint account and certain kinds of payments may be disbursed by cheque. Such arrangements require distinctive forms of management of resources in which there is room for different levels of consultation.

Saraswati Debi, married to a taxi driver and with five dependent children and a combined income of Rs 560, uses her own combined earnings from making cowdung fuel cakes and doing domestic work to finance the daily marketing. More expensive or irregular items, such as meat and fish, are purchased out of her husband's income. Sandhya Sinha, a young hospital aya earning between Rs 100–150 per month, uses her earnings to provide milk and clothing for the two children as well as daily provisions for the household, while her husband pays the rent and other fixed costs.

Among high income couples, women's earnings are most often associated with the purchase of medicine, particularly for their own treatment (this is also the case for some unmarried daughters in higher income households), clothing, school fees, some household consumer goods and the purchase of additional and more expensive food items such as milk and protein foods. Arati Mukherjee's fairly high earnings from her job in a bank are allocated to pay for the two domestic servants, her son's school fees, the household's rice and milk supply and the newspapers and magazines. She also sends Rs 100 every month to her own mother.

In the highest income households, the woman's earnings tend to be seen as providing what are described as 'luxuries' – a fridge or television, entertainments or the fulfilment of social commitments such as gift giving. In one case, a well-paid school teacher also said that her income was partly used to make up her husband's monthly deficit, indicating his role as the main 'provider.'

There is no precise cultural equivalent to the concept of 'pin money' in Bengali, but the clear differentiation between husband's and wife's incomes in some high income households and their respective allocation either to essential/less essential expenditures or to fixed costs/children's additional welfare suggests a concept of women as secondary earners in some households. This is so despite the fact that women are extremely stable earners and that the disparity between male and female earnings narrows in the high income households.

In contemporary bourgeois marriage as in customary practice and cultural understanding, wives are constructed as economic and legal dependents of husbands, particularly through systems of law and taxation. Trade unions, predominantly male in membership, have also constructed the interests of their members within the ideological parameters of men as breadwinners. It is not only because women are generally paid inferior wages that their incomes come to be regarded as secondary, but also because they themselves are constructed as dependants, regardless of their earning capacity.

## Personal expenditure

The extent to which women earners have access to their wages for personal expenditure depends both on the degree of household poverty and on their stage in the life cycle. Table 5.2 shows women's reported personal expenditure broken down by income group and life cycle. By 'personal expenditure' is meant money kept back directly by the earner for expenditure on items for herself or as gifts for others. The implication is not that all women with no reported personal expenditure do not have access to money for at least some of these items – although in some households they do not – but that access may be mediated either by the common fund or by another individual such as a parent or husband. 'Personal expenditure' is then either pre-determined by customary household practice, as in the case of the common fund, or is more open to inspection or policing by other household members. The table is thus a rather crude measure of women's expenditure but gives some indication of whether money is retained personally by women earners.

*Table 5.2*   Number of women reporting personal expenditure by household income groups (all female earners)

| Income group | Unmarried daughters | Wives/mothers with dependent children | Widows and other women without dependent children | Total | As % of women earners in income group |
|---|---|---|---|---|---|
| 500 and below | 8 | 3 | 6 | 17 | 35% |
| 501–1000 | 11 | 4 | 3 | 18 | 43% |
| 1001–2000 | 11 | 6 | 1 | 18 | 69% |
| 2001–3000 | 7 | 12 | 1 | 20 | 91% |
| 3000+ | 7 | 14 | 8 | 29 | 97% |

The proportion of women reporting personal expenditure, predictably, rises with household income. Of those reporting no expenditure, the largest group is wives and mothers with dependent children, the majority of whom are poor, and the women reporting no personal expenditure in the highest income groups are in households where there is a common fund to which all income is contributed or where another member has control of total household income.

In poor households, however, some unmarried daughters, as well as women with no dependent children, do manage to retain an element of their wage for themselves. Beyond their direct employment-related expenses, this is spent mainly on clothing or on trips to the cinema – the major form of entertainment across social class. Half of the women in the sample reported expenditure on clothing and cosmetics, some at least of which is an important employment-related expense for those working in the public arena.

On the whole, women, particularly if they are married and have dependents, have less personal expenditure than men. Evidence on this point is, however, more anecdotal than systematic, as amounts fluctuate widely for given individuals, and women's and men's assessments of what counts as personal expenditure also differ. For women, home-related expenses, such as 'clothes for grandchildren' often appear as personal expenditure. For men, personal expenditure is largely external to the home. Visits to coffee houses or liquor stalls or money spent on hobbies counts as personal expenditure.

The interests of poor mothers are almost wholly submerged with those of their dependents, as is widely reported from elsewhere. (cf. Mencher 1988). Rani Biswas, a home-based tailoring worker, reported that when she earns less than usual she eats only one meal in the day in order to give her children the available food. Betel nut (*pan* – when chewed, this is a mild stimulant) is one of the only personal expenditures which poor women permit themselves.

The eight women counted as single-person households all live in hostel accommodation provided by employers. All are single or widowed, with no immediate dependents, but five have natal families in or near Calcutta with whom they maintain a relationship. Of these, three contribute regularly to the natal household. Vidya Sinha, a 58-year-old widowed nurse, sends half of her wages of only Rs 100 per month to her two married brothers, one of whom is unemployed. Anjali Bose, another widowed nurse, sends Rs 220 of her Rs 620 salary to her mother's household every month. This all-female household (apart from a daughter's son) has no other source of regular income. Despite some substantial commitments and low wages, these single women all have more disposable income, even after taking care of their essential expenditure, than any other group of women. Nor are they answerable so immediately to other family members as to how they spend their income. All have bank accounts and two have been able to purchase land as security for retirement – the only ones in the sample to have done so.

## Remittances and Savings

Fourteen households reported sending money to other households on a regular or occasional basis, six reported receiving remittances and one household both sends out money and receives it. These reported incidences do not, however, include the more hidden intra-household transfers referred to earlier. Nor do they include gifts, which are often substantial contributions to the welfare of relatives. The amounts remitted range from Rs 25 to Rs 250 and involve a fairly limited range of kin, chiefly parents and siblings. Of the fifteen households sending money out, a total of thirteen of the remittances are from employed women to their relatives, four are from male members to their relatives and two destinations were not disclosed. Nine of the thirteen remittances provided by women are on a regular basis and the rest consist of occasional payments. Eight of these remittances are made, on a casual or regular basis, to elderly parents resident elsewhere, and three are made on a regular basis to a brother's (i.e. natal) household. The six remittances coming into house- holds are from non-resident employed sons and, in one case, from an absent husband of a daughter living with her mother. Of these, four are made on a regular basis.

It is not customary for women, and especially married women, to support their own parents financially as this is considered to be a son's primary obligation. The growth in women's employment appears to be altering this pattern and the possible implications of daughters' support for parents are taken up in chapter seven.

Fifty nine – over one-third – of the women in the sample, have bank accounts, of whom four have only joint accounts with husbands. Two more have post office accounts and fourteen hold life insurance policies. Most of the poorer women have no savings at all, but seven women earning less than Rs 200 have bank accounts and two other poorly paid women – an aya and a domestic worker have some savings deposited respectively with an employer and in a locked box. Some married women have jewellery which was given to them at marriage and over which they have very limited rights of disposal. Women with savings saw them either as security for their old age or as a contribution to the dowries of daughters.

## Wages and autonomy

Employed women's access to their wages is mediated both by the different forms in which household income is controlled and managed, and by concepts of need and strategies for investment which vary with class and which must be located within the changing political economy of the family. If 'autonomy', defined in a narrow sense, implies control over money, signified by capacity to determine its use and destination, it can be seen that the women in the sample vary widely in the degree of control which they exercise in this sense, regardless of whether they actually manage household funds. Nor can the degree of control be read off straightforwardly from the class and demographic characteristics of the household. The ideological mediation of the marriage contract, together with complex configurations of household circumstances prevent broad generalizations.

Autonomy could, however, be defined in a wider sense to encompass not just access but self-determination. There is a difference between having the 'right' to decide whether to save money for a daughter's dowry and having the 'right' to decide, on the basis of one's employment status, not to marry at all. To what extent does access to a wage produce autonomy in this sense? The data on single women (and see chapter seven) suggests that in a very few cases where young women have obtained professional qualifications and reasonably well-paid employment, such a choice may be said to exist, if ideological pressures can be resisted. The case of Shanta Ray, a 27-year-old office assistant living in an *asram*, who ran away to Calcutta to escape an arranged marriage, is also an example where the availability of paid employment allowed for such a choice. But the majority of older single women are employed because they are not married, rather than the other way round. Poor remuneration, the ideological unacceptability of unmarried independence for women and the importance of children to long-term security combine to maintain women's dependence on marriage. Even where women can obtain employment therefore, it is likely that they will continue to see their interests and pursue their investments in these terms.

This does not mean that a unity of interests prevails between family members. In the Bengali context, the ideology of the corporate household pooling its available resources in pursuit of a unified set of interests is very strong. This ideology may, however, disguise conflicts of interest over consumption which can have both short- and long-term implications. In some households, food may compete with liquor, while in others, educational and health priorities are a contested issue. These conflicts are often gendered, signifying different social investment priorities for women and men. In the absence of state provided security and in the event of widowhood, children remain, for both proletarian and middle-class women, the major form of social investment, albeit of qualitatively different kinds. Thus, proletarian women's wages go above all to feed and clothe children who will be future wage earners, while middle-class women spend particularly on education and on extra protein foods for children. From the point of view of a wider vision of autonomy, where women's long-term security continues to be bound up with their membership of a family in which male support is guaranteed, their capacity to earn a wage will not, in itself, guarantee greater self-determination.

## Conclusion

This chapter has argued that it is necessary to understand intra-household distribution practices and patterns of financial management both as deeply gendered and as having their own history. Complex processes of ideological mediation mean that it is not possible to predict, from the socio-economic profile of a household, what level of access women may have to income which they have earned and what degree of control they can exercise over its disposal. Women in households at all income levels, however, are likely to merge their financial interests into their households, either as a matter of household survival or as longer term 'investment' in their children. Single employed women emerge as important providers for their natal households, and a few have been able to invest to a limited extent in their own future security.

Chapter six

# Employment and autonomy
## Ideological struggles

> We feel that woman's proper place is in the home and that she is
> unsuited by reason of her sex, temperament and physical structure
> to plunge into the rough and tumble of public life.
>
> (Male respondent to a questionnaire on Hindu public opinion.
> *Census of India 1931*)

> Women must earn. . . .We must first admit that we are not slaves.
> Then we must get jobs like lady clerks, lady magistrates, lady
> judges. We don't get paid for housework.
>
> (Mrs R. F. Hussein, 'Ornaments or Badge of Slavery'
> *mahila* ['Woman'] May 1903)

**Historical struggles**

The outcome of the public debate on the role of Bengali women in the
closing decades of the nineteenth, and for at least the next four decades
of the twentieth century, was essentially conservative. Ideologies of
domesticity redefined and reinforced women's roles as wives and
mothers to match the changing environment of colonial Bengal. The
press, religious reformers and major public figures differed, for the most
part, only on the details of their opposition to women's participation in
employment and public life. For some, any movement of women into
paid employment was to be deplored as a shameful comment on the
respectability of their families. For others, paid work was to be tolerated
only for poor women and for widows in struggling financial circumstances. For yet others, particularly educated women from progressive
bourgeois families, employment strictly in segregated professions such
as teaching and medicine, was desirable both as an end in itself and as a
philanthropic duty. As was pointed out in chapter three, a public
discourse of disapproval surrounded women's presence in most other
kinds of employment.

111

There were, however, dissenting voices which should not be left unattended. In addition, the public discourse was very much that of the upper and middle classes and it was largely a male discourse. The voices of both proletarian women and of *bhadralok* women forced to find employment are largely unheard although the former certainly played an important role in organized labour struggles which began in the early 1920s. The Nationalist struggle and the rise and dominance of left politics in Bengal also drew in large numbers of women activists, for some of whom, the struggle for women's rights was inextricably bound into wider struggles against imperialism and class inequality (Everett 1979, Forbes 1979, Jayawardena 1986, Liddle and Joshi 1986, D. Engels 1986).

While the public debate tended to be dominated by the assumption of an inherent inequality between the sexes which rendered women unfit for the world of employment, there were women and men who challenged this. Mrs R. F. Hussein,[1] whose spirited commentaries are quoted at the head of this and other chapters, provided a turn of the century analysis of women's oppression which turned squarely on social rather than biological causes and would be immediately recognizable to many contemporary feminists. She considered male protectiveness and female dependency to be social constructs and thus ideological guises for oppression rather than outcomes of biological endowment and she castigated religion for perpetuating 'female slavery' through customs such as *sati* (widow burning). She argued that emancipation would be brought about through ideological struggle and by women entering paid employment and cited the example of Burma where 'earning women are not slaves to men' (op.cit.).

Another counter theme, expressed strongly at this period, stressed the 'decline' of women's power from a golden age, located generally in the Vedic period, to a low point of degradation in the Middle Ages when women became secluded within the household. This analysis called upon distinctively Hindu concepts of female power (*shakti*) which emphasized women's unique regenerative powers as mothers and thus did not embody the secular vision of equality of Mrs Hussein, but rather one in which women were considered essentially superior to men (cf. Amodini Ghosh in *mahisya-mahila* Feb/March 1915, Forbes 1979).

Profoundly important as these analyses were in the development of specifically feminist accounts of women's subordination at this time, neither vision spoke particularly to the needs and circumstances of proletarian women. For Mrs Hussein, 'employment' meant the professions for the most part, not an expansion of women's participation in industry and other skilled and unskilled jobs. 'Power through motherhood' is likely to have been at odds with the experiences of wage working women. Of the latter's historical consciousness of their condition as women 'flouting' public morality as well as, and perhaps distinct from, their exploitation as part of a class or regional or religious community, almost nothing is known.

However, women jute mill workers have a long history of militancy which has only recently begun to receive attention. Bose records that on the 16 September 1920, 350 women workers at the Hooghly Jute Mill struck, demanding the dismissal of the European Assistant in charge of the mill for beating a woman worker. Male workers followed and the demand was conceded (S. Bose 1981). Santosh Kumari Devi, a veteran Bengali woman trade union leader in the jute belt in the 1920s, recalled, in a personal interview, the militancy of the women workers in their support for the union (and see Chattopadhyay 1984). Mitra makes a similar observation in relation to the declining numbers of women jute mill workers still employed in 1947 (I. Mitra 1981).

There are, then, traditions of protest and struggle around the right to employment and the terms upon which it is carried out among urban women of all classes, albeit obscured by a dominant discourse and historical neglect. What is, perhaps, most remarkable is the strength and persistence of this dominant discourse despite the contradictions which many sections of the population experience in their daily lives.

Since the 1960s, legislative politics in West Bengal has been dominated by the communist and socialist parties and this has affected both the perception of and the extent of concern for 'women's issues'. Analyses of women's oppression from within these parties have tended to stress its interlinkage with capitalism and with the 'feudal' elements within Indian social life, and have seen the throwing off of 'feudal consciousness' and women's equal participation in public life and employment as critical to their emancipation. However, despite commitment, left dominance has not conspicuously increased or improved such participation. Indeed, female representation in the State Legislature showed a fall between 1957 and 1977 when the current Left Front swept to power. Women have tended to remain the 'rank and file' in left and labour organizations. Similarly, conditions of employment for many women have deteriorated. Recently, and in line with wider developments in Indian feminist struggles, women's groups in Calcutta have begun to develop analyses of the nature of subordination which also encompass ideology and sexual politics, and thus step beyond the left's confinement to the 'Engels answer'.[2]

This chapter is concerned with how contemporary women view some aspects of their situation both as members of families and as wage workers, how their paid work is accommodated within the family and what employment means to them. It also considers employed women's involvement in existing labour organizations and to what extent these are felt to recognize or cater to employed women's priorities.

## The meaning of paid work: employment and the family

The majority of women in the sample are first-generation paid workers. Eighteen households contain two generations of currently employed women and most of these are mothers and daughters. In only four households are a mother-in-law and daughter-in-law both employed. Of the remaining households, the mothers of another ten women and the mothers-in-law of three had been employed. One woman reported that both her mother and mother-in-law had been voluntary social workers. No women had had employed grandmothers and only three of the women whose mothers had done paid work are over 50 years of age.

As the historical profile would suggest, these mothers and mothers-in-law were either very poor or from well-to-do families which encouraged female employment, and the range of employment in which they were involved was very limited. Eight of their daughters or daughters-in-law live in households which are in the lowest two income groups. Employment in this previous generation was restricted mainly to domestic service and home-based employment. The previous generation of middle-class women in paid work were teachers and a doctor. One feature of this intergenerational set of employed women is that five of the women were doing the same jobs as their mothers had done, and in three cases, the job itself had been inherited at the mother's death or when she had been forced to retire.

The movement into paid work is clearly a phenomenon associated with women of the current productive generations and it has taken place against a background of conservatism in relation to the status of paid work for women. As this conservatism is located particularly within familial ideologies of status and respectability, the study attempted to elicit the responses of families to women's employment and the mechanisms by which they adjusted to it. By 'families', is meant the wider circle of effective kin who might influence or exert pressure on a particular household as well as other household members themselves.

Capturing this dimension of meaning raises serious methodological problems which this study has not tried to resolve. Rather, it focuses on views expressed at one point in time. These are inevitably a simplification – views and attitudes have histories. They are also frequently messy, confused and ambivalent but such untidiness may be screened out as a coherent story is sought to be produced. When the question of the dominant response of family members to their employment was explored with each woman, the stories could be systematized as follows:

| Oppose | Appreciate/Support | Envy | Mixed reactions | No effect |
|--------|--------------------|------|-----------------|-----------|
| 8 | 9 | 5 | 6 | 86 |

This presentation further simplifies because it does not capture the differences of opinion between relatives, but it does convey the limited extent to which the women have faced overt hostility. Employment has been accommodated by most families and the opinions of some have been disregarded by the women themselves. Maya Bose, a 20-year-old factory worker from a refugee family who inherited the job from her mother when she became too ill to carry on, said that she did not know what her relatives thought about her employment and nor did she care.

Slightly more families were considered to be sympathetic than hostile, while some were divided among themselves and others had changed their view over time to a more accommodating one. Non-employed female members were the ones generally described as envious. Nirmala Ghosh, a married clerical worker, had experienced a range of responses since she was forced to take up a job in the aftermath of partition: 'My relatives appreciate it, but a few are envious. My mother-in-law made a mild protest in the beginning but she could understand our economic condition.' A few families remain ambivalent. One of the few entrepreneurs in the sample said: 'Sometimes they praise me but sometimes they show slight reservations about my profession. Some relatives dislike it.' In this case, it is the nature of the job rather than employment *per se* which causes the misgivings.

All but three of the women who had encountered opposition were similarly in non-traditional occupations. Krishna Ganguly's mother objected strongly when she took up nursing: 'She thought that no good woman should take up such a profession as no respectable family would take me as a bride.' These fears were not without foundation, as Krishna, now aged 40, has remained unmarried. Monica Ray's family harbours not dissimilar worries about her occupation as an air hostess, despite its very high salary: 'My relatives opposed it and some still do, including my brother. My relatives think it is high time for me to get married and settled.'

A further, and expected, feature of the group which has experienced opposition is that most are from West Bengal-originated middle- or lower middle-class families. This includes one young woman office worker who ran away from her family home in a small town in West Bengal to avoid an arranged marriage: 'My personal experience is very bad. Older family members think that young women should not go out to work.' Only two women from refugee backgrounds (including Krishna Ganguly) experienced any opposition. The other women who reported opposition, Saleha Mahmood and her daughter, are Muslim tannery workers who suffer considerable hostility from their wider family because of their need to do paid work outside the home: 'We never thought of doing outside work, particularly such filthy, low paid work. We are ashamed to visit our relatives as they think we are loose women.' Although it was mainly among the Muslims in the sample that this particular objection was made explicit and did not distinguish between married and unmarried women, the association of paid work with lack of respectability still lurks behind the comments of a few family members, expressed mainly in the fear that certain kinds of paid work can damage the marital prospects of unmarried women.

For married women, initial opposition is most likely to come from a mother-in-law, less commonly from a husband, and marriage can be a point of pressure from the new family to give up paid work. Asha Ganguly worked in the telephone exchange from before her marriage and never considered giving up, but she married a man of her own choice and she pointed out that many of her friends in arranged marriages had been forced by in-laws to relinquish their jobs. Thus, for other families, employment is acceptable for unmarried girls but not for married women who are expected to be full-time housewives.

Neighbour's attitudes are of little significance. The two households which reported opposition from neighbours are balanced by the two which had found them to be very supportive, one of these being the household of the Muslim women whose relatives had been scandalized by their employment. In general, the views of neighbours are discounted as not important and the common response was 'nobody bothers'.

There is a corresponding absence of concern with the social implications of women's paid work for the status of the family as a whole. Only four families had considered, or continued to consider it to have an adverse effect on their status, while one family felt that its status had been enhanced through its 'modern' outlook. The four families were those of the Muslim tannery workers, two nurses and the young woman who ran away to Calcutta and for all of them, the status consideration was that of the family's (sexual) honour and its linkage with what was seen as a loss of female chastity.

For most families, economic necessity appears to have overridden status objections to women's paid work where they existed. This is particularly so in the case of unmarried women, with refugee families being the least likely to raise such concerns. For married women, the situation may change, however, depending on the attitude of the husband's family. This was recognized by both married and unmarried women in their responses to questions on whether being employed is a help or a hindrance to a woman's marriage prospects. Only two women (both older widows) considered it to be an unequivocal disadvantage, while everyone else stressed the economic advantages to the husband's family. Many saw a woman's job as an additional qualification for marriage, stressing that families could no longer manage on only one income. However, almost as many also sounded a note of caution, pointing out that it was up to in-laws to 'allow' a daughter-in-law to do paid work and that in negotiated marriages, women had no freedom of choice if in-laws proved to be 'traditionally minded'.

Here, matters are complex and not easily resolved into neat categories. Economic necessity is itself partly a subjective category, trading class-specific expectations of living standards against wives' socially reproductive work (cf. U. Sharma 1986). The family economy is continually being renegotiated and ideological devices emerge to render changes acceptable. Families in the same economic category may vary considerably in their responses to similar circumstances. Nine women, both married and unmarried, commented that 'modern' young men or 'educated' families want and expect working brides. Economic and social expectations can be made to coincide.

The reasons given by the small sample of non-employed women for not entering paid work reinforce the conclusion that 'status' implications are not of major significance. They were mentioned as a reason by one woman, the 45-year-old wife of a businessman, who said she would feel ashamed of going 'outside' for employment. For the remainder, practical considerations of household management and childcare, absence of what they saw as economic necessity, or lack of qualifications were the reasons put forward.

Women's employment is thus not a cause of great concern to those families already with employed female members from the point of view of its implications for respectability, although lingering worries remain among the more status-conscious, usually West Bengal *bhadralok*, group. The very low presence of Muslim women in the paid labour force, together with the comments of those Muslims in the sample, suggests a greater restriction of Muslim women for such reasons, particularly where employment outside the home is at issue. These reasons continue to be articulated in terms of an 'honour and shame' code of conduct.

For other women, where objections are raised, they are more likely to be in response to the choice of job and this will reflect the extent to which a woman will have to mix with male colleagues or clients or to travel around or accept transfers away from Calcutta. A low-paid factory job in a female-only unit would be preferable, for many families, to a job as an office receptionist, for instance. What is more at issue here is the extent to which more subtle forms of policing and social control of women's behaviour can be expected within the workplace and reinforced from within the family. Where this is reasonably assured, objections which have sexual morality at their core lose much of their force. Mrinal Sen's now classic film of a day in the life of an unmarried female office worker in Calcutta, *ek din prati din* ('one day, everyday'),

117

brilliantly catches the extent of the moral panic and of the policing which is brought to bear when she has to work late and is unable to get a message to her family.

Another idiom which has been pressed into service to accommodate paid work for married women, appeals to the values of 'modernity' (cf. Wood 1975 on a similar pattern in Gujarat). An employed wife or daughter-in-law can be a status asset provided she is employed in a high status occupation. The status element is, however, finely balanced. She will not be expected to agree to career advancement if it entails moving elsewhere or, possibly, acquiring more seniority than her husband.

The question must be raised, however, as to what this accommodation means for women in practice and whether it can be translated into greater control over their lives, particularly in view of the persistence of a gender ideology which associates women so strongly with domesticity.

In the light of the above as well as the earlier findings on domestic workloads, it is arguable that the quality of intra-household relations and the day-to-day reactions of household members are of more significance for employed women. In particular, the relevance of household composition and the perceived advantages and drawbacks of living in complex or single units must be considered.

The question of intra-household conflict over a woman member's employment was discussed within all households in the sample. Such data are necessarily subjective as individuals have both differing perceptions of conflict and varying levels of tolerance for it. However, certain patterns emerge which suggest that there are some structural regularities to these conflicts. Members of forty-eight households reported on what they considered to be significant existing or previous conflicts within their households bearing upon a female member's employment. Neglect of household responsibilities and the envy of non-employed members are the two issues which provoke conflicts.

In the context of the former, mothers-in-law emerge as the main complainants, and half of such conflicts recorded referred to a time when the woman concerned had been living in a joint family which had subsequently fragmented either through death or through conscious decision. A young hospital aya is typical of this category: 'When my mother-in-law was alive she was constantly making trouble. Living in a joint family is difficult for a working woman as the other women are always grumbling.' But others had mothers-in-law who eventually became reconciled, as a telephone operator in her 30s commented, 'previously, both my mother and father-in-law used to complain, but after five years of marriage they had to change.' Her problems did not, however, stop there: 'My husband and I are always in conflict. He thinks that I am not doing my family duties and caring for the children properly.'

While most complaints against employed daughters-in-law are made by mothers-in-law who have never been employed themselves and thus are not accustomed to the practice, this is not always the case. Nila Majumdar, a clerk living with her husband, two children and mother-in-law who is a headmistress, said, 'I don't like joint family living at all. No-one expresses their grievances openly. My mother-in-law doesn't object to my working, but she expects me to fulfil all my household and other duties to relatives as if I weren't employed.'

Daughters-in-law could also create difficulties, however. Sandhya Chatterjee, a widowed school teacher living with her employed son, non-employed daughter-in-law and grandson is in permanent conflict with her daughter-in-law over the latter's view that women should not take up employment unless it is economically essential. She is the respondent whose daughter-in-law has insisted that both the domestic work and the household expenses are divided equally between them on a basis of fifteen days each every month.

Conflicts between women and their non-employed sisters-in-law also figure frequently, but are more often articulated by the wage earner as being prompted by envy rather than disputes over housework. A number felt that the assistance provided by a sister-in-law was given grudgingly. In such households, both the 'glamour' of employment and the additional income which it generates can be sources of tension. However, sister-in-law conflicts are outnumbered in quantity, if not in intensity, by arguments between unmarried siblings over their respective responsibilities. Brothers resent the erosion of customary levels of sisterly attention when older sisters are employed as well as what they regard as the imposition of additional domestic tasks.

The largest number of conflicts, however, are between husband and wife. One woman, who contrasted her previous good experiences of joint family living and the encouragement of her mother-in-law which enabled her to return to college for five years, said, 'Now I quarrel with my husband because he is utterly indifferent to my problems.' As was noted in chapter four, husbands tolerate, or do not openly oppose wives' employment provided that it does not alter the domestic status quo. Joint families can thus, for some women, provide essential support and encouragement.

When asked for their assessment of the advantages and disadvantages of joint family living, a slight majority of those women who felt able to express a view on the matter came out in its favour (64 out of 113). However, the majority of these are currently living in single-unit households and it is the case to some extent that the warmer the approval, the less the woman's experience of joint families. A better guide are the twenty-two women living in fully joint or three-generational families, four of whom are 'completely dissatisfied' with their current situation and five of whom pointed out both advantages and drawbacks. Those women in the sample most strongly disapproving of it are those now living in single units but with previous joint family experience.

Overwhelmingly, the advantage is seen to lie in the reduction of household and childcare responsibilities through sharing with other women. Most feel that this does greatly reduce these burdens and provides greater peace of mind to women with children. But there are dissenters to this view in that several women pointed out that joint family responsibilities can be heavier and involve more elaborate obligations to family members and wider kin and that employed women may be given little licence to neglect these.

The responses are informed by a sense of the costs as well as the practical advantages of living with in-laws and other kin. Psychological problems, jealousies, resentment over unequal incomes and differences of opinion and outlook between the generations can be the price of relief from domestic overload. At the same time the price which married women may pay for freedom from in-laws, in the absence of a renego-tiated conjugal division of labour, is increased levels of conflict with husbands. Ideological support and encouragement to employed women is not the prerogative of any specific family type. If anything, this is even less likely to come from husbands in single-unit households than from in-laws in complex ones.

Women's employment, then, is accepted as legitimate and accom-modated by most families on a spectrum from necessary evil to positive asset. This results in considerable variation in the extent to which family members provide practical and moral support to employed women, however.

What of women's own perceptions of their changing influence in the family as an indicator of the significance of employment in their lives? For two-thirds of the sample, the response was positive. A further quarter felt that being employed had made no difference to their level of influence in their household or control over their lives. Eight said they could not tell or had no experience by which to judge. For those who felt that employment had increased their influence, the fact of their economic contribution to the household was undeniably linked by most to their sense of having enhanced personal influence. A young married clerical worker said, 'I can be much more assertive in my family because they have all benefited from my work. They take advice from me when necessary.' A 20-year-old unmarried garment worker living with her parents said, 'I am now consulted on family expenditure and other important matters. My mother has no decision-making power because she does not earn money.' She was one of a large number of women who contrasted her situation favourably with that of her non-employed mother. More starkly, a widowed aya pointed out, 'Yes, I have influence – I maintain the family. My children realize that if I don't go out to work they will starve.'

Others felt that they had quickly gained more respect from family members. Two unmarried factory workers in their 20s said, 'Our influence has increased. Other household members take special care when we come home. Our parents also take our advice on money matters.' For some, recognition has occurred gradually over a long period. A 45-year-old clerical worker, whose husband has taken over the running of the house since he retired, said:

Although I don't manage the household, every decision is taken by me. My husband never presses his differences. Previously he was all in all. After being displaced at partition, I had to take a job. Now, since retirement, my husband has changed a great deal.

A few specifically mentioned feelings of greater independence. A 34-year-old married teacher said, 'Economic independence gives me a feeling of freedom.' The air hostess said, 'I enjoy personal freedom with no-one imposing decisions on me.'

Of those who felt that little or nothing had changed within their families, some were married women who had been employed before their marriage and so had not experienced a change in their situation in relation to their present household. A 34-year-old clerk said, 'I started work before my marriage and my husband is not dependent upon my earnings so I cannot say I have influence because I go out to work. Still, I do assert my opinions and have influence on my children's education.' Another, who had taken up music teaching since her marriage, said, 'There wasn't any special change. My in-laws are very liberal and progressive anyway.' But for others, no change meant little influence before or after. A college lecturer said, 'It makes no difference. My husband dominates.' Nila Majumdar, the clerk whose unhappy experiences of joint family living are noted on p. 119, feels that her employment, like her marriage, has given her the opposite of any personal control or influence:

I was a very good student and wanted to finish my university education. I did not think of becoming a clerk but partition ruined that dream. I had to give up my education and take this job. I did not want to get married but I had no influence on my parents. Now I am a mother as well as a wife and it is too late to start again but I still feel very frustrated.

The type of employment is also significant. A married tailoring worker said, 'I am only a home-based worker – my influence is neither more nor less.' Another pointed to the importance of regular employment. A 33-year-old unmarried daughter doing casual jobs in radio broadcasting said, 'Until and unless I get a permanent job, my influence will not increase.' Not all employment is equal, therefore, and several women contrasted going outside for employment and doing home-based jobs in terms of a distinction between a 'real' job and work not considered 'proper' employment. Similarly, there is felt to be a great difference between the statuses of regular and temporary work. Indeed, the prestige attached to permanent, particularly organized public sector jobs more than cancels out any misgivings which families may have over an employed female member.

As was emphasized in earlier chapters, almost all the women see employment as a permanent aspect of their lives. Whether for straightforward economic reasons or out of choice, few of them hold out a vision of becoming full-time housewives or dependants and for many, employment does provide independence and self-esteem, albeit in varying degrees. But women do step warily within the labour market. The wage, skill and social barriers which they face are reinforced by pressures located in the family domain. The various barriers to women's labour-force participation have been not so much dismantled as shifted to incorporate some kinds of employment and some measure of economic independence but to foreclose others.

There are points beyond which it is difficult for women to go. Despite the long-term erosion in men's earning power, the concept of men as supporters and women as economic dependants remains deeply entrenched and is reproduced through mechanisms such as the invisibilization of women's employment, especially if it is casual or home based, and the minimization of its economic significance. While fathers and older male relatives are often able to deal with the difficulties posed by a daughter bringing in a wage through the exercise of customary paternal authority, the often high levels of conflict between wife and husband suggest that the latter may have more problems in asserting their conjugal authority. One of the issues discussed with married women was whether they would be prepared to accept a higher wage than that earned by their husband. This question provoked some interesting reflections.

Only three women said that they would not do so, one of them qualifying this by commenting that she would do so only if her husband's wage was insufficient to support the family. Another, a widowed home-based tailoring worker in the lowest income group, said, 'It doesn't arise now for me, but when he was alive I wouldn't have accepted because of the loss of prestige for him.'

All the other married women said they would have no problems about accepting a higher wage but the response of several was typified by the comment of a poorly paid home-based worker who said, 'It is impossible and impractical to think of earning more than my husband.' Of much more concern to married women is the place of work: 'I don't mind getting higher wages but husband and wife must work in different places or the husband will feel insulted by other people's attitudes and I will be embarrassed', said a 46-year-old teacher, articulating a common view.

Anxiety about conjugal competition was very clear in the responses of half of the husbands who were asked the same question. A clerical worker whose wife is a teacher, said, 'I don't think she can get a better paid job than me, but if she is offered one I will not be happy because I think she will feel proud and will ignore me.' Another, who is a low-paid factory worker, said, 'I would welcome it, but I will give her advice not to become very proud of this. She should spend her earnings on the betterment of the family.' Husbands' concern with wives becoming 'proud' is the other side of the coin of wives feeling embarrassed and wishing to minimize the potential for conflict by working in separate places lest they upset the conjugal hierarchy. While the threat posed by a wife's additional income can be neutralized through existing intra-familial distribution mechanisms which ensure that wives do not appropriate it for increased personal consumption, there are no mechanisms for dealing with the contradiction posed by a wife having direct seniority in the workplace. Nonetheless, the varied responses do indicate the potential for disruptiveness which money represents, particularly in conjugal relationships, and suggests that we should look less for immediate and radical changes in employed women's situations, and more to longer term processes of sometimes conflict-ridden negotiation.

Life-cycle changes also affect the meaning of employment and the impact of earnings. Young unmarried daughters earning modest wages are more easily accommodated within familial power structures than older single women whose families are dependent on their financial contribution. The former can be conceptualized as temporarily earning their keep prior to the life-long business of marriage. The latter face families, particularly older male relatives, with more obvious and painful contradictions.

The commitment of almost all the women to paid work nonetheless goes beyond that of immediate economic necessity, despite the difficulties which it may cause. Entering employment is frequently a non-reversible act except through retirement or involuntary redundancy. A 'culture' of women's employment is thus beginning to emerge which is no longer confined to a few upper-middle-class women and the very poor. Its effects are likely to feed back into women's aspirations for themselves and for their daughters, creating changes but also throwing up contradictory responses as women and their families assess and reassess the implications of changing expectations.

As well as discussions about their own job aspirations, all women, employed and non-employed, as well as all husbands in the sample, were asked about their hopes for their daughters, where appropriate. Two aspects of their responses stand out. One is the still very narrow range of employment preferences for daughters, which by and large mirrored the mothers' preferences for themselves were they in a position to choose or to change their jobs. The other is that only one employed woman mentioned marriage as her preference for her daughter instead of employment, although most mothers assumed that their daughters lives would include marriage.

Teaching and any form of academic work is by far the most preferred form of employment and this preference (cited by thirty of the employed women, those of the husbands who wanted daughters to take up paid work and one of the non-employed mothers) cuts across classes. For middle-class women, however, the preference is for college and secondary-level teaching, while lower-middle-class women and a few working-class women aspire more modestly for primary level. The other major preference (fifteen employed mothers and one husband) is for factory work, some stipulating large, established factories, others preferring small-scale units but all hoping for regular jobs. This preference is strong among both lower middle-class women and the very poor, home-based workers and reflects again the importance which women attach to regular employment contracts for both themselves and their daughters. These two preferences account for most of the responses. Four middle-class employed mothers hope their daughters will take up medicine, while only two (themselves a nurse and aya) mentioned nursing. One husband rated nursing an equal preference with factory work. Clerical work was only preferred by one non-employed and two employed mothers. One employed mother (the Muslim tannery worker) went against the trend towards seeing factory work as suitable and desirable and hoped that her daughter would take up home-based employment instead, although the daughter herself is looking for a 'clean' and permanent factory job. Only two mothers responded with unusual aspirations for their school-age daughters, one for engineering and the other for 'something artistic.'

The responses of the employed mothers are informed by two particular understandings. One is that daughters will probably need to do paid work for a range of reasons from satisfaction to dire necessity. The battle for their right to employment is, for them, already won. The other is that women, nonetheless, continue to be extremely limited in the jobs or careers which they may hope to take up. This reflects not so much a conservatism on the part of the present generation of employed women, although elements of that are found, as a realistic assessment of the state of the labour market, what their daughters will be allowed to get away with and the overwhelming importance of job security.

Non-employed mothers and the husbands show both more variety in their responses and, apparently, greater conservatism about women's employment. Two non-employed mothers preferred employment over marriage, one of whom expressed very strong feelings on the matter. The wife of a policeman said, 'My daughter should be well educated and become economically independent. Nobody should ruin her life like me.' But employment was not on the agenda for the rest of these women. Education was emphasized but more with a view to marriage. As the wife of a businessman said, 'She should continue her studies and then marry a boy in a well-to-do family.'

All except two of the husbands also stressed marriage as a priority, while not necessarily excluding employment as well. A clerical worker said, 'We should help her to complete her education and then she should marry. After marriage she can do anything she likes provided her in-laws don't object.' A factory worker said, 'I want to educate my daughter to school final and then she should earn her own expenses in a factory or nursing job until she is married.' The most ambitious of the husbands, a retired government employee, could stipulate the precise nature of the postgraduate qualification he hopes his daughter will obtain, but emphasized that he wanted 'to give her a good marriage.'

Although the samples of husbands and non-employed women are small, they suggest that there may be differences in outlook between these categories and employed women and that these differences may amount to divergent views on the relative status and security of marriage as against employment. One fairly obvious reason for this can be found in the disproportionate number of women in the sample who are either wholly unsupported or insufficiently supported by a husband because of early widowhood, divorce, unemployment or low male income. Their understanding of their daughters' options comes from their own experiences, just as the non-employed married women's understandings come from theirs. For example, Mamata Biswas, a 48-year-old school teacher with a student daughter, had started working thirty years previously while unmarried and when her parents died, leaving herself, a surviving elder brother and an elder married sister. The sister was widowed shortly after and, as she suffered severely from heart trouble, her four children then went to live with Mamata until they were old enough to fend for themselves. However, Mamata continues to support her sister's household as her remaining brother is not prepared to take on the responsibility. Mamata herself married a doctor, but he was forced to give up his job some years ago because of ill health, so she continues to be the only earning member in her household. She believes firmly, and not surprisingly, that her daughter must become employed and that every woman should be economically independent.

Men's understandings of their daughter's options, on the other hand, rarely include what would be a fundamental challenge to their perception of daughters as primarily dependants, first on fathers and then on husbands. This is particularly evident with the employed unmarried daughters in the sample. For their fathers, they are 'earning their expenses' or 'helping the family out' before moving into marriage. In the main sample, only one father, one of the lowest earners, admitted that he will not be able to arrange marriages for his daughters, who run his teastall, because of the family's poverty. For many of their mothers, however, there is tacit acknowledgement that the daughter may not marry; and for the daughters, there may be open recognition of this possibility. It is less painful for a mother to admit her dependence on a daughters' earnings than it is for a father to do so. Most mothers do want their daughters to marry eventually but are much less likely to subordinate the need for employment to this aim, whereas fathers usually reverse the emphasis. For those mothers dependent for their survival on employed daughters, the prospect of their marriage is itself a source of conflict between their own material interests and the daughter's perceived future security. The common complaints of older single women that 'no-one' arranged their marriages reflects this all-too-painful conflict. But material interest in an unmarried daughter is not the only reason for mothers to stress the merits of employment. Mithu Bhadra, a refugee who lost her husband shortly after they settled in Calcutta and who brought up her four children on the earnings from her factory job, said:

> I've become a changed person, very confident and socially established because of working. Some of my neighbours are also working and have remained unmarried. I think if a woman doesn't like to be married she can choose not to. I will not insist on my younger daughter getting married but I must insist on her becoming economically independent.'

The economic forces which lie behind assessments of the relative merits of marriage and employment for young women are weighed in more detail in the next chapter. Here, it remains to consider the views of women themselves on the desirability of marriage.

The single women in the sample who are now in their 40s and 50s belong to a generation in which marriage was more or less the sole expectation for women. Their single, employed status is thus the outcome of factors over which they had no control and which would have been seen, conventionally, as personal misfortune. Is this how they view their own lives? There is no doubt that most had hoped or expected to marry and had resented, at least initially, their lack of opportunity. Krishna Ganguly, who had taken up nursing against her mother's wishes, had done so in default of any arrangement having being made for her marriage by any of her senior relatives – a matter of great disappointment to her. However, she spoke of subsequent bitter experiences in which promises of marriage were made by male hospital staff and later retracted. These caused her to give up the idea of marriage and to reflect on the advantages of having a secure job and economic independence. Another nurse, commenting on similar experiences, said, 'Women can give better company to other women.'

The experiences of the two sets of middle-aged unmarried sisters living together demonstrate the importance of having a viable income and high status employment for the single woman. The four out of the five Chatterjee sisters who are in or retired from professional occupations, expressed little regret about their unmarried status and are articulate on the issue of women's economic emancipation. The five Bose sisters, struggling to maintain themselves out of home-based sewing and selling saris, are acutely aware of their secondary status in society. For them, what is particularly salient is that unmarried women are not treated as, and therefore find it equally difficult to operate as full citizens. As they pointed out, women still need a guardian and a guarantor and their behaviour is continually policed in subtle and not so subtle ways to ensure that they remain asexual, and hence non-threatening beings. It is perhaps significant that almost all of these older single women are active in religious causes to a much greater degree than other women, including widows, and particularly in those cults which hold out a vision of individual self-worth for everyone.

The younger generation of unmarried daughters contains a small number who have actively decided against marriage, including the young office worker who ran away to Calcutta to escape an arranged marriage. Rather more remain unmarried because of a firm commitment to marrying only where there is no dowry demand. But marriage continues to hold its place in the expectations of most unmarried daughters, for emotional and pragmatic as well as for romantic reasons (cf. Roy 1975a, on the culture of romance among adolescent girls). Motherhood is almost unthinkable for unmarried women. Remaining single thus means remaining childless in a context where adulthood and parenthood are closely bound together. The problem of where to live and who to live with is explored in more detail in the next chapter. This poses particular dilemmas for single women, who face both economic and cultural obstacles in securing housing.

Rani Basu, a clerical worker in her early 30s, living with and supporting her widowed mother, confessed to having no desire to marry but feels she should try to do so as she cannot see how she could live alone without a 'guardian' after her mother's death. Her mother is equally concerned about her daughter's future security and has urged her to marry. However, Rani is adamant that she will not accept an offer of marriage which contains a dowry demand. She is also worried about what she considers to be the lack of personal status of wives: 'I am also a person. After I go to my husband's house they should also respect me as a full and complete person, but this has not yet been established.' For Rani, the attainment of the publicly and legally sanctioned status of 'wife' does not compensate for the loss of personhood.

Thus, for a few young women, at least, there is serious questioning of the implications of marriage for their subjectivity, albeit with recognition of the practical and social disadvantages of remaining single. A few, who have access to suitable partners usually through their employment, will resolve the dilemma by marrying men of their own choice. More are likely to remain single by default.

## The meaning of paid work: women in the workplace

Most women enter paid work on a full-time basis. The workplace is thus a major focus of their daily lives. This section explores their levels of satisfaction with their employment and the extent to which workplace organization provides a voice for their concerns.

### Job satisfaction

One-third of the women expressed themselves very or partly dissatisfied with their existing employment. Of the fifty-five who were completely dissatisfied, twenty-four were home-based piece-rate workers, sixteen were workplace-based casual and temporary workers across a wide range of occupations and eight were family labourers. All of these workers cited low (or no) remuneration and/or job insecurity as their grounds. Many also mentioned the corollary of casual employment: the absence of paid leave and their often long working hours. Poor working conditions were also mentioned by seven of these women, but overwhelmingly the issue for this group is low wages and erratic income. Of the remainder, three self-employed women were dissatisfied because of the unprofitability of their business or the difficulties faced by women running their own businesses, a nurse and an aya were dissatisfied both with wage levels and with the attitudes of patients and superiors and two public sector clerical workers found their jobs monotonous and unrewarding. Eight other women were dissatisfied with aspects of their employment, which included remuneration in some cases. The *biri* workers (Muslims) were dissatisfied with the wage rates rather than the employment itself, reflecting their community preference for home-based work. Others mentioned distance or particularly heavy workloads as reasons.

In the main, women in permanent jobs, particularly in the public sector, are the least dissatisfied and teachers expressed the most satisfaction. Apart from the two clerical workers referred to, the only non-manual workers who were actively unhappy with their employment were temporary employees, sometimes of many years standing (fourteen years, in the case of one nurse) and who were still trying to get their status regularized; and the air hostess, who was hoping to move into teaching – despite the drop in salary this would entail – because it was a more 'suitable' woman's job. Home-based workers are by far the most dissatisfied, and workers in small factories expressed levels of discontent almost as great. Altogether, forty-five women are trying actively to find alternative employment, mostly in order to increase their wages and to acquire permanent contracts.

The level of dissatisfaction with home-based work indicates an important feature of most of this large group of employed women; namely their lack of attachment to home-based work as a form of employment. Apart from the *biri* workers, only two other women, both working in small factories/sweatshops and one of whom is a Muslim, actually expressed a preference for home-based work. A self-employed home-based tailor also said she was happy to be 'making money sitting at home'. Other home-based workers, were either looking for alternative employment or were resigned to working at home because of the constraints of domestic responsibilities, ill health or lack of any realistic alternative. Home-based work was not seen particularly as a way of easing the domestic workload, or as having any other advantages, primarily because the appalling levels of remuneration did not permit women to spend any time on domestic commitments except when involuntarily without work. Indeed, as Banerjee shows, home-based workers received, on average, even less domestic assistance from other household members than did outside workers, presumably because they were not recognized as 'proper' employees (1985a: 106).

At the other end of the scale, the satisfaction expressed by public sector workers has to be seen in the context of the strong social approval of 'respectable' employment, of which teaching is paradigmatic, together with the paucity of high-status and reasonably well-paid employment for women. When asked for their aspirations for employment in an ideal world, all but one of the educated women who did not express aspirations in terms of their existing employment, mentioned teaching or lecturing. The lone exception, an office receptionist, had wanted to take up something artistic or creative but considered it, probably correctly, an unrealistic and unfulfillable ambition.

Of the women in permanent jobs, seventeen were seeking promotion to higher grades. Again, better remuneration was a strong incentive to this but was also joined, for some, with a definite sense of career goals and a desire to take on more challenging work or responsibilities. Of the forty-three women who are permanently employed, mainly public sector workers, and not looking for promotion, fifteen were already in more senior positions or were too close to retiring age to expect promotion. A further fourteen had already experienced some promotion but did not plan any further attempts. Fourteen women were thus in very junior positions but not seeking further advancement. Out of these two groups, twenty are married women with dependent children, while the remaining eight are single. For the married women, the decision not to pursue promotion or further seniority was generally related to their domestic situation. A 32-year-old bank clerk with a young child said, 'I don't want promotion as I don't want to change my place of work because of my child's education. I also don't want more responsibility.'

Single women's reasons for not wanting promotion are more complex. Some also have domestic responsibilities which claimed priority. Married and single women in the public sector share the problems associated with transfers. For married women, this creates particular domestic difficulties, as the previous comment illustrates. But there is also an ideological component, both for married and single women, who can face familial censure at the prospect of moving away from home and also difficulties in finding secure accommodation where they will not be the target of harassment. There is also, as yet, no well-developed culture of female careers, as opposed merely to employment, within which women can justify pursuing seniority. As we have seen, 'taking a job' is in itself a relatively new concept for most women in Calcutta. Not surprisingly, for some, the concept of a career structure has little resonance. Single women continue, in many cases, to be in the labour force because of lack of choice or alternative rather than an active commitment to paid work as an avenue to self-advancement.

## Unions and work organization

Trade union membership is restricted to permanent employees in the organized sector and to certain occupations, as Table 6.1 shows.

In addition, one factory worker belongs to a negotiating group and three other factory workers are involved in trying to start up a union in their factories. One executive officer is forbidden by the terms of her contract to be a union member. The level of formal union membership among permanent workers is thus high - only eleven women with permanent contracts are not members. However, this must be balanced against the almost complete absence of union organization in the unorganized sector and among temporary workers.

*Table 6.1*  Union membership by occupation

| Occupation | Members | Total in sample (inc. temporary workers) |
|---|---|---|
| Teachers | 17 | 26 |
| Clerical | 21 | 26 |
| Other admin. and prof. | 6 | 11 |
| Nurses | 4 | 8 |
| Factory workers | 2 | 12 |
| *Total* | 50 | 83 |

*Table 6.2*  Reasons for non-membership of union or work organization

*Unorganized/temporary workers*

| | | |
|---|---|---|
| (1) | No opportunity | 37 |
| (2) | No knowledge of unions | 18 |
| (3) | No union in workplace/for category of work | 13 |
| (4) | Workplace too small to organize | 4 |
| (5) | No time | 2 |
| (6) | No organizing ability | 1 |
| (7) | Religious reasons | 1 |
| (8) | No need | 1 |
| *Total* | | 77 |

*Permanent Workers*

| | | |
|---|---|---|
| (1) | No interest | 8 |
| (2) | No time | 3 |
| *Total* | | 11 |

As Table 6.2 shows, reasons for not joining a union are quite different among unorganized and temporary workers than among those permanent workers who have not joined. Commenting on the complete absence of unionization among home-based workers, Banerjee points out that these women are the most isolated and least socially and educationally equipped group of workers in Calcutta. Their structural isolation reinforces the lack of effort on the part of unions to organize these groups of workers. (Banerjee 1985a: 107–12, and compare her findings on union membership and workers' knowledge). The level of ignorance of unions is highest among this group – none of the outside workers was actually unaware of the existence of unions. However, some lacked any knowledge of particular unions which might represent their interests. A nurse and a clerical worker both said (incorrectly) that there was no appropriate organization for their employment. Temporary workers all thought that trade unions did not cater for workers on temporary contracts.

The largest categories of respondents – those women who either lacked knowledge or who said they had no opportunity to join – also displayed the least knowledge of or interest in the question of worker organization. They were the least likely to express an opinion about workers' rights or whether they would be prepared to participate in a strike or other forms of solidarity. Those women who pointed out that there was no union in their workplace or that the workplace was too small to be organized displayed much higher levels of interest and knowledge. As well as the three factory workers who were involved in trying to start a union, factory workers in general were more knowledge-able and interested and felt that union membership would benefit them. This included the woman who said that she was not a member because she felt unable to take the initiative in organizing the workers in her factory herself.

Only one woman responded that she had no need for membership. She is an aya working for a local doctor who feels a deep sense of gratitude to the doctor for providing her with employment during a difficult time in her life. This is, however, the only expressed example of a personalistic tie in employer–worker relations. Despite the pervasive use, in some workplaces such as small factories, of the idioms of kinship and paternalism, the sense of employers as benefactors or kindly quasi-kin is little in evidence outside the environs of the workplace itself. This may, however, be more common between domestic servants and their employers.

It is clear that levels of knowledge about the relevance and benefits of union organization, as well as membership itself, vary greatly among different occupational groups. Levels of participation in union activity are also very variable. Union office had been held by only three women in the sample, all in local branches. However, forty-five of the public sector employees had taken part in industrial action at least once. Table 6.3 summarizes women's responses to questioning about whether they would join an action in future or if they had an opportunity.

Again, there is a gulf between those women who have no experience or knowledge of worker organization and for whom the question is irrelevant or meaningless, and those mainly public sector unionized employees who have taken part in actions or would do so if called upon by their unions. This includes the small group of non-members among the permanent workers. Those indicating that they would not join are notably women who are afraid of losing their jobs rather than those who object to the concept of withdrawing their labour. Some women do, however, have reservations and this can be for different reasons.

*Table 6.3* Attitudes to industrial action among wage workers

| *Would/may join:* | |
| --- | --- |
| Yes, without qualification | 50 |
| If satisfied with reason | 20 |
| If call is united | 6 |
| Would be forced to | 3 |
| If a permanent worker | 2 |
| *Would not join:* | |
| Afraid of losing job | 8 |
| No scope for action | 2 |
| No quarrel with employer | 1 |
| Cannot say | 40 |

A number of permanent workers feel that their unions call workers out too often and for trivial causes. Of these, some echo a wider social and political perception among sections of the urban middle class in West Bengal that permanent workers, particularly in the State bureaucracy, have become too militant and powerful under the Left Front Government. These women are caught up in the contradictory ideologies of their positions as wage workers and as members of a class segment which articulates its interests in terms of the policing and disciplining of refractory groups of workers who are held responsible for the poor level of infrastructure and services in the city. A woman who was formerly a union activist caught something of this contradiction when she argued:

> There are no women trade unionists. I don't believe that women who participate in salary increase agitations should be called trade unionists. Most of them do not even know the Factory Acts. In my office, some women are either a-political or anti-politics but they are forced to take part in strikes to avoid an unpleasant situation.

Others feel that their unions do not have a proper sense of priorities or sufficient seriousness in their aim of improving workers' conditions. A telephone operator who used to be a union activist said, 'The union must protect workers' rights. That does not mean that it should agitate on every issue. I tried to intervene on these trivial issues but I became unpopular and my subordinates insulted me a great deal.' As a result, she gave up her position and became an ordinary member. A young clerical worker, employed on a temporary basis in a government office and who had not been a union member at the time of the study, had joined one before a revisit in 1985. This was because the union was attempting to negotiate the absorption of all temporary employees, about one-third of whom were women. She was unimpressed with the form of action being taken and felt that the agitation was, at best, half-hearted: 'They come out during break times, eat their snacks and raise a few slogans. When the break ends, they go back to work again.' Nevertheless, this is the only instance noted of an attempt by a union to take up the issue of temporary workers.

There are also women union members for whom the union represents neither nuisance value nor something in which they might be expected to play an active role. An agitation by bank staff taking place during a revisit in 1985, which included two of the women in the sample, provided an opportunity to discuss perceptions of the union and its action with the two women and their female colleagues. The agitation had been called over the dismissal of a number of employees for 'poor work records' and the small group of female employees in the bank – all young married women in junior clerical positions – were taking part in the agitation. They expressed solidarity with the sacked employees and all agreed that the workers were completely solid in the dispute. They saw the union, however, not as a body which included themselves but as the equivalent of a paterfamilias or, to use the Indian idiom, as their *ma-bap* ('mother and father'). The union and its leaders were spoken of with reverence and described as 'taking care of everything. If the women want anything, the leaders take it up.'[3] None had considered the possibility that they could become leaders or activists themselves, considering their main responsibility to lie with their domestic commitments.

Age and status have an effect on women's perceptions. Radical views are more likely to be expressed by younger educated single women, often from refugee backgrounds, whose labour-market experience contrasts markedly with their expectations and who are less encumbered with received notions of deference and respectability and with potentially contradictory class ideologies. For them, employment is less likely to be simply an adjunct to domestic life to which it must be accommodated. Young women factory workers were notable for having a developed sense of the potential to be found in collective organization. The three young single women involved in attempts to start a union in their factories exemplify this pattern.

There are also representatives in the sample of an older generation of politically active, middle-class women whose participation was closely linked to nationalist politics and who come from families with a history of political activism. These women tend to have a history of activity in women's organizations, particularly those linked to a political party, rather than in unions *per se*, and to articulate a wider vision of the contemporary position of women.

Younger married women from middle-class families without a tradition of political activism and with husbands in high status employment are the most likely to experience and express the contradictions of class location and labour market position and to resolve them through apathy or muted hostility to union activities. They are also more likely to be under pressure from domestic responsibilities at this stage in their life as well as to perceive their domestic roles to be more significant in their lives than their experiences as wage workers.

Women's perceptions of the extent to which trade unions represent their interests as women were explored. Table 6.4 provides a condensation of their responses.

*Table 6.4* Do trade unions represent the interests of women workers in particular?

| (1) | Yes – represent men and women equally | 26 |
|-----|----------------------------------------|-----|
| (2) | Yes – own union represents women's interests | 18 |
| (3) | Yes – cannot specify reason | 11 |
| (4) | Yes – fight for equal pay | 3 |
| (5) | No | 14 |
| (6) | *Total responses* | 72 |

For the twenty-six women who responded that unions represent women and men equally, women's interests as workers are inseparable from those of men in that their identities as workers are seen as the main issue. These women used the language of unity, solidarity and collective bargaining to describe the form in which their rights are represented, or would be if they were members. Women who responded that their own union represented the interests of its women members as a distinct category were all members of unions with a high to fairly high female membership - mainly teachers and nurses but also a few clerical workers. Some made this connection quite explicitly, pointing out that their own union may not be typical. Few of the women who felt that unions did represent their interests were able, however, to articulate the concrete ways in which they did so beyond pressing for equal pay and conditions of service. There was a more general sense in which unions were not seen to be connected to the issue of women's needs. As a clerical worker and union member pointed out, 'We don't site our demands separately.'

Those who responded negatively, tended to do so as a consequence of unsatisfactory personal experiences. Several complained that unions are male dominated and both leaders and rank-and-file male workers are uninterested in or hostile to women making separate demands. Another common complaint was that many male workers are hostile to women having employment. A clerical worker said, 'Men in our office think that women have no economic reason to work. They always say that women work just to buy new saris and cosmetics.' She saw this attitude reflected in the 'male-dominated' leadership and its lack of concern with women's interests as employees. A bank worker said, 'Our union doesn't represent women's interests. We don't even have a separate toilet. I think the men can't accept our employment as necessary.' Others had witnessed discriminatory practices within unions. A young factory worker described how her mother, also previously a factory worker, had taken part in a strike and was subsequently victimized. She received no support from her union and her daughter believed this to be because she was a woman.

In general, women's experiences of trade unions appear to be less than satisfactory. The majority, working in poor and often isolating conditions at appallingly low rates of pay, are not reached by union organization and know little about its possible benefits. Although there is a high rate of unionization among organized sector workers, their total presence in trade unions is still small, few are activists and there is little indication that issues such as working hours, childcare facilities or sexual harassment which concern women in particular, are being raised at union level or are considered to be legitimate union concerns.

What has been the response of the unions to women's employment? First, it must be reiterated that women still form a very small part of the organized sector labour force and that most unions have an over-whelmingly or even exclusively male membership. Second, union-ization in India has traditionally been confined to organized sector employees and it is only recently that some attempts have begun to try to reach unorganized sector workers in small units. This still leaves the disproportionately female home-based workers untouched except by some of the women's political and welfare organizations. However, as Banerjee points out (1985a: 108), it is a paradox that in a city with a long tradition of trade unionism and left politics, such workers have been neglected for so long. Its resolution possibly lies in the dominance, within the main left parties, of the vision of the urban industrial (male) proletariat as the major vehicle for political change.

In December 1982, the local committee of the National Federation of Indian Women organized a forum on women's employment as part of a wider campaign to press for increased opportunities for women and improvements in their working conditions. The forum was addressed by male and female speakers from a range of unions and organizations and the meeting revealed a systematic difference in the genders' perceptions of the issue. For men, the problem, if it existed, was located in the workplace. Union speakers from the organized service sector unions emphasized that their sector had achieved equality in the workplace with 'equal pay and equal opportunity' for women. They thus opposed a resolution calling for reserved jobs for women on the grounds that there is no discrimination at work and that there are in any case too many 'minorities' demanding special treatment. No mention was made of the disproportionate numbers of women congregating in junior positions. A bank employees' spokesman also complained that women members are apathetic and do not attend meetings despite the best efforts of organizers. Other male speakers were sympathetic to the demand for reservation but also saw the issue as one of achieving equality of conditions in the workplace.

Women speakers tended to present a much wider analysis. A speaker for the Student Nurses Association emphasized the social location of the problem. She cited the example of a maternity patient who had cried on being told that she had a daughter. She linked this to wider questions of economic and ideological injustice, concluding that unless wider conditions were made to change, women never achieve equality in or out of the workplace. A woman *biri* worker, speaking for home-based women, called for equal pay with men but emphasized the particular implications of starvation wages for young Muslim women: 'Many Muslim girls are left unmarried because they can't raise the Rs 5000 needed as a minimum for marriage.' In a community where few options exist for women outside marriage and where social citizenship depends upon marital status, this was of more pressing concern than working conditions.

There is, then, a gap at the level of perception of the issue and thus at the level of the remedy. For trade union organizers, and this includes those few women who have organizing experience, the solution tends to be seen in terms of 'getting more women into leadership roles'. To that extent, debate focuses on why women do not participate more actively in union affairs or put themselves forward for office. In the left-dominated unions, 'feudal attitudes' on the part of both men and women tend to be blamed. As a prominent male union organizer pointed out, 'It is insufficient to argue that women don't have time because of domestic duties – most union work is done during the daytime.' Also prevalent on the left is the thesis of political backwardness as an explanation. This is symbolized by women's resort to the argument that their domestic responsibilities leave them no time or are of greater importance. A woman teacher and union activist said:

I don't believe it is due to household responsibilities or oppression. It is my experience that when I ask any women to join a union or do anything related to the union, they refuse on the grounds of household responsibilities. But if you offer to take them to a film show of Uttam Kumar[4] they will have no difficulties.

In evaluating these arguments, it is important to recognize that contradictory tendencies and responses are present. As has been suggested, there are groups of women who are indifferent or apathetic towards union activity, whether because of their class location and problematic identity as workers, or because of their actual or perceived domestic responsibilities and orientations. Whether all of this is best described as 'political backwardness' is arguable. Married women's identification with the home is culturally and historically deeply embedded in the consciousness of men as well as women. The disengagement of men from domesticity and its demands is predicated on the primacy of domestic responsibilities for women. An employer, arguing in a personal interview that women took 'too much time off' for domestic crises, said he frequently turned down requests for compassionate leave on the grounds that 'husbands should request their share of leave'. This apparent reasonableness completely ignored the absence of any culture of shared domestic responsibility between husbands and wives.

There are also employed women who want to organize or be organized but lack the resources and they are the least likely to have been approached or canvassed by existing trade unions. Women who have been or are organizers have also had to contend with sexism from male counterparts and from the rank and file. It is often difficult for women to be taken seriously because of pervasive assumptions that women do not need to work or are taking jobs which 'rightfully' belong to men. The subcultures of unions and the terms of the debates, as in most of the advanced capitalist countries, tend to be male (cf. Cockburn 1983). The assumption that formal equality of women and men in the workplace is all that is required is not going to be sufficient to persuade women to take on leadership responsibilities or participate more actively.

The challenge posed by women speakers at the forum and by some of the progressive women's organizations is whether narrowly conceived 'workplace' issues and leadership are the fundamental problems. If women are apathetic to the kinds of concerns taken up by unions, there may need to be some rethinking of the concerns themselves. If women do accord their domestic responsibilities a higher priority than union activism, this suggests a need to place domestic work and the sexual division of household labour and childcare firmly on the union agenda. If 'feudal attitudes' inhibit both sexes from putting women into leadership roles, this suggests the need for education and campaigning on issues such as sexism and sexual harassment. Most importantly, unions would have to take seriously the fact that the majority of employed women are in sectors of the labour force which are wholly unorganized.

What steps would employed women themselves want to see taken to improve conditions for women? A total of 130 women responded to an open-ended question about measures which they felt would benefit women most. Many responded with detailed lists of suggestions and these are summarized in Table 6.5

*Table 6.5* What steps would most benefit employed or job-seeking women?

| | | |
|---|---|---|
| (1) | Better education and training facilities | 71 |
| (2) | More jobs created specifically for women | 32 |
| (3) | Creche facilities | 23 |
| (4) | Women-only transport | 23 |
| (5) | Regularization of employment contracts and working conditions | 22 |
| (6) | Job reservation | 18 |
| (7) | New/better legislation on working conditions | 5 |
| (8) | More jobs created for illiterate women | 5 |
| (9) | Better workplace facilities | 4 |
| (10) | Equal opportunities for jobs and promotion | 4 |
| (11) | Security against harassment | 3 |
| (12) | More information on training and jobs | 3 |
| (13) | Hostels for employed women | 2 |
| (14) | Help with loans and marketing | 1 |
| (15) | Shorter working hours | 1 |
| (16) | Labour-saving devices for the home | 1 |
| (17) | Law to abolish purdah | 1 |

Respondents are not short of ideas. Better education and training was considered by far the most important need. The needs of illiterate women for non-formal adult education were mentioned particularly and most women who wanted more training for women stressed the need for proper technical training to enable them to compete in the labour market on more equal terms. Job creation comes next, with a small number also stressing the need for jobs aimed at illiterate women. Again, the stress was on 'proper jobs' rather than home work, with one respondent suggesting that there should be a quota of guaranteed jobs in all small-scale factory units. Job reservation was mentioned by a smaller but not insignificant number of women, mainly in the public sector, who clearly take a different view from that of their male union organizers.

Two important non-workplace issues for women are childcare and public transport. A significant number of women would like to see the provision of creches, but on a neighbourhood rather than a workplace basis. This is interesting in view of the comment of the personnel officer of a large electronics factory in Calcutta that the take-up level of the factory creche is fairly low. Only organized sector employers with a female workforce of at least fifty are required by law to provide creches and such employers are very rare in Calcutta.

However, women's preference is definitely for local childcare provision – a preference which is not unconnected to Calcutta's chaotic travel conditions.[5]  Not surprisingly, this was also mentioned by a significant number of the women who are faced with long daily journeys. Women-only buses have been operating in Delhi, the capital, mainly as a response to high levels of sexual harassment of women on public transport. In Calcutta, where all citizens suffer from the poor state of communications, the issue for women is not harassment, which is generally absent on city transport, but time which has to be spent on top of domestic duties.

The regularization of employment contracts is, again, a critical issue for women employed on a casual basis. This includes teachers in private schools who are particularly concerned about the absence of regular pay scales. A small number also linked this issue to the need to extend labour legislation into the unorganized sector. A middle-aged home-based worker said simply, 'The government should introduce a law against employers who exploit women workers.'

A temporary worker pointed to the practice of regularly laying off women workers and re-employing them again in order to retain them as temporary workers. She suggested a new law against this practice, unaware, because of the absence of a union to take up workers' cases, that a person who works for 240 days each year is already considered a permanent worker under existing law.  One Muslim respondent also wanted the law extended to abolish purdah restrictions which she saw as the major constraint on her capacity to seek employment. The many appeals to the law are poignant in a context where much progressive legislation exists on the statute book but is persistently flouted.

Nevertheless, the range of individual responses is quite wide and suggests that many women could be mobilized to a more imaginative programme of demands encompassing women across occupational categories.

## Conclusion

Despite a long history of labour-force participation among some proletarian and high status women, the dominant discourse has placed Bengali wives and mothers in the home. The growth of women's employment in the last decade has only partially dislodged this discourse. It is acceptable for women to take paid work, provided it is of a certain kind, is amenable to policing by authority figures and by self-policing mechanisms, does not interfere unduly with women's primary responsibility to the domestic life of the family, and does not radically disrupt existing power relations between the generations and the genders. This has meant that some potential contradictions could be absorbed or reduced, particularly for married women.

As workers, women's capacity to act individually or collectively to change their conditions is limited by their preponderance in the unorganized and non-unionized sector and by ideological barriers to greater participation in both the organizational structures and the debates within the labour movement.

Chapter seven

# Dependence and autonomy
Women's employment and the family in Calcutta

After her marriage, she (the Bengali woman) must try to be
accepted by the elders of her father-in-law's household. The wife
must be respectful in a Hindu household.

(*mahila* July 1902)

What is a woman's home? Always either her father's or her
husband's or her brother's or her son's. Men won't be free till
women are free.

(Mrs R.F. Hussein 'Ornaments or Badge of Slavery'
*mahila* July 1903)

## Gender, employment and family

The question which this book set out to answer – what is the effect of
women's employment on the household? – now seems, in its initial
conceptualization, to have been posed too narrowly. The effects themselves are embedded in a history in which women have been constructed
at different times as familial dependants and as workers.

This chapter is an attempt to make visible the wider issues which
have become apparent in the course of the argument. The meaning of
employment for women must be sought in the context of the ways in
which women's lives are bounded by the family, in which those
boundaries change historically, developmentally and with class, and in
which the family itself is constructed. Women's lives must be situated
in their histories, and the histories of women are, to a greater extent than
is true for men, embedded in their families. The family is a critical site
in the construction of female dependency.

The ways in which this dependency is structured have implications,
first for which women enter the labour market and which are withdrawn
from it at particular historical moments, and second, for women's

142

capacity to secure their short- and long-term material circumstances. Structures of dependency are related to, but do not reflect mechanically, changing demands for female labour, or class position. The family is an arena of intense ideological mediation and women's access to paid work is constrained by historically and culturally specific concepts of familial dependency and what are considered appropriate behaviours and occupations for women.

A fuller understanding of women's dependency must therefore take into account a set of gendered processes which operate interactively. Dependency is multi-faceted and inheres in mental as well as material structures. In the previous chapters, the concept of dependency has appeared, loosely, in five analytically distinguishable ways.

First, it has appeared most obviously as an economic category, in the sense of a dependence on the financial support of male kin, including husbands. The extent of this dependence varies, not only with the level of female employment but also with the extent to which 'real' jobs offering viable incomes are available to women.

Second, it has a legal aspect. Legal systems in India, as elsewhere, construct forms of female dependency through the legal regulation of marriage and family life. Employment legislation may directly or indirectly restrict women's access to certain kinds of paid work, such as by placing limitations on, for example, shift working. Third, customary practice gives superior rights of access to property and housing to male family members.

Fourth, ideologies of domesticity, expressed within a particular cultural idiom, constitute women as dependants. Women are naturally inscribed with the attributes of carers and homemakers. Their 'place' is primarily, if not wholly, in the home. Such ideologies have a more general provenance in capitalist societies. Where 'the economic' is fetishized as that which is paid, the non-valorized 'female' attributes of domesticity are not the ideological equal of the 'male' attributes of breadwinner and supporter.

Fifth, gender identities are constructed psychically and socially in such a way that women may experience themselves, for all or much of their lives, as dependent emotionally upon and subject to male and older female authority figures.

Gaining access to employment may thus challenge directly only certain aspects of dependence. It may also result in the reconstitution of other aspects within the workplace and the home through such practices as gender stereotyping of jobs, paternalism, legal restrictions and the policing of employed women by senior family members. Further, low-paid work may hold out little prospect of financial independence.

This chapter focuses primarily on material structures of dependency and their relationship to family forms. It looks particularly at women who lose their source of familial economic support and who have, historically, been the ones most likely to enter the labour market. It first explores some aspects of the historical relationship between the availability of paid work for women and changing concepts of familial dependency. It then examines, by means of case histories from the sample, the different trajectories of those categories of contemporary women rendered vulnerable through the loss or withdrawal of alternative means of support. Finally, it considers whether the households of employed, 'non-dependent' women are more susceptible to poverty than households with male breadwinners.

The chapter concludes with an examination of women's access to property and related resources. It argues that wider understandings of female dependency render that access problematic and that the issues of housing and 'ideological placement' are as important for modifying dependence as command over wages.

## Women's employment and changing concepts of economic dependency

As was pointed out in chapter three, the recorded labour-force participation rate of women in Bengal has not been uniformly low throughout the century. Women were employed in substantial numbers in the earliest established manufacturing industries such as jute and textiles. Between 1920 and 1970, however, female employment in manufacturing declined dramatically and there are now very few women left in jute, which was the single largest employer of female industrial labour.

The reasons for this decline are still debated. Protective labour legislation on hours, shift work and health provisions for women employees on the one hand, and mechanization of tasks mostly performed by women on the other, are generally blamed. But labour legislation was implemented patchily in Bengal and frequently flouted by the simple expedient of describing female labour as 'temporary'. Mechanization, similarly, has been uneven in its effects on the labour force and it is unclear how many women's jobs were lost as a direct consequence of this (cf. Savara 1981). Social and ideological explanations for women's displacement from manufacturing industry have received less attention although they have particular significance for understanding the changing ways in which women have been constructed either as dependants or as a potential labour force.

When the first mills were set up in Bengal, mostly in the vicinity of Calcutta, in the 1860s and 1870s, labour was drawn from the local Bengali population, notably from displaced artisans and low caste landless labourers or marginal cultivators. Whole families were generally employed, with men and women engaged on complementary processes. Children's labour started at around the age of eight years. Women labourers during this early period were either married women working along with their husbands, or widows. There was no equivalent to the young single female workforce found in industrial towns in Britain at a similar period and indeed, such a workforce only began to appear in West Bengal very recently.[1]

Early factory labour fairly soon underwent a major change in ethnic and regional composition. From the 1890s, and accelerating from 1910, the predominantly local Bengali labour force of men, women and children was increasingly replaced by single male migrant labour from outside Bengal. According to the Royal Commission on Factory Labour of 1931 (henceforth, the RCFL), by 1921, only two out of eleven unskilled labourers and a quarter of skilled labourers in Bengal were Bengalis. As recently as 1958, a government inquiry into the living standards of industrial workers and their families in Calcutta found that only 23% of the families were Bengali in origin (Report on Family Living Survey 1958–9, Government of India 1960). This declining trend in the Bengali industrial labour force was much commented upon in successive commissions and inquiries and usually explained as a consequence of the Bengali disdain for manual work.[2]

The substitution of non-Bengali for local labour raises many issues. At one level, the argument that Bengal's early industrialization caused a scarcity of local labour is a reasonable one.[3] Jute undoubtedly had to compete for labour with the developing engineering, pharmaceuticals and mining industries. This by itself, however, does not account for the particular positioning of ethnic, regional and gendered categories of labour in the different industries. Nor can it explain the persistently low wages in the jute industry. A range of factors, including ethnic and gender stereotyping of 'suitable' categories of labour, were probably implicated here.

In terms of the economics of labour supply, single male migrant labour was almost certainly cheaper to employ than local labour. It is clear from the RCFL that employers in Bengal saw 'up-country' labour as an ever abundant and cheap source. This was so much so that the apparent lowness of wages in the jute industry elicited some sharp questioning of employers by the Commissioners as to whether they were paying a 'living wage' which would enable a (male) worker to 'raise a family'. The employers' response was to argue that workers were either an unstable labour force of single men living cheaply in factory lines who could still afford to remit large amounts to their villages and to which they returned for long periods; or that whole families were employed (RCFL, Evidence: 149–51).

Regardless of the truth of this perception (in fact by 1930, 90% of factory labour was permanent and female and child labour was declining), it was the case that, at least for unskilled labour, reasonable survival was only possible if the entire family brought in wages or if a worker had some other source of livelihood such as land on which his family could partially subsist. It was recognition of this which partly prompted the general concern expressed by the Commission over the decline in the female workforce and their decision not to recommend a reduction specifically in women's working hours in case this should lead to further job losses.[4] The decline in women's factory employment would seem to be connected to the decline in the employment of whole families in the mills and their replacement by predominantly single male migrant labour.

The significance of ideological forces in shaping the responses of the Bengali population to industrial labour, particularly in relation to the employment of women requires further analysis (cf. also Banerjee 1985b). Evidence given to the Indian Factories Commission of 1890, which inquired extensively into the conditions of female labour, shows that even by this early date, few married Bengali women were going for factory employment. Of the six adult women interviewed in the Bengal inquiry, the only married woman was a Bihari working along with her husband. The other five women were all Bengali widows ranging in age from 20 to 40 and from artisan and cultivating castes, who had gone to the mills as a consequence of their widowhood. When asked if they would send their daughters into the factory they all replied that they would expect their daughters to marry and go to their husband's house: 'As a rule, Bengali women never come to work in the mills unless they are widows' (Evidence of Taroni, Barnagore Branch Mill, Report of the Recent Commission on Indian Factories 1891: 89).

While traditional norms enjoining some degree of seclusion upon married women may have been implicated in their absence from the factory, this does not explain why the employment of, first, married Bengali women and then Bengali women generally, appears to decline from this period onwards. As has already been pointed out, however, the issue of women's employment in Bengal, and particularly in metropolitan Calcutta, from the late nineteenth century onwards was shot through with strong moral and ideological preoccupations. For most segments of the emerging Bengali middle class and those aspiring to it, the idea of women entering the public domain of employment was highly shameful and considered equivalent to a loss of chastity. Much of the early Bengali labour force came from those middle-ranking artisan and agricultural castes (such as the Mahisyas) which were also making determined efforts to raise their social status during this period. The withdrawal of women from public activities was an important element in this process.

Employed women thus became increasingly equated by many prominent moralists with prostitutes. By 1930, the Assistant Director of Public Health felt able to assert confidently that 'among female workers, one out of every four owns to being a prostitute.' (RCFL op. cit. 6). A contemporary study of prostitution in Calcutta suggested that the majority of women jute workers were prostitutes, especially if they owned jewellery (Ghosh 1923).[5] Whether or not these assertions bore any relation to the real level of prostitution, at least in Calcutta where it was said to be very high, it was certainly necessary for a woman factory labourer to have male protection both in the workplace and in the living quarters, if she was domiciled there (cf. Curjel 1923, Report of Indian Factory Labour Commission 1908, vol. V, part 2: 6).

Single women labourers were particularly vulnerable to sexual harassment and women without husbands were thus forced to find a male worker with whom they could cohabit, often forming semi-permanent liaisons which also gave them some access to a male wage for raising any children. Unless they were much older widows with no dependants, therefore, women factory workers were dependent on male protection as well as on male wages if they were to avoid destitution. Factory employment for women was generally casual and piece-rated and vulnerable to substitution by child or young adult male labour. Bengali women found working in the factories by the 1920s, as Curjel pointed out, were generally widows abandoned by their husbands' families or women who had 'lost their reputation.' I. Mitra (1981) argues that the militancy of women jute workers in the 1940s was a consequence of the double oppression which they faced as women workers. As well as their economic oppression, they constantly faced the moral opprobrium of the wider society and of their male fellow workers which constituted them as 'loose women'.

There seems no doubt that those Bengali women remaining in the industrial labour force faced strong pressures to withdraw from it if they had access to a male income. Giving evidence to the RCFL (1931), a skilled Bengali labourer in the Burma Shell refinery near Calcutta told the Commission 'my wife does not work; in Bengal our wives do not work' (vol. 2: 115). Having no land or property he could only maintain his family by doing overtime and a second job in a grocery shop. Bengali women were firmly domesticated.

There was a slight rise in women's employment in manufacturing industries in the Second World War when labour shortages arose, and the results of a family budget survey between 1943–4 on jute workers in Howrah found that families consisted of an average of 4.2 persons, of whom 1.6 were earners (Labour Investigation Committee [Jute] Government of India 1946). By 1958, however, the Family Living Survey (Government of India 1960) revealed that in a sample of 833 industrial workers in registered factories in Calcutta there were only fourteen women earners and 90% of families had only one earning member.

Did the decline in women's employment in Bengal coincide with changes in official discourses about the family? In her study of women workers in the Bombay textile industry between 1919 and 1939, Kumar (1983) analyses official attempts by agencies of the colonial state to define the 'natural unit' of the working-class family in order to legislate on issues of employment, housing and morality. In Bombay, this began with the first Family Budget Survey in 1922. Ignoring both the major contribution of wives to family income and the existence of complex family forms, the FBS defined the family as that of a male breadwinner, dependent wife and children.

The next survey in 1932 made quite explicit the principle of the 'family wage' as the basis for the setting of industrial wage levels, and Kumar argues that this was not fortuitous in the light of the rationalization that was increasingly causing job losses among women textile workers. Savara (1981) notes also that trade unions and other organizations in Bombay increasingly supported the principle of the family wage, both to restrict competition for jobs and to establish the notion that a non-employed wife should be included in the calculation of a worker's living costs.

The picture in Bengal appears less clear cut. The evidence for Bengal given to the RCFL (1931) does not reveal any clear image either of the basis upon which wages should be calculated or of what constitutes a family or a dependent relative. Faced with the array of different cultural and regional backgrounds of the workforce and the lack of any systematic inquiry into family composition and family budgets, members of the Commission alternated between the assumption that a worker was a male breadwinner with a dependent wife and children and a firm appreciation of the importance of the wage contributions of women and children (see esp. vol. 2: 52, 126, 149, 150, 181–92). They were equally clear that the principle of a family wage was yet to be conceded and that the increasing loss of women's jobs in the factories meant an increase in the poverty of families (ibid: 126).

The operation of official dependency rules in respect of who was entitled to receive a worker's compensation or death benefit also showed no uniformity of view as to what constituted a 'dependant'[6] and their operation was admitted to be arbitrary. The Commissioners recommended simultaneously that dependency should be 'presumed' but 'rebuttable' in the case of widows and children, and that widowed sisters and widowed daughters should, in future, be included as dependants (ibid: 70). They concluded that 'the joint family system would make it very difficult to assess the degree of dependence' but, expediently, wanted to restrict the number of dependants to the minimum which could be considered 'just' (ibid: 76).

The testimonies of the two trade union officials interviewed by the Commission do reveal, however, something of the basis of these various and apparently conflicting judgements. Both were Bengalis representing respectively jute mill workers and white-collar employees in the government printing press. Both took the view that wages should be set by reference to the cost of living of the social category of the worker. Krishna Chunder Ray Chaudhuri, the President of the Kankinarah Labour Union, argued that 'the standard of living of a sardar is different from the standard of living of a weaver and the standard of living of a weaver is different from that of a spinner' (ibid: 125 and see also 124 for a similar view on a caste basis from a factory manager). Significantly, Chaudhuri's own computations of a living wage were based on the cost of living of skilled labour, which was more likely to be Bengali. Prohlad Chandra Ray, his Bengali white-collar counterpart, produced his own family budget as evidence for his claim that the (predominantly Bengali) middle class was unable to maintain itself without going into debt or selling off family property. His own budget included allowances for non-employed female dependants and children's education.

Skilled and white-collar workers were not only more likely to be Bengali but were also most likely to be non-migrants and to have non-employed female dependants to maintain *in situ*. In that sense their establishment costs were undoubtedly higher than those of single male migrants and their 'customary expectations' included the concept of adult female dependency. Although not formulated explicitly as a demand for a 'family wage' based on a male-breadwinner/dependent-wife conceptualization of the family, the complaints of the Bengali trade unionists over wage levels certainly involved the assumption that the typical worker was a married male with a range of non-employed dependants whom he had increasing difficulty maintaining.[7]

The historical picture is both complex and incomplete but the decline in women's employment in Bengal does seem to have been accompanied by some renegotiation of familial dependencies which was in part played out in the struggles between organized labour, employers and, to a lesser extent in the Bengal case, the state. Further research would be necessary to determine whether the demands of trade unionists for some form of family wage are seen as a defensive strategy to protect living standards (cf. Humphries 1977), as part of an increasing attempt by organized male labour to restrict competition for scarce employment, or as part of the differentiation and demarcation of the Bengali petit bourgoisie. What is not in doubt is that women's access to paid employment became, particularly from the 1920s, both more contingent and hedged around with ideological restrictions. For both working-class and middle-class Bengali women, loss of access to a male income and the right to maintenance in either a brother's, husband's or son's household had serious consequences. Thus, to understand women's vulnerability to poverty, it is necessary to take into account both class position and familial circumstances. Chapter five has already touched upon the ways in which increased dependence on a male wage or salary earner brought about a narrower definition of that earner's responsibilities for dependants. While in principle, unmarried sisters, brothers' widows and widowed mothers could expect support from their households, in practice, low incomes together with a growing sense that an earner's own wife and children commanded a prior claim to that income meant that women who did not have or who lost such a claim were potentially vulnerable, and these were the women who would have to find employment.

Historically, it is widows who have formed the major category of vulnerable women, as the testimonies of Bengali widows working in the jute mills indicate. This vulnerability has not been confined to working-class women. A study on prostitution in Calcutta in the 1920s gives the case histories of several Bengali widows from *bhadralok* backgrounds, the families of whom were unable or unwilling to support them and for whom few other options existed which would have ensured a living income (Ghosh 1923). The very large numbers of widows in Calcutta[8] was partly a consequence of the near universality of marriage at very young ages, often to much older men; but the perception of widowhood as a social problem at that period reflected a growing concern with the issue of dependency. While public debate in the 1930s was almost completely hostile to the employment of married women, the need to find 'suitable' employment for widows was generally conceded (cf. Government of India 1933, *Census of India 1931*, vol. V, part 1, appendix 1).

For both widows and for married women with unemployed or low-waged husbands, the extreme scarcity of what was considered to be suitable employment for women posed severe problems. Unless they possessed educational qualifications enabling them to enter teaching or other segregated occupations, they were confined to very ill-paid domestic service and home-based cottage industries or personal services.

More recently in West Bengal, the combination of a rising age of marriage, declining real wages and the growth of 'women's jobs' in the newer manufacturing industries and in the clerical sector has put a new category of young single women into the labour force. The implications of this must now be considered.

## Women's employment and contemporary family forms

The point at which women enter the labour force and what jobs they are able to do are thus an outcome of the relationship between the wider processes which structure poverty, changing demands for labour, historically produced concepts of dependency and ideologies sanctioning appropriate work for women. This section examines the trajectories which have brought women in the sample into the labour force as a result of changes or uncertainties in access to male support and their implications for women in terms of familial dependency and material security.

Case histories show that the most significant factors which precipitate women into the labour market who would not otherwise expect to be employed, are marital status and low male incomes. Single women may be either daughters supporting or helping to support parents, or older women wholly or mostly maintaining themselves. Widows and women whose marriages have terminated continue to form a significant group of self-supporting women. Inadequate incomes or unemployment among husbands cause some married women to seek employment.

It was pointed out that certain features of the demographic and social composition of the sample distinguish it from the general population. First, the proportion of single women is very high. In the general population sampled in the 1976 Calcutta Poverty Survey, 29% of women between the ages of fifteen and forty-four were never married, while the comparable percentage for this sample is 48%. Of these, almost half are aged over twenty-five. The proportion of women from refugee households is also high. The particular economic and social crisis confronted by displaced Bengali Hindus in the aftermath of 1947 has probably been responsible for the much higher rates of female employment in the refugee population, and the general economic crisis in Calcutta has brought young unmarried women increasingly into the labour force. It is thus particularly among these groups that changes in the ways in which familial dependencies are constructed might be expected.

*Case histories*

Single women

Of the eighty-one never-married women in the sample, sixty-four are living with one or both of their parents in a total of forty households of which twenty-three are refugee in origin. The current composition of these households is as follows:

| | |
|---|---|
| Parent(s)/unmarried children | 27 |
| Parent(s)/unmarried children/married sons | 7 |
| Parent(s)/unmarried children/married daughters | 3 |
| Other 3-generational | 2 |
| Other 2-generational | 1 |

The average financial contribution of unmarried daughters to the household budget (excluding work seekers and unpaid family helpers) is 67% of the total wage income with a range from 18–100%. Four households are entirely supported by the wages of unmarried daughters.

The diverse fortunes of refugee families tend to be laid out architecturally in the colonies on the southern outskirts of the city where many refugees were granted housesites. Some of the housing is *pakkha* (brick), two- or three-storeyed and reflects the achievement or recovery of prosperity. Some houses are in various stages of construction and transition to *pakkha* status. Others, small, neat and constructed of wood and tin, are still the temporary shacks which went up in 1947.

The Basu family's house is one that is in transition. The main interior walls of their two rooms are of brick, and they have managed to build a kitchen and bathroom. Otherwise there are few signs of prosperity. The father has worked since 1947 as a retailer's clerk and earns only Rs 350 per month. In 1982, their three daughters were studying at intermediate level and an only son was employed as a trainee in an electrical works. The mother had changed from making paper bags for a local supplier to stitching children's garments for the local market. In a good month, with her daughters helping, she could earn Rs 125. A revisit to this family in 1984 revealed the tragic precariousness of their existence. The son had lost his job the previous year after suffering from typhoid. Unable to obtain other employment and in a state of depression, he had committed suicide. The eldest daughter was therefore searching for employment and the family has ceased to look for marriage partners for the daughters as they are not able to meet the dowry demands of prospective bridegrooms.

The Das family's experience has been less traumatic although, like many refugees, they suffered economically. The family consists of a widow, her unmarried daughter, Ira, an unmarried son, two married daughters and three married sons. Only Ira and her unmarried brother remain with their mother. One brother has moved to another part of West Bengal and retains little contact with the household, while the other two brothers now live in separate houses with their wives and children, but in the same compound. Ira is a 25-year-old graduate employed temporarily as a clerk in a government office. Since 1981 she has moved from one temporary position to another, hoping for a permanent vacancy eventually. Ira helps to support her widowed mother who has a small pension but who would otherwise be dependent upon her two married sons. Some years previously, her mother had taken the decision to split the housesite between the three units. She foresaw the possibility of quarrels and wished to forestall this. The two sons contribute to her expenses but not on a regular basis. Ira's mother mentions the subject of marriage to her 'practically every day' but as they are not prepared to give dowry there have been no offers and Ira hopes for a permanent post so that she can support her mother more adequately.

Shanta Dey's family live in a half-constructed three-roomed house in a colony. Her father, who died in 1977, had been a low-paid government school teacher and Shanta and her sister Jaya are the youngest of eight children. Their eldest sister has remained unmarried and looks after the house for their elderly mother. Three married sons have left the family home, and two other daughters have also married. Shanta and Jaya give private tuition at home and supplement their mother's pension of Rs 150 with another Rs 90. Their married brothers send money irregularly about every three months or before festivals.

The family of Deepali and Sita Majumdar, who are aged 27 and 24, also came to Calcutta in the wake of partition having lost all their property, but did not obtain a housesite in a colony. The family, which consists of parents, three sons and two daughters, rents a one-room house in a bustee in north Calcutta. The father has been ill and unable to work for some years. As a consequence, Deepali and Sita, the two eldest children, left school after completing primary level and found employment in a leather and an electronics factory respectively. The eldest of the sons, who had completed intermediate-level schooling, is employed as a clerical worker. Another son is unemployed and the youngest son is still studying. The daughters' wages together provide two-thirds of the family income of Rs 400 per month.

Savitri Dhar's family has been in Calcutta for three generations. She is 36 years old, the second eldest of nine children, and had expected to marry after her graduation in 1972. However, her father, who was a businessman, died the same year. As the eldest of the sisters she felt obliged to look for a job and has been teaching in a local school since 1974. Savitri and two of her brothers provide the family's income.

The ten households of unmarried women not living with a parent or parents are constituted as follows:

| | |
|---|---|
| Single-person households | 5 |
| Unmarried sisters | 2 |
| Unmarried sister with married brothers | 1 |
| Other sibling-based combinations | 2 |

Apart from the unmarried sister living in her natal joint family, all the single women are financially self-sufficient. Two of the women living alone contribute one-third and one-half of their monthly wages to their natal households respectively.

For some single women, their entry into employment took place, again, as unmarried daughters. Malati Ray lives with her widowed mother's sister and her married sister's young son who is a student in Calcutta. She is 36 years old and is employed in a milk-distribution depot. Her father, who died in 1970, had been a skilled worker in a local firm but was laid off and her mother had then taken a job in a government department to enable them to survive. She died in 1975 leaving Malati, her unemployed elder brother and a younger sister without any income. The following year, after a lot of searching, Malati obtained her present job. Her brother has since left the house and her remaining sister has married.

Sudha Mandal, who is 45 and the matron of a hostel where she has accommodation, originally entered employment of her own personal wish. She was the youngest of six children and her father was a lawyer in Midnapore District. After graduating, she taught in a school in another district but when her mother died some years later, she returned to her father's house. All her brothers and sisters were married and living elsewhere and there was no-one to care for the elderly father. One of her brothers subsequently returned to live in the house, but in 1978, the father died. Sudha did not want to live with her brother and came to Calcutta to find employment.

Swasti Chatterjee was born in East Bengal in 1942 and came to Calcutta with her family at partition. She has worked as a nurse for nearly twenty years and lives permanently in a quarter. Her widowed mother and three unmarried brothers live elsewhere in Calcutta and she visits them but does not contribute financially on a regular basis. She has a younger sister, whose marriage expenses of Rs 8000, she paid out of her savings. As the elder sister and second child, she was unable to marry as no-one in the family made any attempt to arrange it.

The five Bose sisters live in the house built by their father when he was a young man. The eight-roomed house is subdivided three ways with a tenant occupying the ground floor and their married brother living with his family in a partitioned-off part of the upstairs. The house is full of reminders of a wealthier past. One room preserves the image of a well-to-do middle-class household with polished old furniture, ornaments and paintings. Their father had worked for the post office and died in 1968 having failed to marry any of his daughters because of the dowries being demanded. The sisters survive by doing tailoring work at home and selling saris in the neighbourhood. Relations with their brother are poor because of their continuing occupation of the family property. Since their parent's death, their relatives have also ceased contact with them.

**Table 7.1** Costs in last five years, or expected costs of daughters' marriages by income group (in rupees)

| Household income group | Less than 2000 | 2000–5000 | 5000–10 000 | 10 000–20 000 | 20 000–30 000 | 30 000–40 000 | 40 000 + |
|---|---|---|---|---|---|---|---|
| <500 | 2 | 16 | 6 | | | | |
| 501–1000 | 1 | 8 | 9 | 1 | | | |
| 1001–2000 | 2 | 1 | 4 | 6 | 1 | 1 | |
| 2001–3000 | | | 3 | 6 | 4 | 3 | 1 |
| 3001 + | | | | 2 | 5 | 2 | 4 |
| Total | 5 | 25 | 22 | 16 | 11 | 6 | 5 |

*Note:* 90 households responded

Employed unmarried daughters are important to the economic survival of a significant number of households in the sample. Typically, these daughters have either replaced fathers as main earners or are supplementing low male wages. A number have unemployed brothers. In refugee households particularly, daughters can be found in a range of non-traditional occupations. This phenomenon raises the question of whether such employment is a temporary expedient for most daughters, prior to marriage or to a return to dependency on another male family member who subsequently obtains employment. The case histories suggest that the act of entering employment of itself renders either of these outcomes less likely.

The histories of older unmarried daughters and single women show that employment tends to be an alternative to marriage in families which both need the extra income a daughter can provide and are unable or unwilling to afford the high levels of dowry payment (see Table 7.1) which have been customary among West Bengal Hindus since at least the 1930s.[9] Enforced dependence on the daughter's wage in cases where she is a major earner then further inhibits parents from trying to arrange a marriage. Some married women in the sample took matters into their own hands by finding husbands for themselves, but the great majority of marriages in Calcutta continue to be arranged and daughters generally require the social and financial intervention of parents or other family members such as older brothers to enable them to marry.

Sibling order is also significant for marriage and employment prospects. Eldest daughters are the ones most likely to look for employment if a crisis arises and younger siblings are in school. While several elder sisters had then been able to finance the marriages of younger sisters, their own prospects for marriage disappeared. In other cases, whole families of sisters have remained unmarried, either supporting parents or, after their death, remaining together and pooling their incomes.

The presence and the nature of relationships with brothers is equally significant for unmarried women. In eight families there are daughters only and their income contribution takes on particular importance. In other families, the crisis of male unemployment is such that sisters may be substituting for unemployed brothers and taking on, or sharing their customary role of supporting parents. When brothers marry this may set up a dynamic whereby the new unit either moves out altogether, perhaps because of employment elsewhere, or lives separately under the same roof with separate budgets which may or may not involve a financial transfer from the new household to the parental one. The support of parents by married sons, particularly where there is an employed daughter, is thus becoming more contingent and sons who separate after their marriages move to less regular forms of support. Unmarried daughters also expressed strong feelings of responsibility towards parents, thereby making it less difficult for a brother to withdraw support. This sense of responsibility also extends to some married daughters. In five households in the sample, married daughters live with a parent or parents and seven other married daughters remit money to a parent or parents.

For single employed women, relationships with brothers take on renewed importance after the death of parents. Both have legal or customary rights to the parental home if owned or to the tenancy if rented. In practice, as the histories of the single women show, where brothers remain in the family home, unmarried sisters tend to move out or separate, as in the case of the Bose sisters. In only one case does an unmarried woman continue to live with her married brothers. In one other – almost the poorest household in the sample – six unmarried, Muslim sisters and brothers who all work in the *biri* industry, live with a father's sister and have no expectations that any of them will be able to marry.

## Divorced and separated women

Only four women were, or admitted to being, divorced or separated. Three, of whom two are childless, have returned to their families of origin and one lives alone with her son since her husband's desertion. All are poor, the highest earner getting only Rs 180 per month. Two other households reported separations between daughters and husbands which had resulted in daughters returning to their parents' houses temporarily. In both cases, the marriages had subsequently been resumed.

Indumati Saha, who is 27, now lives with her parents in the small shack which they built in the refugee colony more than thirty years previously. She had married her husband against the wishes of her family when she was 17 years old. After several years of systematic cruelty she was thrown out of the house by her mother-in-law and had to return to her parents leaving her children behind. She has since been unable to regain access to the children and now works as a machinist in a small tailoring shop nearby, having lost her previous job in a mica factory when it closed down. Her natal family, which consists of her parents, five brothers and one brother's wife and child, is extremely poor. Her father is self-employed with a low income, her mother makes paper bags at home, and the only other breadwinner – the elder married brother – had deserted the family at the time of a revisit in 1984.

Divorce or separation remains a fairly rare occurrence and a very difficult option for women. In all cases, women had endured considerable ill treatment before either leaving or being deserted. There is a great deal of pressure on married women to suffer in silence rather than end a marriage; pressure which comes partly from ideology – it is shameful and ignominious for a marriage to be ended, whether by the wife herself

157

or by the husband's family – but also for the profoundly practical reason that her alternatives are fairly dismal, especially if she is poorly qualified and has children to support. Remarriage is very uncommon for women. Finding employment is thus the only alternative, especially as the right of a divorced or separated woman to remain in her parent's home is one that is customarily considered to be terminated by her marriage settlement.

Widows

The sample contains twenty-two widowed women living in twenty-two households. The relationship of the rest of the household members to the widow is as follows:

| | |
|---|---|
| Unmarried children | 8 |
| Married sons/unmarried children | 6 |
| Married daughters/unmarried children | 2 |
| Deceased husband's joint family/own son | 1 |
| Sibling/unmarried or married children | 2 |
| Living alone | 3 |

Widows contribute an average of 25% of total household income (excluding single-person households), the range of variation being from 3–62%. Two of the widows living alone contribute respectively one half and one third of their incomes to their families of origin. The third receives some income from a piece of property left to her by her mother's father. The three living alone are childless or have lost children.

These three, all of whom live in quarters provided by their employers and are in their 40s and 50s, have similar histories. Panna Chowdhury was widowed at the age of 15 after 18 months of marriage. She then entered nursing training in order to support herself. Suchitra Ray and Sumita Ghosh both left their in-law's homes because of ill treatment some years before the deaths of their husbands and went in search of employment. In Sumita Ghosh's case, she also cut off relations with her natal family because they harassed her to return to her husband's house. Suchitra Ray left her only son with her parents while she trained as a nurse and found employment to support them both. The boy disappeared in tragic circumstances at the age of 15. Suchitra now helps to maintain the household of her widowed mother and divorced younger sister. She has no brothers.

Mariam Joseph, a Christian convert whose mother had been a school teacher, was widowed after only two years of marriage and returned to live with her mother, who died only recently. She obtained a teaching job in the same school and brought up her daughter, who is now a lawyer and who continues to live with her after her own marriage.

Uma Chandra is 42, has a young son and lost her husband in 1975. One month after his death she obtained a clerical job which entails working outside Calcutta for periods of time. She continues to be based with her parents-in-law and her husband's two brothers and their wives and children but supports herself and her son out of her monthly salary of Rs 900.

Mithu Bhadra, who came to Calcutta at partition, was widowed at the age of 27 and left with four young children. Her husband had worked in a factory producing sewing machines and when he became ill he persuaded her to take a training course in the factory school. After his death, the company offered her a job and after twenty-seven years she has worked her way up to floor supervisor. All her children are now married and she lives with her only son, his wife and child in the house which her husband had started building before his death.

For widows, long-term security lies as much in having employed adult children with whom to live as being able to obtain employment. For most of the widows in this sample this has been possible, and their much lower average contributions to family income reflect the presence of other, better paid earners in the household. Nevertheless, younger widows face insecurity. Mithu Bhadra faced a hard struggle to bring up her children on a wage much lower, initially, than that which her husband had earned. Case histories show the importance also of being able to obtain some kind of training before or just after widowhood. Suchitra Ray commented that without the support of her mother, who looked after her son while she trained she would have had to take employment as a domestic servant as there was no other unskilled work available to women at that time.

Young widows cannot assume an automatic right to support from their husband's relatives. Uma Chandra's first move after her husband died was to look for a job, despite living with her husband's reasonably well-to-do family. Childless widows, like single and divorced women are an anomalous category whose difficulties stem less, at the present time, from lack of employment opportunities than from lack of place. They do not belong properly to any household, nor can they easily live alone, as women without male protection are, or are considered by their relatives to be, a target for other males to harass. It is not fortuitous that a high proportion of these women are employed in jobs with living quarters attached.

Increased employment for women is affecting the construction of familial dependencies, most notably where young single women are concerned. A set of factors, which include a rising age of marriage, high male unemployment and changes in ideological perceptions, as well as changes in the demand for female labour have brought unmarried women into the labour force. At the same time, legal and ideological trends have narrowed the range of dependants which individual (male) wage earners expect to support, particularly if they are married. Unmarried sisters and the widows of male relatives have increasingly fallen outside this range. Support for parents, customarily a son's responsibility is beginning to devolve, in a few families, upon daughters.

The longer-term consequences of this trend cannot easily be foretold, but their profundity is likely to be limited by the continuing disabilities which single women experience both in the labour market and in the family. The significance of women's employment must first be set against its implications for female poverty and for women's access to resources other than just wages. The right to property and the provision of shelter is as crucial to the restructuring of female dependency as the capacity to find employment.

## Poverty, shelter and autonomy

Poverty is ubiquitous in Calcutta. The questions to be considered here are whether poverty also has a gendered aspect and whether, and in what ways, women in general are disadvantaged in relation to men in their access to living space. Data on wage levels of men and women in the sample show that women are disadvantaged in all income groups and this disadvantage is particularly severe among the lowest income groups in the sample where the poorest women are earning an average of 28% of the wages of the poorest men. It is also the case that while all illiterate women are poor, not all poor women are illiterate and some are highly educated. The poverty of their households, then, appears to be a function of gender rather than of class. Table 7.2 (which excludes job seekers) gives the average income levels of particular categories of female earner.

Table 7.2 shows that widows and unmarried daughters have lower-than-average wages. Single women are slightly below average. These differences appear to reflect the fact that it is these categories of employed women who are most likely to be precipitated into the labour market by crisis or dire necessity and to have little choice about the employment which they take.

Total household incomes are also significantly lower. Households with no male earners at all have much lower average incomes, and if the one all-female professional household were excluded from the calculation, the average wage of women in wholly female-supported households would come down to Rs 204 and the average household income would be only Rs 553. What many of these households lack, then, is an established male breadwinner and the poorer the household the more likely it is to be one which is dependent upon female earners.

*Table 7.2* Average monthly wages of selected women earners/average incomes of households

|  | Own income | (n) | Household income | (n) |
|---|---|---|---|---|
| Female wages (whole sample) | Rs 448 | (156) | Rs 1606 | (114) |
| Widows' wages | Rs 390 | (22) | Rs 1236 | (22) |
| Unmarried daughters' wages | Rs 244 | (61) | Rs 1068 | (40) |
| Single-women's wages | Rs 431 | (18) | Rs 963 | (10) |
| Wholly female-supported households (excl. single-person households) | Rs 340 | (27) | Rs 834 | (11) |

*Note:* Household categories are not exclusive

Lower household incomes may be a consequence of the developmental phase of the household. Employed widows tend to be living with children whose earning power could be expected to grow rather than diminish. Unmarried daughters, on the other hand, are more likely to be substituting for male earners or supplementing erratic or declining male incomes. Further, as they are less likely to marry, both because of the family's difficulties with raising dowries and its dependence on daughters' wages, such households may then remain or become permanently more impoverished.

The exceptions are those single women who have been able to obtain additional qualifications and training. The father of the five professional sisters who live together, knew he would not be able to afford dowries, so paid for them to be educated in order that they might get jobs. In default of such opportunities, marriage remains, overall, the best economic option for women. Such reasoning, doubtless, lay behind the financing of younger sisters' marriages by two of the employed single women. However, for families already in economic crisis, this option may be ruled out by its cost.

Another important aspect of the process of downward mobility is the fragmentation of kin relationships among poorer families. All of the poor households in the sample are comparatively isolated in terms of the existence of, or capacity to mobilize assistance from, wider kin. The fracturing of kin networks may have taken place over several generations, as remaining links with rural origins have ossified. It has also been a consequence of the severing of ties between wealthier and poorer kin where economic and demographic factors have intervened in the fortunes of families. Predominantly female-supported households are particularly vulnerable to this. As the Bose sisters said of their prosperous maternal and paternal kin, 'Who can be bothered with five unmarried sisters?'

For women without a marriage partner, the issue of access to housing is as significant as access to employment. Where property is owned, the issue for single, divorced and widowed women turns upon their capacity to acquire or maintain access through inheritance rights. Where housing is rented, single women must be able to enforce a claim to remain in the house, or room, after the death of a parent or relative who had the tenancy. Very few of the sample households have claims to land or other non-residential property. In all, ten households reported shares in joint family property consisting of either agricultural land or urban real estate, mostly outside Calcutta. Twenty-seven households own and live in their own houses and a further four, living in rented houses, own houses or house sites elsewhere in Calcutta. Four households, three of which are female supported, receive rent from tenants, all except one of whom lives on the same premises.

The experiences of women in the sample suggest that their capacity to press claims is variable, particularly in a situation of severe housing shortage. As U. Sharma (1984) points out, in north India, women's shares in parental property are conventionally considered to be met by the provision of dowries at marriage. In default of marriage they retain a right to shelter under their father's roof and they have, in law (if Hindu), a right to an equal share in the estate with their brothers, whether they marry or not (but see Agarwal 1988 for legal variations which recognize customary differences). As we have seen, however, few of the single women remain in the parental home if there are married brothers also living there. The asymmetrical access of women to property is derived less from contemporary legal disabilities than from customary and ideological practices which disadvantage women.[10]

For married women, fairly strong moral sanctions as well as post-marital residence tend to prevent further claims to joint family property and to the parental home if occupied by a married brother. A number of married women commented that it would be 'shameful' to ask for a share when large amounts had been spent on their marriages and they were living in their husband's house. However, for single women also, maintaining a claim can create difficulties and tensions. The five professional sisters, still living in the house which their father had rented for many years before his death, have shares in the joint family property in a town some distance from Calcutta. After their father's death, his brothers tried to cheat them out of their share by forging the ownership documents. Being in a position to do so, they fought several long court cases and finally won a settlement. However, one of their difficulties has stemmed from their inability to utilize their share of the land by building a house on it, and they will otherwise have to wait for their settlement until the property is sold and the proceeds divided.

Despite the law, single women's property rights are seen as less legitimate. The Bose sisters have a poor relationship with their only brother as he resents their occupation of what he considers to be 'his' house. Single women tend to leave, particularly if they are the only unmarried sister, rather than provoke tensions. In this respect, single women who do not have brothers or whose brothers have settled permanently elsewhere, or who have, through demographic accident come from a generation or two of sonless families, are in a much better position to maintain property claims.

In a number of families it is precisely the absence of male claimants which has produced a number of co-resident mother–daughter combinations. Mariam Joseph's household has been based on three generations of women – widowed mother, widowed daughter and married granddaughter – passing on the tenancy of their rented house. Suchitra Ray currently lives alone in hospital quarters, but she helps support her widowed mother and will be able to return to her mother's house after retirement. Her father died when she was very small, leaving her mother with three young daughters, a son who also died shortly afterwards and a housesite and small piece of paddy land which he had purchased but not built on. Her father had been one of nine children, four of whom were sons, and after his death her mother had been unable to secure any of the joint family estate. One daughter had been married before his death and the other two were subsequently married after selling off the mother's jewellery. However, the marriages of two of the daughters failed and they both found employment, one returning to live with her mother. Over many years, the daughters have been able to finance the building of their mother's house and live partly off the agricultural produce of the paddy plot. The remaining daughter was recently widowed and has also returned with some of her children to live with her mother.

Given the difficulties of ensuring longer-term security of residence, it is not surprising that single or separated women will invest in land purchase and house building if they are in any kind of financial position to do so. Aruna Brahmachari and Krishna Ganguly, both unmarried nurses in their 40s and 50s, have each purchased small plots of land outside Calcutta to provide for some future security, despite having a formal entitlement to property occupied by married brothers.

Even in a situation of high male unemployment, access to a viable income remains poorer for women. The expansion of female employment opportunities in Calcutta has been largely an expansion of the worst-paid forms of employment which cannot underwrite any real economic independence. For both working-class and middle-class women, employed or not, marriage remains a more viable economic strategy. The lowness of women's incomes is compounded by the ideological importance of marriage for their capacity to act as full citizens in a context which traditionally has no role for single women. As importantly, women's independent access to property, particularly housing, is circumscribed by their continuing role as 'ideological dependants' of their male kin.

The rise in female employment, especially among young women and if accompanied by the emergence of more daughter-supported households, could be significant in the longer term for the social investment strategies of families in relation to their daughters, particularly in education and training. However, the significance of such changes for women's capacities to act in a more autonomous way in relation to employment, marriage and residence may not necessarily be radical.

Commenting on the attitudes of young American immigrant women workers at the turn of the century, Eisenstein (1983) points out that strong cultures of familial loyalty often generated contradictory ideologies and a conflict of priorities for unmarried working daughters. While marriage was held up as the real goal, daughters were also expected and socialized to be more compliant and obedient to their parents than boys and hence to hand over more of their earnings to support their families and not to move away from home. This resulted in 'the placing of greater claims on her loyalty and the denial of individual goals' (ibid: 138), including the goal of marriage.

There are interesting parallels with the situation of unmarried working daughters in Calcutta. One result of a rise in the number of unmarried women supporting parental households could be a reinforcement of ideologies which locate women primarily within their domestic and familial roles, but this time as devoted daughters, rather than a fuller acknowledgement of their roles as wage workers or a respect for the possibility of choices which may conflict with familial dependency.

## Conclusion

This chapter has sought to open up the discussion of the impact and meaning of employment for women by situating it within a wider understanding of female dependency. It has looked particularly at the economic and cultural forces which have determined women's level of labour-force participation in Bengal and attempted to link them to changes in the family, both at the level of public and private discourses about dependency and at the level of social relationships.

A strong ideology and practice of female dependence upon male kin for economic support has been shown to produce vulnerable categories of women who enter a restricted range of jobs which frequently cannot provide adequately for the longer-term security of themselves or their households. As importantly, women without husbands are disadvantaged in their access to other material resources such as housing. Women's poorer command over economic resources means that marriage and motherhood remain the most reliable route to security.

Chapter eight

# Conclusion

This book has attempted to examine the impact of women's employment on family-based households in a particular setting in order to explore its implications for women's autonomy. As was pointed out in the introduction, the issue is not a new one. Revolutionary socialist theory and practice have been concerned with the relationship between women's subordination and their exclusion from the labour market since the question was raised by Engels.

More recently, the debates of the UN Decade of Women have placed the question firmly in the context of policy issues and strategies. Some of this debate has been about 'economic realism'. Women's skills and potential constitute a wasted human resource if they are not incorporated into the labour force. Social equity arguments – that women have as equal a right to employment as men – have also gained currency. In the women and development literature these two perspectives have often combined into a general concern with women's 'status'. Is it improved by entering employment? Is employment creation thus a useful general policy prescription for improving the status of women? (cf. USAID policy paper, 1982)

The argument of this book has been twofold. First, it has suggested that there can be no general answer to these questions because the terms upon which women enter the labour force and engage in employment are variable, are subject to gender disadvantage, and operate differentially among women. Second, it has argued that the terms of the debate need to be widened, first to include women's access to a range of resources, of which the wage is only one; and second, to encompass a historical understanding of different social constructions of female dependency. What these arguments imply is that we must move away from universalistic models of 'women's status'. There is no universal standard for measuring this – nor one standard to measure up to – which transcends all contexts.

This does, however, raise the question of whether it is possible to make any kind of judgement of the impact of women's employment which does not simply collapse into particular instances. There have been a number of attempts to provide a more general theoretical and conceptual framework for understanding this impact. At risk of over-simplification, these fall predominantly into two kinds of approach.

The first may be described as 'developmentalism'. I use the term to describe those models of change which are based on a concept of successive stages or cumulative changes leading to a desired outcome. Developmentalism has exercised a powerful hold over western thought. It has its adherents among socialists and among supporters of the capitalist path to development, as well as among liberal thinkers. It has also been influential in mainstream sociology (e.g. Goode 1963). It thus appears in various guises as evolutionary steps towards socialism, as stages of modernization culminating in a mature market economy and as liberal notions of an incremental accumulation of individual rights guaranteed by the state.

Despite the very different discourses within which the politics of these positions are embedded, there is another underlying unity in that all are driven by a dynamic of rupture: the expansion of the market and its accompanying individuation. For socialist developmentalists, the market is important for breaking down and destroying 'backward' practices and ways of thinking, which is necessary for socialism to develop. Wage labour thus enables women to break free from the patriarchal family. For capitalist modernizers, the market brings every-one into the formal economy and opens up freedom of choice by 'equalizing' them as individual consumers. Employment thus enables women to participate as consumers on equal terms. For liberal develop-mentalists, employment integrates women into the public domain where individual rights are guaranteed legislatively.

These are the scenarios of progress, and in the light of the previous analysis some of their limitations should be fairly obvious. Familial power structures may be reinforced or reconstituted rather than broken down. Choice is not a very meaningful concept for women struggling to meet their daily survival costs from inadequate wages. Economic participation does not guarantee legal and social citizenship.

The second kind of approach stresses continuity rather than rupture. When confronted with the market, individuals and families make decisions which accord with their existing ('pre- or non-market') values and which thus reinforce the interests of the collective over the indiv-idual.[1] Scott and Tilly's pioneering work on women's employment in nineteenth-century Europe (see esp. 1975) contains one of the clearest statements of this position. They argue that the employment of young single women in industrializing economies was both a consequence of the persistence of familial values and operated to reinforce them.

Families controlled the sending of daughters into wage work and the proceeds went directly to maintain the family economy. This was both a financial and a moral unit, organized through hierarchies of gender and generation to maximize the economic contributions of its members.

The work of Salaff (1981) on young single women workers in Hong-kong, and other accounts of women factory workers in the 'new' industries of Asia echo this theme strongly (e.g. Kung 1983, Mather 1985). Daughters work to maintain their natal families, while employers collude with family patriarchs in the policing of young women's behaviour. The employment of daughters, far from enabling choice and autonomy, reinforces their dependence and subordination.

These are persuasive arguments for which the Calcutta findings provide some support, but they are not adequate to stand as a general theorization of the impact of women's employment. This is partly because they deal almost exclusively with the employment of young unmarried women and it is necessary to look at the effects of women's employment over the whole life cycle. The biggest difficulty arises over how to conceptualize change. Scott and Tilly do acknowledge the occurrence of change as the wage economy expands. Change is seen as a consequence of the development of individualist and instrumentalist values which displace the values of the family economy.

The term 'values' is a rather blunt instrument for understanding the complexities of change. First, it suggests a set of ideas, beliefs and cultural artefacts more unified and encompassing than those by which life is really lived. Second, it is too external to its subjects to capture the meanings, interpretations, emotions and other mental activities which enter into decisions and codes of conduct.

To take Scott and Tilly's (1975) own example; young working girls are seen as the major site of the development of instrumentalist values in that they increasingly try to keep their wages for personal consumption rather than give them to their families. But young working girls also become wives and mothers who, as the literature continues to confirm, subordinate their personal consumption to the needs of the household. Have their values changed? Or do we need a more nuanced understanding of these processes?

Third, values themselves beg explanation. Where do they come from? While for developmentalist models, they require no explanation, being simply a reflection of economic processes or stages of development; in 'continuity' approaches, they tend to acquire an autonomy of their own. Neither is satisfactory. People do persist in acting in the world in accordance with values, ideas and beliefs which resist or contradict 'economic rationality'. But they do not always act passively within those values. The problem with both kinds of approach is that they remove political and personal struggle, and hence human agency, from the agenda.

Recent feminist approaches to conceptualizing gender and the labour market offer an alternative. Two particularly important contributions have been to point out, first, that the domestic and the public, the family and the economy, should not be treated as separate structures. Just as capitalism restructures the family and gender relations, so capitalism is itself shaped by familial and gender relations. The workplace may be fetishized as the site of economic rationality. It is also premised upon gender divisions. Reconceptualizing the family/economy split helps to overcome the false dualism implied in opposing 'family' values to 'market' values.

Second, women are not an eternal category of surplus, and therefore cheap, labour but are constructed as cheap labour through processes which must be problematized. This means that we must look both at the ways in which inter-generational transfers of resources operate to create female labour of a certain kind, and at the production of discourses of dependency around gender. Any judgement of the impact of employment must, therefore, ask what kind of employment is being provided, for which women, and accompanied by what ideas and stereotypes about women's place in society.

Third, while recognizing the force of material and ideological constraints on women's lives and choices, the potential for transformation through personal and collective struggle should not be disregarded. Whether this is constituted by a decision to leave home and find employment to avoid an enforced marriage, or by organizing for better conditions for workers, these are experiences which cannot be rolled back.

The issue of autonomy is, however, a vexed one. How is it to be defined and measured? If the concept of status has to be contextualized, is this not also true of a concept like autonomy? The answer is both yes and no. Such concepts operate at different levels. At one level they embody political visions – ideas of a just society for both women and men which can transcend the specificities of time and place. On another level, as goals, they are forged by the politics of the situation and by what are judged to be political priorities at any given moment. This does not just mean that 'western' feminism will have different goals and priorities from 'Indian' feminism. This may or may not be so. Neither western nor Indian women are homogeneous in race, class, culture or generation and women are not in any case endowed with solidarity as a straightforward consequence of biology or nationality. There are many feminisms in India as well as in the west and thus there can be a variety of goals and orders of priorities.

## Conclusion

In this account, the idea of autonomy has moved back and forth between these two levels. In the former sense, autonomy has meant not just the capacity to obtain control over economic resources adequate enough to enable certain choices to be exercised over the direction of one's life, such as whether and whom to marry; but also the capacity to act and be treated as a full social citizen in the home, the workplace and the world at large, whatever choices one has made. In the latter sense, and recognizing the social realities of contemporary India, greater autonomy can inhere in being able to take a job in non-traditional forms of employment or moving around without a family chaperone or being listened to by members of the family.

In neither of these two senses is autonomy to be equated with 'individualism'. As Ursula Sharma points out, to advocate a politics of separate lifestyles for women in Third World contexts where there is heavy dependence on familial support of some kind by everyone, is wholly unrealistic (1986: 197–9). But it should also be added that one of the goals of feminism is to reconstitute family relationships in more democratic forms which do not submerge and subordinate the needs, desires and alternative visions of one gender.

# Appendix

What measures would help employed women?

One of the arguments which has been stressed in this book is that women do not form a natural community of interest either by virtue of possessing certain biological characteristics or necessarily as a consequence of being subject to a common gender disadvantage. Women's interests are defined (and may be overridden) by their social positioning across a range of relationships – such as class, race, religion – as well as gender.

The problematic which is contained in the notion of 'women's interests' has been insightfully discussed by Maxine Molyneux (1984) in relation particularly to socialist transformation. She points out that a general theory of women's interests can only consist of a specification of the ways in which different categories of women are differentially affected by their social positioning. However, there may be common interests defined by gender which, in given contexts, cut across other positions. She then distinguishes usefully between gender interests which are strategic, in that they derive from a theoretical analysis of women's subordination and entail a vision of an alternative and less oppressive society; and gender interests at a practical level which arise out of the struggles of women in concrete circumstances such as food shortages or the withdrawal of services in which women as carers have a particular interest. These latter may be class specific or they may entail temporary alliances between women who are differently positioned. They are generated by the immediacy of shared adversity, rather than by an analysis of and struggle towards a common 'feminist' goal.

This distinction is a useful one to maintain when considering policy implications. It should be clear from this account that the meaning and consequences of employment differ for women of different classes, marital and life-cycle statuses. While the women's movement in India has developed a range of analyses of strategic gender interests, the responses which most women give to the question of what measures would improve their lives tend, understandably, to reflect the concrete disadvantages which they face. They are thus articulated for the most part as practical gender interests. In these terms, it follows that there are relatively few policy prescriptions which can be set forth which would benefit women as a general category, but there are a number of broad issues which affect most women to some degree. Four major issues in particular have appeared salient in the context of this inquiry. These are environmental hazards, labour-market discrimination, domestic work and childcare and sexual harassment.

All Calcuttans suffer from the poor environment and absence of civic services. Women carry a disproportionate burden because of their additional responsibilities in household servicing. Poor transportation, polluted and inadequate water and fuel supplies mean that many women have a very long and often arduous working day if they are to get household tasks accomplished. This almost certainly has consequences for their health and labour productivity. The generally poor environment causes high rates of infectious disease which particularly strike children and the elderly. Women carry the burden of care. There is no doubt that improvements in the urban environment and infrastructure would bring about major benefits in the lives of women, employed or not.

Labour-market discrimination appears in various forms at all levels. Wage discrimination is particularly apparent in the unorganized sector where there is a surplus of illiterate and unskilled female labour desperate for employment and a narrow range of occupations within which they can compete. For organized-sector workers, discrimination tends to be more indirect, appearing in the clustering of women at the lowest levels of the hierarchy. Gender stereotyping of jobs is ubiquitous throughout the labour market.

Tackling the magnitude of discrimination, especially in the unorganized sector, is a long-term political issue which depends on more than administrative measures. Many women cited the need for laws to prevent wage discrimination and to regularize employment contracts. They were unaware of the existence of already quite comprehensive employment laws which, if implemented, would provide some degree of protection. The reasons for their non-implementation are complex but a first step could be taken to inform women and raise their awareness of their existing legal rights. There could be an important role for trade unions here in relation to the unorganized sector.

One of the problems emerging from women's experiences in the labour market, is the gulf between organized and unorganized sector working conditions. While legislative measures may achieve some success within the organized sector (and particularly within the public sector where protective legislation and concepts such as job quotas and 'equal opportunities' already have some purchase - albeit not without opposition), their relevance to the unorganized sector, where the majority of the urban poor is located, is limited precisely by the fact that much of this sector lies beyond legislative scope. It may be that the poverty of the worst remunerated workers is in the shorter term best addressed remedially by directing resources into public health and nutritional programmes targeted particularly at the poorest women, rather than by attempting to 'legislate' better employment practices.

More training headed the list of measures which women felt would improve their employability. Again, interventions in relation to education and skill acquisition would benefit at least some women whose labour-market disadvantage appears to be a direct reflection of their non-competitiveness as workers. However, this has to be set against the fact that in some areas of the labour market the attractiveness of women workers is a consequence precisely of their non-competitiveness and hence cheapness and disposability. Better knowledge and awareness of labour-market conditions and rates of remuneration are pre-requisites for any improvements in women's collective strength in negotiating improved terms for their labour.

The labour market is deeply imbued with sexual divisions. The future of women's employment in Calcutta will depend to a great extent on trends in those sectors of employment which are already 'feminized', such as the organized and unorganized service sector; or which may become feminized. Further growth in manufacturing assembly work and the rise of new areas such as computer data processing are likely to produce more 'women's jobs'. Cheapness, adaptability and disposability are the hallmarks of employers' demands; women are the persons to whom these characteristics are attributed. The social and economic impact of a disproportionate growth in female jobs in a context of chronically high rates of male unemployment would be an urgent task for any future study.

In the longer term, only a much higher rate of employment creation in the West Bengal economy is likely to produce more general improvements in working conditions and remuneration for a significant proportion of the labour force, male as well as female.

In Calcutta, the issue of domestic work and childcare both unites and divides women. They are unified by a sexual division of labour which allocates these tasks to women. They are divided in class terms by the solutions. Middle-class women depend a great deal on both kin and domestic servants. Poor women contribute to the provision of this solution and have no resort to it themselves. Lack of alternative employment continues to keep many poor women in domestic service, enabling middle-class households to reproduce their own conditions of existence (including the existing, sex-segregated division of labour) while confirming the impoverishment of their own.

In the absence of more employment opportunities, a more equitable domestic division of labour and greatly increased socialized childcare facilities which would be accessible and acceptable to poor women as well as the better off, it is difficult to see how this will be changed. Those women expressing a need for creches were almost entirely middle-class public sector employees. Poor women did not consider this a priority, partly because many were home-based workers but partly perhaps because the concept of children as a category requiring specialized care and attention has less salience for the poor in the daily battle for survival.

It is likely that any significant increase in childcare facilities will be through private provision, in that further growth in employment among middle-class women will eventually generate a demand for solutions which the market will provide. Those women who are faced with the necessity of purchasing such a solution may then be able to mobilize to demand tax or other concessions from employers and thus to recover some of the costs of their employment. Market solutions will do little for the poor. The needs of poor children require comprehensive public investment in health, nutrition and educational programmes.

Vulnerability to direct forms of sexual harassment is a feature of certain jobs such as nursing and some kinds of factory work. In these contexts, it must be treated by trade unions and labour organizations as a legitimate workplace issue if it is to be tackled effectively. This will not, however, help the majority of women workers who have no access to any form of grievance procedure. It is necessary to treat sexual harassment as part of a much wider long-term issue of women's security outside as well as inside the workplace. The provision of secure housing for single women would be a useful public measure. The security of women on the streets is a concern which is probably best tackled through women's groups through the development of appropriate defensive techniques which could be made accessible to a wider constituency of women.

# Notes

## Chapter one
## Introduction: issues, methods and empirical background

1. Jaggar (1983) provides a thorough account of the various (western) feminist perspectives on the concepts of autonomy and agency. The Indian feminist journal *manushi* (published from New Delhi, and see also Kishwar and Vanita 1974) is an important source for the variety of different views among Indian activists. See also Omvedt (1975) for a Marxist-feminist view of women's emancipation in the Indian context and Jayawardena's historical discussion of Indian feminism (1986).

2. In a recent overview of demographic trends in India, however, Dyson (1987) suggests that since the 1970s female death rates have improved overall at a faster rate than those of males. Disaggregated data are needed in order to know whether this indicates a general improvement or a greater degree of differentiation within the female population.

3. See Alavi (1973) for an exposition of this point in the context of political mobilization, which is excellent apart from its gender blindness.

4. For full details of the sampling method, see 'Calcutta 1976: A socio-economic survey of households with municipal address', Tables with notes, and 'Calcutta 1976: A socio-economic survey of pavement dwellers', Indian Statistical Institute, Calcutta.

5. In 1976, the total number of households in Calcutta was estimated to be 872 708.

6. The 'household' was defined in approximately the same way as in the 1976 survey, that is, either on the basis of regular commensality or/and regular budgetary contribution. Thus, persons absent because of employment but contributing regularly to the budget and considering that household to be their primary residence were counted as members, but those permanently resident elsewhere, albeit making financial contributions to a sample household were not. It follows that many houses contained several households and single-person households show greater prevalence than in the Indian census figures.

175

7. There are a number of accounts of Calcutta and of aspects of its history from different standpoints. For the British period, see Cotton (1909), Blechynden (1905), A.K. Ray (1902). More recent sociological accounts include N.K. Bose (1968), A. Mitra (1963), S.N. Sen (1960), S. Sinha (1972). A general overview from a British travel writer's pen can be found in Moorhouse (1971). Lubell's (1974) account of employment in Calcutta contains a useful summary of the pre- and post-independence economy. McGuire (1983) contains an analysis of the nineteenth-century political economy of Calcutta.

8. The Indian state of West Bengal came into being at independence in 1947 when undivided Bengal was partitioned and its eastern districts became the eastern wing of Pakistan. The term 'Bengal' referred administratively to the old British provinces of Bengal, Bihar, Orissa and Assam until 1874, when Assam became a separate province. The 1905 partition of Bengal created two provinces, with Assam reattached to East Bengal. This was rescinded in 1912 after Nationalist pressure. Bihar and Orissa became separate States in 1936.

9. For clarification of administrative and planning divisions in the CMD, see Lubell (1974: 3).

For an account of the composition of early factory labour in Bengal, see

10. Das Gupta (1976) and also chapter seven of this volume.

## Chapter two
## Employed women: the social and economic background

1. The terms 'organized' and 'unorganized' sectors have a specific administrative meaning in India in that they relate to size of establishment and the official regulation of premises by the factory inspectorate. In practice, there is much overlap with the familiar distinction between the formal and informal sector. See chapter three for further discussion.

2 Bose (1968) and Pakrasi (1971) describe the background and characteristics of the refugee population in Calcutta. Moorhouse (1971, 1983 edn: 115–17) gives a case study of a downwardly mobile refugee family. A more sympathetic account is given by Mitra 1977: 21–9).

3. See Caplan (1985: 52) for a similar use of this term in south India.

4. See A.K. Sen (1982) for a succinct discussion of these issues. On measuring poverty in India see, among others, Dandekar and Rath (1971), Srinivasan and Bardhan (1974).

5. As reported in the Telegraph, Calcutta, 29 December 1982.

6. Borthwick (1984) discusses the informal ways by which women acquired education in the nineteenth and early twentieth century. Some were taught by husbands and *zenana* (women's quarters) teachers were also appointed at a later stage.

7. Figures are abstracted from the 1971 Census District Handbook of Calcutta Part X-A and B. The categorization of households by religion does not imply that members actively practise that religion.

8. Owens and Nandy (1977) contains an interesting discussion of the rise of

Mahisya dominance in the engineering industry in Greater Calcutta and the 'work cultures' associated with different castes.

9. See for instance, Nirad Chaudhuri (1951) and the many fine novels of Rabindranath Tagore. The rise and nature of the *bhadralok* in nineteenth-century Bengal is discussed in Broomfield (1968), S.N. Mukherjee (1970), Franda (1971), McGuire (1983) and B. Chakrabarty (1985). Owens and Nandy (1977) comment on its contemporary significance.

10. See Kapur (1974) for a detailed analysis of the reasons for educated women's entry into the labour force in India, drawing on studies from the early 1960s onwards. Liddle and Joshi (1986) also analyse middle/upper middle class women's employment strategies. All the findings are broadly similar.

11. All the names used in this book are pseudonyms.

# Chapter three
## Working lives: women in the labour force

1. The following is just a selection of references on the subject. De Souza (1969), Nath (1970), Gulati (1975), Mitra, Pathak and Mukherjee (1980), G. Sen (1983), Thorner (1984). Excellent overviews can be found in the *Towards Equality* Report (Government of India 1974) and in Kabeer (1987).

2. This sector resembles, but is not entirely contiguous with the more familiarly termed informal sector. On the genesis and utility of this term, see Hart (1973), Bromley and Gerry (1979), Moser (1978), Connolly (1985). For Calcutta see Lubell (1974). For Calcutta and West Bengal, A.N. Bose's study of small sector industries (1978) is a forceful plea for seeing the formal sector as parasitical upon the informal sector rather than as a separate or parallel sector. It should be noted, though, that Bose restricts his use of the term 'informal sector' to small-scale unregistered industries with backward and forward linkages to large-scale registered enterprises.

3. But see Chakrabarty (1989a) on early support networks among jute mill workers.

4. This imagery echoes that of class and gender in Victorian Britain (cf. Hall 1979, Walkowitz 1980).

5. The real extent of prostitution in Calcutta is unknown but there is some suggestion that it may have increased recently with greater impoverishment and limited employment opportunities for women. No attempt was made to examine prostitution in this study, but Banerjee included a small number of prostitutes in her study (1985a) and Bandyopadhyaya (1983) has written on contemporary prostitution in Calcutta, drawing upon her own research.

6. For more detail on conditions for unorganized sector women workers in Calcutta see the very thorough discussion in Banerjee (1985a). Piece-rate workers interviewed for this study were compensated for the time spent in talking to us.

## Chapter four
## Working lives: the domestic arena

1. A similar point is made by Bujra (1978) in relation to non-capitalist economies. See also Papanek and Minault (eds) (1982), U. Sharma (1978) and Jeffery (1979) on 'public and private' in South Asia. However, this does not, in my view, imply that the spheres of men and women were complementary in the 'separate but equal' sense, rather that women's subordination took a different form under non-capitalist relations.

2. Widows were in some ways the Bengali equivalent of the bothersome single woman in Victorian Britain (Vicinus 1985). While virtually every woman was married, very early marriage for girls to often much older husbands, high mortality rates and a social taboo on widow remarriage left many women widowed and socially redundant at very young ages. See chapter seven for further discussion.

3. Mies makes a similar point when she draws attention to the parallels between concepts of womanhood in Brahmanical Hinduism and the bourgeois concept of womanhood arising with capitalism (1980: 185).

4. The influence of the Brahmos in the restructuring of gender roles and identities in Bengal bears comparison with the influence of the Evangelicals in early nineteenth-century Britain. Both arose at a 'crisis of conjuncture' – the restructuring of class relations under early capitalism and the need to fashion a distinctive morality – in the case of the Evangelicals, in opposition to the prevailing 'degeneracy' which they saw all around them, and in the case of the Brahmos, as a response to the challenge posed by imperial ideologies. In so far as both pursued the path of moral reformism with a puritan Christian flavour, the results show many similarities (cf. Hall 1979, Borthwick 1984).

5. For more details of the circumstances of this household, see Standing (1985b). See Salaff (1981:269) on the trade-off for young women in Chinese families between housework and employment.

6. Cornuel and Duriez (1985) make a related point in the context of French households. They point out that the time spent by middle-class parents on a child's milieu and education is worth more that that of a working-class parent because the child's career prospects are greater.

7. This is known in Bengali as *adda*, a culturally resonant term which has no precise equivalent in English but means a kind of meeting for discussion. It is a typically male activity – women described their conversations with neighbours as *golpo*, which is usually translated as 'gossip'. Only two women used the term *adda* and this was in the context of describing leisure-time conversations with husbands and children.

8. The work of John Bowlby in Britain in the 1940s and 1950s (cf. particularly 1953) gave both impetus and the sanction of science to such ideologies of motherhood. It is quite possible that college-educated Indian mothers who have done psychology courses have encountered these ideas.

## Chapter five
## Employment and autonomy: women's wages and the distribution and management of household income

1. The elision of these two arguments conceals a major shift in the way in which married women's earning power may be conceptualized. In earlier sociological writing, and for many economists, women's inferior earning power is taken for granted or ascribed to their lesser 'human capital' endowments (experience, skills etc.) because they opted for marriage. Feminists have pointed out that all women, not simply the married, are disadvantaged in the labour market and this in itself propels women into marriage because they must join their inferior earning power to that of a superior male earner (cf. Westwood 1984).

## Chapter six
## Employment and autonomy: ideological struggles

1. Mrs Hussein was an educated Muslim woman from East Bengal who accompanied her brother to England and later married a junior government official, settling in Bihar where he was posted. Her writings appear in several issues of *mahila* during 1903.
2. For example, the organization *sachetana*, which was set up in 1982 and has a membership drawn mainly, although not exclusively, from women academics and college students. It campaigns on a broad range of feminist issues.
3. Dipesh Chakrabarty (1989a), writing on the question of culture and class consciousness among Calcutta's jute mill workers in the period 1890 to 1940, notes the use of this idiom in political discourses of the time and makes a forceful plea for understanding the non-capitalist elements in workers' consciousness as part of the culture and history of their struggles.
4. Uttam Kumar is a famous Bengali cinema idol.
5. The Government Committee on the Status of Women makes a similar point (Government of India 1974: 228) and also points out that the International Labour Organization considers such provision to be the responsibility of governments to co-ordinate.

## Chapter seven
## Dependence and autonomy: women's employment and the family in Calcutta

1. This was partly because young never married women scarcely existed as a category. Witnesses to the 1908 Factory Labour Commission commented upon the very young age of girls at marriage in the context of arguments against any raising of the age at which children could legally work in the factories: 'Many of our girl employees are married at the age of ten. Much valuable work is done by these girls and if the age is raised ... the work must necessarily suffer' (cotton mill employer, Report of the Indian Factory

Labour Commission vol.2: 242–3). In other words, girl children turned straight into married 'women' and the cheapest child labour would be lost as married women either left the labour force or worked on different operations at higher wage rates than child labour, although at rates still considerably lower than those of male labourers.

2. Ranajit Das Gupta (1976) points out, however, that in 1946 the majority of labour in the engineering industry in Calcutta was Bengali. But see also Owens and Nandy (1977) on the rise of Mahisya dominance in this sector from the 1940s at the expense of high-caste Bengalis who preferred white-collar employment.

3. Nirmala Banerjee has pointed this out to me (personal communication).

4. This was not, however, their only concern. They were particularly exercised by the effects on 'morality' of the low ratio of women workers to men and thought that an increase in the employment of women would combat rather than exacerbate this, thereby underlining the role of female factory workers as providers of sexual services.

5. The writer does not consider the likelihood that women who had married would have jewellery from their marriage settlement. Some of the widows interviewed by the 1890 Commission certainly owned jewellery.

6. Significantly, though, the worker in question is always assumed to be male. As most female employees were categorized as 'temporary' they appear not to have had any right to these benefits.

7. If this interpretation is correct, there is a certain disingenuousness in the demands of these trade unionists for a restriction in the working hours of women because of their 'domestic duties'. This demand was firmly rejected by women textile workers in Bombay on the grounds that it would lead to job losses (cf. Savara 1981). When this objection was put to the President of the Kankinarah Union, his response was that he had not given serious thought to the matter (RCFL 1931, vol.2: 129).

8. Widowhood was a major social problem. The 1921 Census gives the following table:

*Table N.1* Civil condition of 1000 females by age period (Calcutta)

|  | Unmarried | Married | Widowed |
| --- | --- | --- | --- |
| 0–5 | 990 | 9 | 1 |
| 5–10 | 962 | 36 | 2 |
| 10–15 | 615 | 368 | 17 |
| 15–20 | 134 | 809 | 60 |
| 20–40 | 46 | 752 | 202 |
| 40–60 | 23 | 423 | 554 |
| 60 and over | 13 | 163 | 824 |
| All ages | 302 | 475 | 223 |

*Source:* Government of India 1923, vol. V1 part 1, Calcutta, Report: chap. 1

9. The rise in dowry demands is discussed in the 1931 Census, vol. V, part 1 Report (Appendix 1: 412–16). Evidence from women in the sample about the dowries of their mothers or grandmothers shows considerable regional as well as caste/class variation in the extent and amount of payments. Also, some Calcutta families, involved in nationalist and socialist politics in Bengal in the 1930s and 1940s, had repudiated dowry in their own marriages. The rise in demands is presumably associated with the absence of viable economic activity for women for several decades.

10. Writing of middle-class women in Britain in the eighteenth and early nineteenth century, Davidoff and Hall point out, appositely, that:

> It was never the laws of property alone which prevented the myriad middle class women who owned capital from using it actively. Rather, it was the ways in which the laws of inheritance and the forms of economic organization. . . intersected with definitions of femininity.

(1987: 451)

## Chapter eight  Conclusion

1. In her discussion of the impact of industrialization, Salaff (1981) distinguishes between two main approaches to conceptualizing economic change, which she terms disjunctive and convergence theories. She suggests that women's employment is seen in terms of one or the other. My use of continuity is similar to Salaff's concept of convergence but the term disjunctive is used in a more encompassing way than 'developmentalism'.

# Bibliography

Agarwal, B. (1986) 'Women, poverty and agricultural growth in India' *Journal of Peasant Studies* 13: 165–220.

—— (1988) 'Who sows? Who reaps? Women and land rights in India' *Journal of Peasant Studies* 15, 4: 531–81.

Alavi, H. (1973) 'Peasant classes and primordial loyalties' *Journal of Peasant Studies* 1: 23–62.

Anthias, F. (1980) 'Women and the reserve army of labour: a critique' *Capital and Class* 10: 50–63.

Bandyopadhyaya, B. (1983) 'Prostitutes in Calcutta' *South Asia Research* 3, 1: 28–34.

Banerjee, N. (1985a) *Women Workers in the Unorganized Sector* Hyderabad: Sangam Books.

—— (1985b) 'Modernisation and marginalisation' *Social Scientist* 13, 10–11: 48–71.

Bardhan, P. (1984) 'On life and death questions: poverty and child mortality' in *Land, Labour and Rural Poverty: Essays in Development Economics*, Delhi: Oxford University Press.

Barrett, M. (1980) *Women's Oppression Today: Problems in Marxist Feminist Analysis*, London: Verso and New Left Books.

—— and McIntosh, M. (1980) 'The family wage: some problems for socialists and feminists' *Capital and Class* 11: 51–72.

Barron, R.D. and Norris, G.M. (1976) 'Sexual divisions and the dual labour market' in D.L. Barker and S. Allen (eds) *Dependence and Exploitation in Work and Marriage*, London and New York: Longman.

Becker, G. (1965) 'A theory of the allocation of time' *The Economic Journal* LXXX, 200: 493–517.

—— (1974) 'A theory of marriage' in T.W. Schulz (ed.) *The Economics of the Family*, Chicago: Chicago University Press.

Beechey, V. (1978) 'Women and Production: a critical analysis of some sociological theories of women's work' in A. Kuhn and A. Wolpe (eds) *Feminism and Materialism*, London, Boston and Henley: Routledge and Kegan Paul.

Ben-Porath, Y. (1982) 'Income distribution and the family' *Population and Development Review* 8 (Supplement): 1–13.

Bhowmick, P.K. (1969) *Occupational Mobility and Caste Structure in Bengal*, Calcutta: Indian Publications.

Blechynden, K. (1905) *Calcutta Past and Present*, revised edn, 1975, Calcutta: General Printers and Publishers.

Borthwick, M. (1984) *The Changing Role of Women in Bengal, 1849–1905*, Princeton: Princeton University Press.

Bose, A.N. (1978) *Calcutta and Rural Bengal: Small Sector Symbiosis*, Calcutta: Minerva Associates (on behalf of ILO, Geneva).

Bose, N.K. (1968) *Calcutta: A Social Survey*, Bombay: Lalvani Publishing House.

Bose, S. (1981) 'Industrial unrest and growth of labour unions in Bengal' *Economic and Political Weekly*, Special Number 16, 44–6: 1849–59.

Bowlby, J. (1953) *Childcare and the Growth of Love*, Harmondsworth: Penguin.

Brannen, J. and Wilson, G. (1987) *Give and Take in Families*, London: Allen and Unwin.

Bromley, R. and Gerry, C. (1979) *Casual Work and Poverty in Third World Cities*, Chichester: John Wiley and Sons.

Broomfield, J.H. (1968) *Elite Conflict in a Plural Society: Twentieth Century Bengal*, Berkeley and Los Angeles: California University Press.

Bruegel, I. (1979) 'Women as a reserve army: a note on recent British experience' *Feminist Review* 3: 12–23.

Bujra, J. (1978) 'Female solidarity and the sexual division of labour' in P. Caplan and J. Bujra (eds) *Women United, Women Divided*, London: Tavistock Publications.

Caplan, A.P. (1985) *Class and Gender in India: Women and their Organizations in a South Indian City*, London: Tavistock.

Chakrabarty, B. (1985) 'Political radicalism and middle class ideology in Bengal: a study of the politics of Subhas Chandra Bose 1928–40' Unpublished PhD thesis, University of London.

Chakrabarty, D. (1989a) *Rethinking Working Class History: Bengal 1890–1940*, Princeton, New Jersey: Princeton University Press.

—— (1989b) 'Colonial rule and domestic order: 'home' and 'woman' in Bengali nationalist thought', draft paper, University of Melbourne.

Chatterji, R. (1984) 'Marginalisation and the induction of women into wage labour: the case of Indian agriculture' *World Employment Programme Working Paper*. No. WEP10/WP.32, Geneva: International Labour Organization.

Chattopadhyay, M. (1984) Santosh Kumari Devi: a pioneering labour leader' *Social Scientist* 12, 1: 62–73.

Chaudhuri, N. (1951) *Autobiography of an Unknown Indian*, Macmillan: London.

Cockburn, C. (1983) *Brothers: Male Dominance and Technological Change*, London: Pluto Press.

Connolly, P. (1985) 'The politics of the informal sector: a critique' in N. Redclift & E. Mingione (eds) *Beyond Employment: Household, Gender and Subsistence*, Oxford: Basil Blackwell.

Cornuel, D. and Duriez, B. (1985) 'Local exchange and state intervention' in N. Redclift and E. Mingione (eds) *Beyond Employment: Household, Gender and Subsistence*, Oxford: Basil Blackwell.

# Bibliography

Cotton, J. (1909) *Calcutta Old and New*, revised edn, 1980, Calcutta: General Printers and Publishers.

Cunnison, S. (1966) *Wages and Work Allocation*, London: Tavistock.

Curjel, D. (1923) 'Enquiry into the conditions of employment of women before and after childbirth in Bengal industries' Calcutta: Government of Bengal Commerce Department, File no. 2R-20.

Dandekar, V.M. and Rath, N. (1971) *Poverty in India*, Poona: Indian School of Political Economy.

Das, V. (1976) 'Indian women: work, power and status' in B.R. Nanda (ed.) *Indian Women: From Purdah to Modernity*, New Delhi: Vikas.

Das Gupta, R. (1976) 'Factory labour in eastern India: sources of supply 1855-1946. Some preliminary findings' *Indian Economic and Social History Review* XIII, 3: 277-329.

Davidoff, L. and Westover, B. (1986) *Our Work, Our Lives, Our Words*, Basingstoke: Macmillan Education.

—— and Hall, C. (1987) *Family Fortunes: Men and Women of the English Middle Class 1780-1850*, London: Hutchinson Education.

De Souza, V.S. (1969) 'Changing socio-economic conditions and employment of women in India' *Trends of Socio-Economic Change in India 1871-1961* vol. 7, Simla: Indian Institute of Advanced Study.

Delmar, R. (1976) 'Looking again at Engels' origins of the family, private property and the state' in J. Mitchell and A. Oakley (eds) *The Rights and Wrongs of Women*, Harmondsworth: Penguin Books.

Delphy, C. (1979) 'Sharing the same table: consumption and the family' in C.C. Harris and M. Anderson (eds) *The Sociology of the Family: New Directions for Britain*, University of Keele, Sociological Review Monograph 28.

Desai, I.P. (1956) 'The joint family in India: an analysis' *Sociological Bulletin* 5: 146-56.

Dex, S. (1985) *The Sexual Division of Work*, Brighton: Wheatsheaf Books Ltd.

Dwyer, D. (1983) 'Women and income in the third world: implications for policy' *International Working Paper* no. 18, New York: Population Council.

—— and Bruce, J. (1988) *A Home Divided: Women and Income in the Third World*, Stanford: Stanford University Press.

Dyson, T. (1987) 'An overview of recent demographic trends in India' Paper presented to the British Association of South Asian Scholars Conference, York, March 1987.

Economic Intelligence Service (1984) *Standard of Living of the Indian People*, Bombay: Centre for Monitoring Indian Economy.

Edholm, F., Harris, O. and Young, K. (1977) 'Conceptualising Women' *Critique of Anthropology* 3, 9 & 10: 101-130.

Eisenstein, S. (1983) *Give us Bread but Give us Roses*, London: Routledge and Kegan Paul.

Elson, D. and Pearson, R. (1980) 'The latest phase of the internationalisation of capital and its implications for women in the Third World' *Discussion paper* no. 150, University of Sussex: Institute of Development Studies.

—— (1981) 'Nimble fingers make cheap workers: an analysis of women's employment in Third World export manufacturing' *Feminist Review* 7: 87-107.

Engels, D. (1986) 'Sex, marriage and social reform: Bengal in the 1920s' Paper given to the Ninth European Conference on Modern Asian Studies, Heidelberg.

Engels, F. (1884) *The Origin of the Family, Private Property and the State*, 1985 edn, Harmondsworth: Penguin Classics (new introduction by M. Barrett).

Everett, J. (1979) *Women and Social Change in India*, New Delhi: Heritage Publications.

Forbes, G. (1975) 'The Indian women's movement: a struggle for women's rights or national liberation?' in G. Minault (ed.) *The Extended Family: Women and Political Participation in Indian and Pakistan*, Delhi: Chanakya Publications.

—— (1979) 'Women and modernity: the issue of child marriage in India' *Women's Studies International Quarterly* 2, 407–19.

—— (1982) 'Caged tigers: "First wave" feminists in India' *Women's Studies International Forum* 5, 6: 525–36.

Fox, B. (ed.) (1980) *Hidden in the Household: Women's Domestic Labour under Capitalism*, Toronto: Women's Educational Press.

Franda, M.F. (1971) *Radical Politics in West Bengal*, Cambridge, Mass: MIT Press.

Fruzzetti, L. and Ostor, A. (1976) 'Seed and earth: a cultural analysis of kinship in a Bengali town' *Contributions to Indian Sociology* (New Series) 10, 1: 97–132.

Ghosh, J.N. (1923) *The Social Evil in Calcutta and Methods of Treatment*, Calcutta: private printing.

Gluckman, M. (1962) 'Les Rites de Passage' in M. Gluckman (ed.) *Essays on the Ritual of Social Relations*, Manchester: Manchester University Press.

Goode, W. (1963) *World Revolution and Family Patterns*, New York: Free Press of Glencoe.

Gore, M.S. (1968) *Urbanisation and Family Change*, Bombay: Popular Prakashan.

Government publications and reports, see p. 190.

Gulati, L. (1975) 'Female work participation: a study of inter-state differences' *Economic and Political Weekly* 10, 112: 35–42, 11 January.

Hall, C. (1979) 'The early formation of Victorian domestic ideology' in S. Burman (ed.) *Fit Work for Women*, London: Croom Helm.

Harris, O. (1981) 'Households as natural units' in K. Young, C. Wolkowitz and R. McCullagh (eds) *Of Marriage and the Market*, 1st edn, London: CSE Books.

Hart, K. (1973) 'Informal income opportunities and urban employment in Ghana' *Journal of Modern African Studies* 11: 61–89.

Hershman, P. (1977) 'Virgin and Mother' in I.M. Lewis (ed.) *Symbols and Sentiments*, London: Academic Press.

Heyzer, N. (1986) *Working Women in South East Asia*, Milton Keynes: Open University Press.

Humphries, J. (1977) 'Class struggle and the persistence of the working class family' *Cambridge Journal of Economics* 1, 3: 241–258.

Hunt, P. (1980) *Gender and Class Consciousness*, London and Basingstoke: Macmillan.

Inden, R. (1976) *Marriage and Rank in Bengali Culture*, New Delhi: Vikas.
—— and Nicholas, R. (1977) *Kinship in Bengali Culture*, Chicago and London: Chicago University Press.
Jaggar, A. (1983) *Feminist Politics and Human Nature*, Sussex: Harvester Press.
Jayawardena, K. (1986) *Feminism and Nationalism in the Third World*, London/ New Delhi: Zed Books Ltd/Kali for Women.
Jeffery, P. (1979) *Frogs in a Well*: Indian Women in Purdah London: Zed Press.
Jephcott, P., Seear, B.N. and Smith, J.H. (1962) *Married Women Working*, London: Allen and Unwin.
Kabeer, N. (1987) 'Women's employment in the newly industrialising countries: a case study of India and the Philippines' Report for the IRDC, Sussex: Institute of Development Studies.
Kapoor, S. (1965) 'Family and kinship groups among the Khatris in Delhi' *Sociological Bulletin* 14: 54–63.
Kapur, P. (1974) *The Changing Status of the Working Woman in India*, Delhi: Vikas.
Kishwar, M. and Vanita, R. (1974) *In Search of Answers: Indian Women's Voices from Manushi*, London: Zed Press.
Klein, V. (1965) *Women Workers: Working Hours and Services*, Paris: Organization for Economic Cooperation and Development.
Kolenda, P. (1968) 'Region, caste and family structure: a comparative study of the Indian "joint" family' in M. Singer and B. Cohn (eds) *Structure and Change in Indian Society*, New York: Wenner-Gren Foundation.
Kumar, R. (1982) 'City lives: women workers in the Bombay cotton textile industry 1919–39', MPhil thesis, Centre for Historical Studies, Jawaharlal Nehru University, New Delhi.
—— (1983) 'Family and factory: women workers in the Bombay cotton textile industry, 1919–1939' *Indian Economic and Social History Review* 20, 1: 81–110.
Kung, L. (1983) *Factory Women of Taiwan*, Ann Arbor: UMI Research Press.
Liddle, J., and Joshi, R. (1986) *Daughters of Independence: Gender and Class in India*, London/New Delhi: Zed Books Ltd/Kali for Women.
Lubell, H. (1974) *Calcutta: Its Urban Development and Employment Prospects*, Geneva: International Labour Office.
Malos, E. (ed.) (1980) *The Politics of Housework*, London: Allison and Busby.
Mather, C. (1985) ' "Rather than make trouble, its better just to leave": behind the lack of industrial strife in the Tangerang region of West Java' in H. Afshar (ed.) *Women, Work and Ideology in the Third World*, London: Tavistock Publications.
McGuire, J. (1983) *The Making of a Colonial Mind: A Quantitative Study of the Bhadralok in Calcutta, 1857–1885*, Canberra: Australian National University Monographs on South Asia, no. 10.
Mencher, J. (1988) 'Women's work and poverty: women's contribution to household maintenance in South India' in D. Dwyer and J. Bruce (eds) *A Home Divided: Women and Income in the Third World*, Stanford: Stanford University Press.
Mies, M. (1980) *Indian Women and Patriarchy*, New Delhi: Concept Publishing.

Misra, B. (1975) 'Factory labour during the early years of industrialisation: an appraisal in the light of the Indian Factory Commission, 1890' *Indian Economic and Social History Review* 12, 3: 203–28.

Mitra, A. (1963) *Calcutta India's City*, Calcutta: New Age Publishers Private Ltd.

Mitra, A. (1977) *Calcutta Diary*, London: Frank Cass, Calcutta: Rupa and Co.

Mitra, A., Pathak, L.P. and Mukherjee, S. (1980) *The Status of Women: Shifts in Occupational Participation 1961–71*, Indian Council of Social Science Research, New Delhi: Abhinav Publications.

Mitra, I. (1981) 'Growth of trade union consciousness among jute mill workers 1920–40' *Economic and Political Weekly*, Special Number, 14, 44–6: 1839–48.

Moitra, T. (1983) 'Some reflections on the women's problem in India', paper given at the Workshop on Women and Poverty, Centre for Studies in Social Sciences, Calcutta, 17–18 March 1983.

Molyneux, M. (1984) 'Mobilization without emancipation? Women's interests, state and revolution in Nicaragua' *Critical Social Policy* 10, 1: 59–75.

Moorhouse, G. (1971) *Calcutta: The City Revealed*, revised edn, 1983, Harmondsworth: Penguin Books Ltd.

Moser, C. (1978) 'Informal sector or petty commodity production? Dualism or dependence in urban development?' *World Development* 6, 9/10: 1041–64.

Moser, C. and Young, K. (1981) 'Women of the working poor' *Institute of Development Studies Bulletin* 12, 3: 54–62.

Mukherjee, S.N. (1970) 'Caste, class and politics in Calcutta 1815–38' in E.R. Leach (ed.) *Elites in South Asia*, Cambridge: Cambridge University Press.

Munslow, B. and Finch, H. (1984) *Proletarianisation in the Third World*, London: Croom Helm.

Myrdal, A. and Klein, V. (1970) *Women's Dual Roles*, London: Routledge and Kegan Paul.

Nath, K. (1970) 'Female work participation and economic development: a regional analysis' *Economic and Political Weekly* 5, 21: 846–9, 23 May.

Omvedt, G. (1980) *We Will Smash this Prison! Indian Women in Struggle*, London: Zed Press.

——(1975) 'Caste, class and women's liberation in India' *Bulletin of Concerned Asian Scholars* VII, 1: 47.

Owens, R. and Nandy, A. (1977) *The New Vaishyas*, New Delhi: Allied Publishers Private Ltd.

Pahl, J. (1980) 'Patterns of money management within marriage' *Journal of Social Policy* 9, 3: 313–35.

—— (1983) 'The allocation of money and the structuring of inequality within marriage' *Sociological Review* 31, 2: 237–62.

—— (1984) 'The allocation of money within the household' in M. Freeman (ed.) *The State, the Law and the Family*, London: Tavistock.

Pahl, R.E. (1980) 'Employment, work and the domestic division of labour' *International Journal of Urban and Regional Research* 4, 1: 1–20.

Pahl, R.E. (1984) *Divisions of Labour*, Oxford: Basil Blackwell.

Pakrasi, K.B. (1971) *The Uprooted: A Sociological Study of Refugees of West Bengal*, Calcutta: Editions Indian.

Papanek, H. (1979) 'Family status production work: the "work" and "non-work" of women' *Signs* 4, 4: 775–81.

Papanek, H. and Minault, G. (eds) (1982) *Separate Worlds: Studies of Purdah in South Asia*, Delhi: Chanakya Publications.

Ray, A.K. (1902) *A Short History of Calcutta*, revised edn, 1982, Calcutta: RDDHI-India.

Redclift, N. (1985) 'The contested domain: gender, accumulation and the labour process' in N. Redclift and E. Mingione (eds) *Beyond Employment: Household, Gender and Subsistence*, Oxford: Basil Blackwell.

Roldan, M. (1985) 'Industrial outworking, struggles for the reproduction of working class families and gender subordination' in N. Redclift and E. Mingione (eds) *Beyond Employment: Household, Gender and Subsistence*, Oxford: Basil Blackwell.

Ross, A.D. (1961) *The Hindu Family in its Urban Setting*, Delhi: Oxford University Press.

Roy, M. (1975a) *Bengali Women*, Chicago: Chicago University Press.

—— (1975b) 'The concepts of "femininity" and "liberation" in the context of changing sex roles: women in modern India and America' in D. Raphael (ed.) *Being Female*, The Hague: Mouton.

Salaff, J. (1981) *Working Daughters of Hongkong*, Cambridge: Cambridge University Press.

Savara, M. (1981) 'Changing trends in women's employment: a case study of the textile industry in Bombay', PhD thesis, University of Bombay.

Sayers, J., Evans, M. and Redclift, N. (1987) *Engels Revisited: New Feminist Essays*, London: Tavistock Publications.

Schultz, T.W. (ed.) (1974) *The Economics of the Family*, Chicago: Chicago University Press.

Scott, J. and Tilly, L. (1975) 'Women's work and the family in nineteenth-century Europe' *Comparative Studies in Society and History* 17, 1: 36–64.

Seccombe, W. (1974) 'The housewife and her labour under capitalism' *New Left Review* 83, 3–24, Jan–Feb.

Sen, A.K. (1982) *Poverty and Famines: An Essay on Entitlement and Deprivation*, Oxford: Oxford University Press.

——and Sen Gupta, S. (1983) 'Malnutrition of rural children and the sex bias' *Economic and Political Weekly* 28, Annual Number: 855–62, May.

Sen, G. (1983) 'Women's work and women agricultural labourers: a study of the Indian census' *Working Paper* no. 159, Centre for Development Studies, Trivandrum.

Sen, S.N. (1960) *The City of Calcutta: A Socio-Economic Survey 1954–5 to 1957–8*, Calcutta: Bookland Private Ltd.

Shah, A.M. (1974) *The Household Dimension of the Family in India*, Berkeley: California University Press.

Sharma, J. (1980) *Caste Dynamics among Bengali Hindus*, Calcutta: Firma KLM Private Ltd.

Sharma, U. (1978) 'Women and their affines: the veil as a symbol of separation' *Man: Journal of the Royal Anthropological Institute* 13: 218–33.

—— (1984) 'Dowry in North India: its consequences for women' in R. Hirschon (ed.) *Women and Property Women as Property*, London and Canberra: Croom Helm.

—— (1986) *Women's Work, Class and the Urban Household: A Study of*

*Shimla, North India*, London: Tavistock.

Sinha, S. (1972) *Cultural Profile of Calcutta*, Calcutta: Indian Anthropological Society.

Srinivas, A.N. (1977) 'The changing position of Indian women' *Man: Journal of the Royal Anthropological Institute* 12, 2: 221–38.

Srinivasan, T.N. and Bardhan, P.K. (1974) *Poverty and Income Distribution in India*, Calcutta: Statistical Publishing Society.

Stack, C. (1974) *All our Kin: Strategies for Survival in a Black Community*, New York: Harper and Row.

Standing, H. (1979) 'Women workers in the Calcutta Metropolitan District' End of Grant Report to the Social Science Research Council.

—— (1985a) 'Women's employment and the household: some findings from Calcutta' *Economic and Political Weekly* XX, 17, Review of Women's Studies: 23–38, 27 April.

—— (1985b) 'Wages, resources and power: the impact of women's employment on the urban Bengali household' in H. Afshar (ed.) *Women, Work and Ideology in the Third World*, London: Tavistock Publications.

Tagore, R. (1964) *Two Sisters*, Calcutta: Viswa Bharati.

Thorner, A. (1984) 'Women's Work in Colonial India, 1881–1931' in K. Ballhatchet and D. Taylor (eds) *Changing South Asia: Economy and Society* Hongkong: Asian Research Service.

Timberg, T.A. (1978) *The Marwaris: From Traders to Industrialists*, New Delhi: Vikas.

Ul-Awwal, I. (1982) 'The problems of middle class educated unemployment in Bengal 1912–42' *Indian Economic and Social History Review* 19, 1: 27–45.

(USAID) United States Agency for International Development (1982) *Women in Development* Policy Paper, Washington: USAID.

Vatuk, S. (1972) *Kinship and Urbanization: White Collar Migrants in North India*, Berkeley: University of California Press.

Vicinus, M. (1985) *Independent Women: Work and Community for Single Women 1850–1920*, London: Virago Press.

Walkowitz, J. (1980) *Prostitution and Victorian Society: Women, Class and the State*, Cambridge: Cambridge University Press.

Westwood, S. (1984) *All Day Everyday: Family and Factory in the Making of Women's Lives*, London: Pluto Press.

Whitehead (1981) ' "I'm hungry, mum": the politics of domestic budgeting' in K. Young, C. Wolkowitz and R. McCullagh (eds) *Of Marriage and the Market*, 1st edn, London: CSE Books.

Wilson, E. (1977) *Women and the Welfare State*, London: Tavistock.

Wood, M.R. (1975) 'Employment and family change: a study of middle class women in urban Gujarat' in A. de Souza (ed.) *Women in Contemporary India*, New Delhi: Manohar.

Yalman, N. (1963) 'On the purity of women in the castes of Ceylon and Malabar' *Man: Journal of the Royal Anthropological Institute* 93, 1: 25–58.

Yanagisako, S.J. (1979) 'Family and household: the analysis of domestic groups' *Annual Review of Anthropology* 8: 161–205.

Young, K., Wolkowitz, C. and McCullagh, R. (1981) *Of Marriage and the Market*, London: CSE Books.

## Government publications and reports

Government of India (1913) *Census of India 1911*, vol. V, Bengal, Bihar, Orissa and Sikkim, part 1, report, Calcutta: Bengal Secretariat.

—— (1923) *Census of India 1921*, vol. IV, City of Calcutta, part 1, report, Calcutta: Bengal Secretariat.

—— (1933) *Census of India 1931*, Vol. V, Bengal and Sikkim, part 1, report, vol. VI, Calcutta, parts I & II, Calcutta: Central Publication Branch.

—— (1946) Labour Investigation Commission Reports, New Delhi: Government of India Press.

—— (1960) Report on Family Living Survey among Industrial Workers 1958–9, Labour Bureau: Ministry of Labour and Employment.

—— (1974) *Towards Equality: Report of the Committee on the Status of Women in India*, New Delhi: Department of Social Welfare.

—— (1983) *Census of India 1981*, part IIB (i) Primary Census Abstract, General Population, Government of India: New Delhi.

Report of the Recent Commission on Indian Factories, London: HMSO, 1891.

Report of the Indian Factory Labour Commission 1908, vol. II, Simla: Central Branch Press, 1908.

Report of the Royal Commission on Factory Labour in India (RCFL), vol. 5 part 1 (Bengal), London: HMSO, 1931.

# Name index

# Subject index